Love for Cooking

Also by Uta Hagen
Respect for Acting (with Haskel Frankel)

Love for Cooking

UTA HAGEN

Collier Books
A Division of Macmillan Publishing Co., Inc.
New York

Collier Macmillan Publishers
London

Macmillan Publishing Co., Inc.
866 Third Avenue, New York, N.Y. 10022
Collier Macmillan Canada, Ltd.

ILLUSTRATIONS BY BARBARA FIORE

Library of Congress Cataloging in Publication Data
Hagen, Uta, 1919-
    Love for cooking.
    Includes index.
    1. Cookery.   I. Title.
TX715.H126   641.5   76-12538
        ISBN 0-02-547380-8
        ISBN 0-02-009710-7 pbk.

First Collier Books Edition 1978

Printed in the United States of America

For my daughter Letty
Long may she cook!

Contents

Introduction: A Way of Life

In the beginning there was Hungarian goulash! It was my first successful dish. I'm not sure it was really authentic, although it was heavily sprinkled with Hungarian paprika, but I was proud of it and made it so often that friends expected nothing else when they came to dine.

Anyone who believes he can't cook should start by learning to make one thing really well. Once you've seen faces light up and heard oohs and aahs at the first bite or just the contented sound of chewing when conversation stops and concentration is turned to tasting the food you yourself have brought to the table, you too will become addicted to the kitchen in search for more such rewards.

Obviously my repertoire developed. As in the pursuit of any adventure there were successes and failures, but my love of entertaining grew. I can now claim that few people leave my house without asking for a recipe. I love that, and I love giving it to them or showing them how to prepare a specialty. I've never understood the desire to keep a recipe secret.

Before I step into the kitchen for you, I'd like to explain that what I cook and how I entertain is tied to my way of life. I've devised ways of preparing food days in advance not only because of my work in the theater and at my studio, but because for many months of the year I commute between Montauk, Long Island, and New York City. I also enjoy my company and want to spend more time with them than with the pots in the kitchen.

I love my life! I particularly love my life at home, in the kitchen, in the garden, at the dinner table, in front of an open fire, on a patio in the sun, or in the fields picking fruit and berries. I love to be alone in the fields, the garden, or the kitchen or at the dining table preparing for the time when I can share these places with my family and friends and serve them the surprises I made for them when I was alone.

At this moment, I'm sitting at my typewriter outside on the back deck of my house by the sea. It's the kind of mid-September day on eastern Long Island that reminds me of an Italian autumn. The breeze is soft and cool but the sun is toasting. My three poodles are cavorting with a bedroom slipper. The black pines look silky and silver in the light. At the edge of the hill, goldenrod, partridge peas, and Poor-Robin's-Plantain glisten with yellows. Around the deck the marguerites are like parasols of yellow bending in the breeze, and the green leaves of budding Nippon daisies give off a pungent aroma. Monarch butterflies are at their peak as they flutter by, in army proportions migrating to another sunny region. Occasionally a bird dips his belly and wing tips into the bird bath despite the clattering of the typewriter. This morning I put up sixteen quarts of tomatoes and relish with the fruit of my own vines. What more could I possibly ask for?

I've never been able to identify with the average career woman and her complaints about the tedium of being a housewife. Almost my greatest sense of fulfillment has come from "home-making." Although I always attack my work in the the theater with my whole being, it has often given me a schizophrenic pull of resentment by taking me away from my pleasures at home. I once acted in an extraordinary play at our studio with a fabulous cast. When the production was delayed it became a personal crisis that my spring planting had to be put off. It nearly ruined the early vegetable crop!

Taking a play on tour, living on trains and in hotels, is my idea of hell. I tried to make my last long tour tolerable by traveling with a hot plate. People laughed when I tried to conceal perishable groceries on the window sills of elegant hotel suites or rushed to close the transom as sizzling food odors escaped down the hallways of the Ritz or the Ambassador or the Barclay.

My parents and my husband always insisted that talent bears with it the responsibility to fulfill it. To them my work in the theater was my duty. My work at home was viewed as a game. Who could argue? It's true that I've never lost a sense of playing when I cook, bake, set a table, put up fresh curtains, or even wax a floor. I can work ten hours in the garden hardly aware that time is passing. I almost "take a trip" when the intensity of nature moves in on me—the feel and smell of clean earth or compost, the sound of insects and birds or the breaking surf, the brilliance of color, the changing light. When you *do* something with nature you become a hundred times more aware of it. And so it is with food.

My mother, who always brought food to the table like a festival of joy, was probably responsible for my own need to turn every meal into an event. When there's no actual birthday, anniversary, reunion, or holiday to celebrate, I invent something. I set the stage. The room and table are decorated with flowers from garden or fields. Dried flowers and leaves, even clover, dandelions, grasses, and reeds can be amusing. I never tire of hunting for new ideas in place mats and table linen, elegant ones for Washington Square and informal, fanciful ones for the country. My idea of bliss is a meal that begins with hors d'oeuvres around six o'clock and gradually works its way through many courses, accompanied by wines, liqueurs, and delicious conversation. My elegant orgies are saved from becoming pretentiously bourgeois by the fact that I do the serving and the guests help with the dishes, and someone usually sits down to the splendor in a T-shirt and blue jeans. Menus depend on the preferences of the guests, the season, my budget, and availability of foods at the market.

I hope to pass on the short cuts and easier cooking methods I've acquired and offer you recipes for all occasions with my whole heart. If you like them and they give you pleasure, you will obviously become my friend.

The "Herbert" for whom I've named a number of recipes and to whom I refer in numerous anecdotes, is Herbert Berghof, a fabulous actor, director, teacher, human being, and . . . my husband.

I. Getting It Together

ORGANIZATION

I'm impatient by nature. I want quick results, preferably sensational ones, and this can lead to kitchen chaos. Actually, the garden taught me how to curb impatience. The first time I stuck a few shoots of vine into the ground and was told that it would cover the given area in four or five years, I laughed aloud and almost yanked it out again. Then in about four years, there was my vine, lush and beautiful just as I'd hoped it would be. Cooking has a similarity to gardening; planning ahead and laying the groundwork didn't take years, but it did take time.

Now when people ask how I manage so many activities, I can claim I've finally learned to organize. I make lists for everything. There are lists all over the house. Sometimes they even make *me* laugh. They're subject to change and I try not to be pedantic about them, but I get enormous satisfaction from crossing out what's accomplished.

I plan all menus a week in advance and do one weekly marketing. When traveling between Montauk and Manhattan I market once a week in both places. It saves time.

Many foods can be prepared ahead and some dishes two or three days before they're served. If I'm cooking something elaborate, I often double the recipe and freeze some of it to thaw and reheat for another occasion.

On the day of a dinner party in the city, I set my table in the morning and in the country I do it soon after lunch so this part of the fun doesn't get mixed up with the cooking. Flowers are picked and arranged early in the morning, usually with the rising sun.

The kitchen used to be a mess after I'd finished cooking, so the clean-up was a major chore. Then I began to wash and rinse utensils as I went along, incidentally using only half as many bowls, whisks, pots, and pans. Now when dinner goes on the table, my kitchen is clean except for the saucepan or skillet I may have used last. It's also easier to wash dishes between courses as long as the company is chatting and doesn't notice. If they become aware of it, they might get uncomfortable and feel they should be helping. It's easier to wash off the hors d'oeuvre plates and forks before putting out the first course and to wash soup bowls right after they've been used, rather than waiting till later when they're all gummed up. Try the same method with the dishes from the main course and the salad plates and forks, the guests are usually ready for a breather then anyway. When it's all over, let the company help you with the glasses and dessert dishes and then go happily to bed with a clean kitchen.

My city kitchen is large and old-fashioned. In the country it's compact and modern with room for about two people to move around. I prefer the country kitchen, in which I don't have to take more than a step between sink, stove, refrigerator, or chopping block. In Manhattan my cabinets sprawl all over the place, rather than being conveniently placed overhead or under the counters. There's not much I can do about it. I still dream of working in one of those gorgeous kitchens with a central chopping block, wall ovens, and concealed bins for staples. I *have* acquired a self-cleaning oven, which is a joy; I no longer dread the clean-up job that followed a roast lamb or the Christmas goose.

Pegboards are marvelous for hanging up small pans and utensils that are used a lot. I keep a tall metal vase next to the stove in which to prop whisks, wooden spoons, scrapers, bulb basters, etc. so I don't have to hunt for them in drawers. Wall brackets are handy for ladles, spatulas, measuring spoons, and strainers. You can get a marvelous magnet bar fitted on the wall to which all your knives will cling. Ideally there should be enough counter space to hold equipment like the blender and Mix-Master so they don't have to be lugged in and out of cabinets. The chopping board should always be at hand, not stored away.

You can get used to the inconvenient placement of your kitchen equipment, so I re-examine mine once a year, usually when I'm cleaning cabinets and drawers, to see how to improve the layout.

EQUIPMENT

Even someone who has done only a little cooking has a favorite knife, spoon, pan, or casserole he couldn't do without. I'll try to avoid stressing my preferences in listing necessary equipment. You may already have the essentials, but here they are. As a start you will need the following pots, pans, casseroles, and skillets made of cast iron:

> a 6-quart oval Dutch oven with lid
> a 3-quart round casserole with lid
> a 1½-quart round casserole with lid
> a shallow 10-inch casserole (lid optional)
> 3 skillets, 12, 10, and 8 inches respectively.

If you're buying new ones, get the best enameled ones from Europe or Scandinavia. The enamel often chips on the cheaper varieties. Try the ones lined with glazed porcelain, which solve your sticking problems and are easy to wipe sparkling clean. (Mine come from Waterford, Ireland, and are Teflon lined. Sadly enough they're no longer available. If you find other Teflon-lined cast ironware, grab it.) Most of this ware is pretty enough to bring to the table, and can also go from the refrigerator to the stove or oven with no problem. This eliminates the need for special omelet pans or soufflé dishes and is almost a lifetime investment.

Other pots and pans should be made of stainless steel or enameled metal. They should include:

> a double boiler
> 3 saucepans ranging from 1 to 3 quarts
> a 4-quart pot with lid
> a 6-quart pot with lid and
> a lobster pot with lid (4-gallon capacity).

The lobster pot can double for jam and jelly, which requires a "rolling boil." If you don't like lobster, jam, or jelly, you obviously won't need it. Try to get the pots and pans with black or white Teflon lining. You'll love them.

You need a

> roasting pan with a rack.

The rack can double for cooling cakes and pastries. You'll also want

> 2 white glazed earthenware ovenproof dishes 8 by 12 inches and
>   5 by 9 inches. They are about 2 inches deep.
> soufflé dishes (optional)

They also come in glazed earthenware in a variety of sizes and although they're very pretty, I find I can do without them because I use the cast-iron casseroles instead. And be sure to have

> serving platters that take oven heat.

I never seem to have enough bowls. You should at least have a nest of

> 3 Pyrex, glass, or metal mixing bowls
> 1 extra-large bowl.

You might as well throw away this book unless you have

> an electric blender or food processor.

The next item may be considered a luxury but it saves time and elbow grease and encourages seemingly difficult recipes. It also comes with two nice bowls;

> a Mix-Master.

Then if you can afford an electric beater that can be held in one hand you're lucky. Otherwise an essential item is

> a hand rotary beater.

For beating you'll also need a variety of

> French wire whisks.

For baking:

> 2 baking sheets (Teflon lined, if possible)
> 2 muffin tins, holding 12 and 6 muffins respectively
> 2 9-inch pie plates
> 2 8-inch spring-form cheesecake molds (to double for all tortes)
> 4 loaf pans (2 standard size and 2 small ones)
> a flour sifter
> a rolling pin, long, skinny, and nonsticking
> a pastry blender
> a pastry brush (try a kitchen supply store for those made of goose
> feathers).

You can't be a cook without

> a chopping block or cutting board.

The one I have in the country fits over the sink and has a hole at one corner to scoop leavings right into the sink. It's great for large quantities of fruit and vegetables or for making ravioli or manicotti.

On to the heart of kitchen matters:

> paring knives
> a carving knife
> a medium-sized knife
> a large chopping knife.

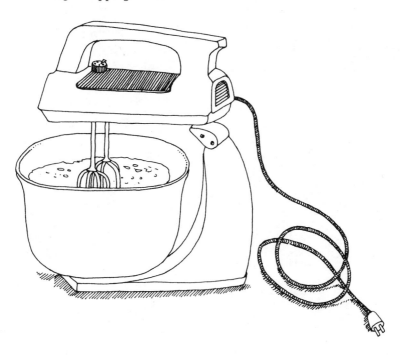

A friend once gave me a huge knife made by Kentucky mountaineers that is perfect for big chopping jobs. Its counterpart in New York has a round blade with a small handle on each end to rock back and forth. In your knife collection include

>a serrated knife for bread and cake
>a carborundum.

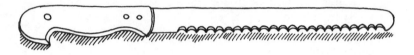

This is a long abrasive slab invaluable for keeping knives razor sharp. It works better than an electric sharpener and is available at most hardware stores. Be sure to grind the knife up and down moving forward along the slab; never use a circular motion. Some of the newer knives from Japan and Germany come with instructions for sharpening on the back of a porcelain plate. They work!

For many recipes you will want

>a foodmill or ricer
>a Mouli grater.

The latter is a luxury item that can make the difference between light, fluffy ground cheese and nuts or mealy ones. Also,

>a whistling kettle

is important, especially if you're absent-minded;

>wooden spoons

are essential in all sizes. I still have some of my mother's, bent, slightly charred antiques I couldn't part with. My newest acquisitions are large, perforated ones that I use more and more, even for serving. Then I have tiny ones for sauces or for scooping out the grooves in the blender.

On a wall rack hang:

>stainless steel ladles
>a spatula
>a slotted spoon and/or a slotted skimmer
>a two-tined fork.

Everyone should have:

> 2 rubber scrapers
> a vegetable peeler
> a winged corkscrew
> a four-sided grater
> a beer-can opener
> a sturdy can opener, electric if possible
> a garlic press
> a metal colander
> a nest of 3 strainers or sieves
> a funnel
> a bulb baster
> measuring spoons
> measuring cups.

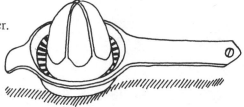

I have the cups in all sizes ranging from a Pyrex 1-cup to a plastic 2-quart capacity. Get

> a fruit-juice squeezer
> a small lemon squeezer.

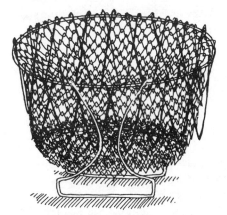

The latter has a handle and can be balanced over a cup, bowl, or the blender while squeezing the juice. Of course,

> a lettuce basket

can be used to swing-dry washed lettuce, but it can double as a decoration filled with fruit. There's also a collapsible kind that can double as a rack in the bottom of a pot or skillet for boiling vegetables or for deep frying.

You'll need:

> a timer
> poultry shears
> a deep-fry thermometer that can double for candy
> a good peppermill
> a nutmeg grater.

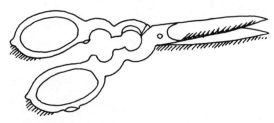

The last item is inexpensive, and the difference between prepared nutmeg and freshly grated is enormous.

Give away your metal pot or percolator to someone you don't like and get

> a glass or porcelain coffee maker.

Whatever system you use, drip, filter, or steam—don't perk the coffee. Never boil it. Don't use instant. As you can see I'm dogmatic on the subject.

If you have these things or their equivalents, there won't be much you can't make. Special items for preparing snails, making pasta, etc. will be listed under specific recipes.

Whenever my husband gives me a new utensil he calls it a toy. Certainly no new doll when I was little could have excited me more. I try to keep my "toys" clean and shiny and maintain them as any good craftsman would his tools.

THE INGREDIENTS

I've been acutely aware of scarcities and the actual disappearance of certain foods, of spiraling costs and the consequent influence on my budget, all a direct result of global food problems. Still, I look for the best food available within my range. Using second-rate substitutes guarantees disappointing meals and ends up costing more.

If you buy everything at the same store the quality of some of the food will suffer. Take the time to find a good butcher, fish market, cheese store, and greengrocer. A specialty store for condiments and unusual imported or domestic food is a bonanza. Use the supermarket for staples. I don't pretend to be an authority about the best cuts of meat or the freshest fish. I'm not even sure how to pick out the best melon, so I've learned to make friends with the tradesmen. I lean heavily on their advice.

Fruit and Vegetables

I realize I'm lucky to have a fine greengrocer in the neighborhood. Year round he carries a wide variety of loose-leaf lettuce and herbs. He has such delicacies as field lettuce and rugola, that beautiful Italian cousin of watercress. In season he carries garden-fresh fruit and vegetables and when my garden isn't producing, I buy them from him to transport to the country. Unless canned or frozen vegetables come from my own garden, I forget about them. You don't save money when the "cheaper" lettuce at the supermarket has to be stripped of so many wilted outer leaves. If you're used to those tacky boxes or dry, brownish garlic, try the huge, juicy white ones at a good vegetable store. Big, firm mushrooms that haven't yet unfurled to let their brown gills hang out are always waiting for you. Even a standard product like celery seems crisper. By the way, always use *freshly squeezed* lemon juice in any recipe calling for it.

Dairy Products

I use unsalted butter, jumbo eggs, fat-free milk, and, obviously, the freshest cream in all my cooking. Try to find a good cheese store and sample the hundreds of surprises (not all at the same time!) from Europe, Scandinavia, and many sections of America. I like the American Boursin better than French, for example. If you're in a rut with the average supermarket Swiss cheese or the one they label Switzerland Swiss (?), experiment with their superior counterparts, French Gruyère, Austrian Emmenthaler, Finnish Swiss, etc. Try using Monterey Jack for grating and melting. When possible get a freshly made mozzarella. The difference between it and the prepackaged brand can't be described.

Oil and Vinegar

The aroma of a good olive oil is unmistakable as it heats up in the skillet to flavor your food. A few excellent Spanish oils aren't nearly as expensive as their French or Italian counterparts.

When olive oil is too heavy for a given recipe, you have a large option of cooking oils. If you've been using only one kind, experiment with others. Corn oil, safflower, peanut are all pleasant, as well as soybean oil. Try the excellent sesame oil, which is lighter in color and consistency than its Oriental cousin.

A good vinegar is equally important. Try malt vinegar. Experiment with special white and red wine vinegars that are bottled with or without tarragon until you find your favorite. The same is true for bottled mayonnaise. Once in a while I get a gorgeous German import but it's very expensive. My favorite mayonnaise recipe is on page 42.

Flour

Using the correct flour for a specific dish can make the difference between something good and something ordinary. When I simply specify *flour* in a given recipe, I mean *unbleached* flour. Give away your bleached or "fortified" flour that has been spoiled by chemical additives. Superfine cake flour appears in only one of my recipes, but there's a nonlumping, quick-mixing flour that I use a great deal. Either Wondra by Gold Medal or Pillsbury's can be purchased at any supermarket and comes in a shaker. Buy the shaker first and next time you can buy it less expensively by the bag and refill your shaker with a funnel. In my opinion this flour is the best for blending and making lumpless sauces, lighter pancakes, better crêpes. It also clings to food that should be dusted or breaded with an evenness that's not matched by regular flour. I will refer to it throughout the recipes as *quick-mix flour*. Measure it in the same proportion as regular flour.

Salt, Sugar, and Seasoning

Use sea salt instead of the salt that tastes of chemicals. If you think it doesn't matter, put a few grains of each on separate fingers to taste the difference. For many recipes you'll want Kosher or coarse salt. Use freshly ground pepper and nutmeg. Avoid all additives like monosodium glutamate, meat tenderizers, and synthetic sweeteners—they're *poison*. I also believe that people who use prepared seasoning salt or monstrosities like garlic salt simply don't have any taste buds. Use fresh herbs whenever possible and get a nice variety of dried ones for your spice shelf.

If you're a health nut, raw sugar is awfully good and can be used in the same way as processed sugar. Superfine sugar is expensive but excellent for the quick blending and absorption required in so many desserts, meringues, and pastries.

A fine tea or coffee is not just for fancy people. Buy some and drink less.

An unusual cracker or biscuit can make your guests' eyes light up when served with the hors d'oeuvres.

I realize not everyone lives in a region where all these goodies are available, except perhaps by mail order. I also believe the awareness of fine food is growing throughout the country by leaps and bounds, and if you demand it loudly enough the suppliers will see that you get it.

My doctor gets cross about my cooking because both my husband and I have a tendency to high cholesterol. Unfortunately many of the things I enjoy making include, butter, olive oil, eggs, cream, and cheese. Even a fresh vegetable doesn't taste as sensational without a little butter. Fatty meats I can do without. Once in a while, as a gesture of appeasement, I squeeze lemon juice on the vegetables and salads and dress them simply with herbs. I cut down on cheese and eggs and use margarine in sauces or as a cooking base whenever the taste can be disguised with other flavors. I substitute yoghurt for sour cream and find it works well in many recipes. I use peanut or vegetable oil in place of olive oil and evaporated skim milk in sauces or recipes that call for cream.

This special advice is only for those who worry about their diets.

FOLLOWING A RECIPE

Herbert once told a friend, "Uta does everything dangerously, even cooking!" It used to be true. I literally stormed a recipe, grabbing for the first ingredient and utensil and plunging into action. More often than not I ended up with a disaster. Since I know I'm not the only one to make this mistake, I want to stress the importance of *reading the recipe through from beginning to end* before doing anything else. *Organize the equipment and ingredients and consider the timing involved.* Only a few weeks ago someone told a story of cooking an elaborate dish for a dinner party. The guests arrived as the hostess, having finished the preparation, came to the last line of the recipe: "Cook for 6 hours." They went out for dinner.

Try to understand each step of the recipe before beginning. I've attempted to write the recipes in such a way that they have to be read first instead of placing the ingredients at the beginning and then describing what to do with them. Short cuts have been incorporated, so it's best not to try any of your own. Long ago I read a recipe calling for browning meat "a few pieces at a time." I thought it would be faster to throw them into the pan all at once. They didn't brown, they stewed.

Timidity, fearfulness, or pedantry can be almost as destructive as rashness. I've watched someone measuring out an eighth teaspoon of salt with a trembling hand. Take courage, and learn from failure as well as success, just as in any other art form. If cooking is new to you or you prepare a real dinner only once a fortnight, remember that a new recipe can take three times as long the first time you make it. When someone marvels at my ability to produce an "effortless" meal, I love to tell the joke about the big Texan visiting New York who stops a little old lady on the street to ask, "Could you-all tell me how I can git to Carnegie Hall?" and she answers, "Practice! Practice! Practice!"

Except for seasoning, don't omit any ingredients from a recipe. A friend of mine making yeast bread once decided to omit the sweetening, not understanding that it helped to activate the yeast.

MEASUREMENTS AND EQUIVALENTS

Flavoring and seasoning are often a matter of personal preference. I started to improve when I learned to taste everything I made. When I ask you to add salt and pepper "to taste," for example, I mean just that. I'm an undersalter, not just because it suits my taste buds but because an oversalted dish can rarely be saved. If I've added too little, it can always be sprinkled on later. When I specify "a pinch" of something, I mean just that; as many grains of salt, pepper, etc. as can be pinched between two fingers.

While I'm dealing with measurements it may help to know equivalents for certain ingredients, items I sometimes question when only one of the measures is listed.

> Butter: 1 pound = 4 sticks = 2 cups
> 1 cup = 2 sticks
> 1 stick divides into 8 tablespoons.

Your eye will soon get accustomed to cutting a stick in half when you need 4 tablespoons.

1 pound granulated sugar	= 2 cups
1 pound brown sugar	= 2¼ cups
3 teaspoons anything	= 1 tablespoon
4 tablespoons anything	= ¼ cup
5 large whole eggs	= 1 cup
4 egg whites	= ½ cup
1 pound cheese	= 4 cups grated
1 pound unshelled nuts	= 4 cups shelled
1 envelope gelatin	= 1 tablespoon
1 medium lemon produces	= 2 tablespoons juice

The recipes I will present are the favorites and *specialités* of my *maison*. They are predominantly European, adapted to American ingredients and measures. You will find no hot or highly spiced dishes because I believe they burn out your stomach lining. I have a few personal dislikes. Squid and mussels simply give me a belly ache and I'm ashamed to admit that I find bouillabaisse for the birds. Certain English food should not be discussed. Have you ever had suet pudding?

In any event, I hope you will love making, presenting, and eating my dishes as much as I do!

II. Basic Cooking Terms and Methods

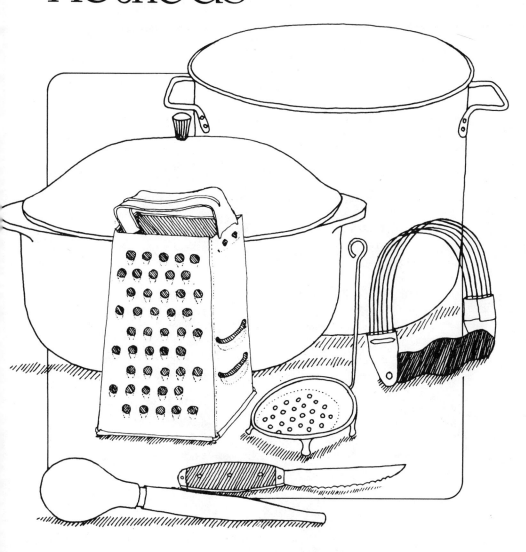

Professional chefs often disagree about the meaning of the terms they bandy about. The words themselves can often conjure up images that are inaccurate. For instance, when I hear "blanching" I immediately envision something turning pale. In cooking this can only be applied to a blanched almond after having been immersed in boiling water to rid it of its brown skin and reveal the pale flesh. But let me begin with the procedures that seem to be at the very heart of cooking:

SLICING, CHOPPING, DICING, MINCING, AND GRATING

It seems that at the best haute cuisine schools the first weeks are spent exclusively at the chopping board. A food processor from France can do all these things and more with the flick of the wrist. If you have a rich relative, ask for one for Christmas. I own a slicer from Europe which stays in the drawer because I'm afraid I'll slice off my fingertips. For most of us sharp knives are still the best tools.

Slicing and chopping are self-explanatory. They are tedious jobs that can be more fun if you know a few tricks. When slicing a round object like a potato, or if you want to slice a carrot lengthwise, cut off one side so it will lie flat for the rest of the slicing. To chop parsley or herbs, hold down the tip of the knife with one hand while you bounce the handle up and down with the other. It's ten times faster than lifting up the entire knife for each chop.

To *dice* vegetables means to cut them into cubes of half an inch or smaller. Slice them lengthwise first, then hold the slices together with your left hand while cutting straight across them with your right. To chop or dice an onion, peel it and cut a thin slice from the bottom all across the onion. Make thin slices downward to within half an inch or less from the bottom all across the onion. Turn it halfway around and repeat the process, criss-crossing the previous slices. Then place the onion on its side and slice downward for perfect little dice. The same thing works for a large shallot.

Mincing means chopping food very fine indeed. However, to mince garlic, use your garlic press.

Grating seemed unnecessary to explain until a friend tested my Lemon Mousse recipe (page 324) and used the coarse side of the grater to make the "grated lemon rind." The mousse was inedible.

One side of the grater usually has two wide slits for slicing, which I rarely use, preferring a knife. The next side has pea-sized slits which are ideal for coarsely grating cheese, onion, etc. The next-smaller-sized holes are perfect for grating orange or lemon rind and for finely grating hard cheese by hand. The smallest holes are good for grating something like whole nutmeg by hand.

The Mouli grater, for large quantities of nuts or things like Parmesan, is advisable for best results.

PRECOOKING FOOD BY PARBOILING OR BLANCHING AND REFRESHING

These confusing terms are simply methods of preparing food a step ahead of their final recipe. For example, I *parboil* or *blanch* green vegetables to retain both color and texture by popping them into an open boiling-water bath for a few minutes until tender crunchy. Then they are *refreshed* under cold water to stop the cooking and to maintain color before being dolled up with butter or sauces for cooking in a final recipe. Tomatoes, peaches, almonds, chestnuts, etc. are *blanched* in boiling water for a minute or less to facilitate removing their skins. Smoked food such as bacon is sometimes *parboiled* or *blanched* in water to remove saltiness or smokiness.

BOILING, SIMMERING, POACHING, AND SCALDING

These are all a matter of degree of heat. *Boiling* uses high heat to create a turbulent bubbling in the pot. *Simmer* over medium or low heat, allowing the liquid to bubble very gently in the pan. Not just eggs but poultry and fish are often *poached* in a liquid maintained below a simmer. Almost no little bubbles should be visible. I like to think the water or liquid shivers a little now and then. *Scalding*, as with milk, usually means that the liquid is brought almost to the boiling point until bubbles appear around the edge of the pot, then removed from heat.

REDUCING LIQUIDS

Boiling down sauces, gravies, fruit juices, etc. to thicken them, intensify their flavor, and reduce them in volume is a frequent procedure. The pan is left uncovered to allow moisture to evaporate and hasten the reducing.

BAKING, ROASTING, AND BROILING

You can *bake* or *roast* in a covered dish or an open one. Preheat the oven about fifteen minutes before needed to ensure correct timing for the dish you're cooking. *Broiling* means that only one side of the food is exposed to direct heat at one time. When using the broiler section of your oven, always leave it ajar at least an inch to guarantee proper ventilation and even heat which doesn't escape into the oven above the broiler.

BRAISING, POTTING, AND STEWING

Food experts can be fiendish in their apparent attempts to confuse. *Braising* is a term for food that has been browned or precooked before finishing it off in varying amounts of liquid or fat in a covered pot. The final cooking usually takes place in the oven but can also be achieved by simmering on top of the stove. *Potting* means almost the same, a good example being the good old-fashioned American pot roast. Generally less liquid is used. *Casseroling* also means the same thing and is a term I refuse to use except as a noun: casserole, describing a heavy, covered pot. *Stewing* differs slightly in that the food is usually cut into bite-sized chunks and often goes right into liquid in the pot without prebrowning.

SAUTÉING, FRYING, DEEP-FAT FRYING, PAN FRYING, PAN BROILING, AND STIR-FRYING

Sautéing and *frying* are often used interchangeably and mean cooking in an uncrowded open skillet in varying amounts of fat, tossing and stirring the food until it's cooked and never leaving it unattended. I think I use the term *frying* more for breaded or floured food. I've never understood the expression *pan frying*. Where else would you fry anything? In the air? *Pan broiling* means heating food in a skillet on the stove using little or no fat.

Deep-fat frying is quite simple if you use your deep-fry thermometer. The only times I goofed I played the temperature by ear and the fat was either too hot or too cool for the recipe. The fat will not spatter if you don't fill your skillet or casserole more than half-way with vegetable or peanut oil. Butter or margarine will smoke and burn and olive oil is usually too heavy for deep-fat frying. Lower the food gently into the fat, don't toss it in. When the food is cooked, remove it with a slotted spoon, or use a deep-fry basket and simply lift out the basket. When frying

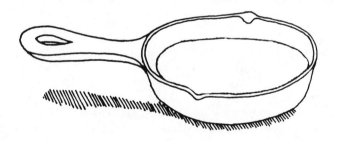

food in several batches, be sure to let the fat return to the correct temperature between batches. One thing more. The oil or fat used for this purpose can be reused again and again. I keep one container of oil for vegetables, another for poultry, and another for fish and shrimps. After use, remove the bits of food or crumbs that have accumulated by placing a fine strainer over a funnel in the container to pour back the clean fat. Throw it out only when the oil has turned dark and murky.

Stir-frying food means briskly tossing and stirring bite-sized pieces of food in a small amount of cooking oil over high heat for a few minutes. Recently a famous Chinese chef demonstrated this method on TV and I was relieved to hear that he too preferred using a heavy, round-edged skillet to that teetering, crazy Oriental utensil, the Chinese wok.

RENDERING FAT

Fat from a chicken or a goose (yum yum) or from beef or lamb can be *rendered* to be used as a marvelous base for many recipes. Cut up the fat into large pieces and place it in the top of a double boiler with a tablespoon of water until it has dissolved and turned clear. Then strain it through a double layer of cheesecloth placed over a can. Cover and keep it on hand in the refrigerator. It keeps almost forever.

BASTING

To *baste* use a spoon or bulb baster to keep food moist with fat or liquid during cooking.

DEGLAZING

After browning food in a skillet or pan *deglaze* the pan by adding liquid. Stir and scrape over high heat to loosen any particles of food that are stuck to the pan to incorporate them in the liquid. If you don't do this you may leave the best flavor behind.

DEGREASING

Removing unwanted fat from roasts, soups, sauces, stews, etc. can be achieved in several ways. The easiest method wherever possible is to allow the food to cool so the fat will rise to the surface and congeal, when it can easily be lifted off. Reheat the food. Or allow the food to rest for a few minutes. Much of the fat will rise and can be skimmed off with a spoon or sucked up with a bulb baster. If there's only a film of fat, draw a piece of paper toweling across the surface to absorb it. When a pan or roasting pan must be degreased during the cooking period, use pot holders to tip it slightly, then suck the fat from the corner with a bulb baster.

DOTTING

"Dot with butter" means to put little flat dime-sized or round pea-sized dabs of butter over the surface of the food. I usually pinch the dots right from a bar of butter with my fingers.

MARINATING

Foods are covered by seasoned liquids such as wine, vinegar, brine, or syrup —a *marinade*—for a period of time to tenderize and add flavor.

PURÉES

A *purée* is a food that has been reduced to a mash by being put through a sieve, food mill, or blender.

STIRRING, BEATING, WHIPPING, WHISKING, BLENDING, AND FOLDING

Stirring means to mix food with a spoon using a circular motion. *Beating* is an energetic form of stirring and can be achieved with a spoon, a fork, a whisk, or an electric or hand rotary beater. The hand method always involves the wrist and hand, never elbow or shoulder. If you're using the electric Mix-Master, you can walk away from the beating. *Whipping* by hand, as in the case of egg whites or cream, usually implies a circular lifting motion of the utensil to incorporate more air for fluffiness. *Whisking* is used a good deal in these recipes to make sure you'll use wire whisks to stir, beat, or whip the food. *Blending*, when used as a term *not* employing your electric blender, means to mix the food gently with less vigor than used for stirring. *Folding* a mixture of ingredients should be done as gently as folding a baby in your arms. Once in a while you can be briskly gentle. To fold cream, egg whites, and even flour into other ingredients, use a rubber spatula, drawing the edge down through the center of the bowl and scooping along the bottom, then bringing the mixture up on the sides with a circular swish. Continue doing this as you turn the bowl with your left hand until everything has been folded together without loss of fluffiness.

THE PASTRY BAG

I almost gave up decorating cakes, pies, and meringues, because the pastry bag gave me such trouble. Whenever I filled it with icing, cream, or meringue and squeezed, the filling squooshed from the wrong end onto my wrists and arms, or landed on the floor in great glops. Finally a friend showed me what to do. Place the empty bag over a bowl, nozzle side down. Fold back the sides across the rim of the bowl and pour in the filling. Pinch the top seam together and fold it over an inch deep several times. Then fold each corner toward the center, forming a triangular peak. Roll up the peak several times again. Squeeze the bag from the top as you would the end of a toothpaste tube, but use both hands.

If you prefer, you can substitute a metal icing tube which has a plunger and may seem easier to control. It takes longer, because of the small tube and constant refilling. Both the bag and the tube come with different-shaped nozzles for decorating. I most often use the large, plain round one and the star-shaped one for making rosettes.

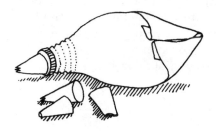

THICKENING WITH FLOUR, CORNSTARCH, AND ARROWROOT

Blending flour with butter to make a *roux* for thickening the base of sauces, gravies, soufflés, etc. is covered in the chapter on sauces as well as in individual recipes. However, when you want to add flour to thicken a soup or gravy *after* the liquid has cooked, always mix one or two tablespoons of quick-mix flour with about a quarter cup of the liquid you're using in a separate bowl. Make a smooth paste and add *that* to the larger amount of hot liquid before continuing to stir until the food has thickened.

Many recipes are thickened by adding cornstarch or arrowroot. Again, in order to avoid lumps, make a paste of either starch with double the amount of *cold* liquid before adding to the food you want to thicken. For example, you should stir till smooth

> 1 tablespoon cornstarch or arrowroot with
> 2 tablespoons cold water, milk, wine, or broth.

Arrowroot allows the food you're thickening to remain translucent. Cornstarch clouds it. Cornstarch is cheaper and more readily accessible and the cloudiness rarely matters. But arrowroot is blander and doesn't need a high temperature to lose a starchy taste. It's better in fruit puddings, for example.

SOFTENING AND DISSOLVING GELATIN

There are Escoffier-like ways of making natural gelatin from meat bones and fish skeletons. When my beef, chicken, or fish broth jells, I'm pleased as punch, and am sure to make good use of it. But if I need gelatin for sauces, puddings, glazes, or aspics, I don't fool around with anything except the commercial powdered gelatin. A few rules may be helpful. Before dissolving it, soften the gelatin by sprinkling it over a quarter cup of cold liquid and letting it rest for five or ten minutes. To dissolve use very hot, not boiling liquid. Stir until the liquid is clear with no remaining granules and then chill till set. Don't use more gelatin than required by the recipe or the food may get rubbery. To hasten setting, the dish can be set over a large bowl of ice cubes. Refrigerate, but don't freeze it or the gelatin will crack like crystal.

MOLDING AND UNMOLDING GELATIN AND ASPIC

I used to be intimidated by the entire notion, but it's easy. Unless the recipe asks that a mold be lightly oiled, dip it in cold water and knock out the excess before filling it and setting it gently in the refrigerator.

To unmold, run a sharp knife around the edge of the food in the mold. Fill the bottom of the sink or a larger bowl with very hot water and quickly dip in the mold just up to the brim for a *few seconds*. Place the serving dish on top of the mold and, keeping your fingers firmly on the mold as well as the plate, turn the whole thing upside down. The food will slip out to quiver like a jewel on its platter.

BREADING TECHNIQUE

For poultry, fish, veal, etc. *breading* before frying is almost identical. It is accomplished by dipping first into flour, then coating with a beaten egg, and finally with coarse, dry bread crumbs. I use three shallow plastic breading dishes that fit together with grooves. They can be ordered from a good kitchen catalogue. As a perfectly acceptable substitute, from left to right line up a piece of wax paper, a shallow bowl, and another piece of wax paper. On the dish or wax paper at the left spread about

> ¼ cup quick-mix flour.

In the dish in the center, lightly beat

> 1 whole egg

and on the last dish or paper sprinkle

> ½ cup bread crumbs.

These amounts should suffice for a dozen small chicken pieces, 6 veal scallops, or 6 small fish filets. If you need more of any of it, add it as you proceed. Wipe and dry the food, sprinkle it with a little salt and pepper. Then coat lightly with flour, dip to coat with egg, and finally roll in bread crumbs. The food can be prepared up to this point and covered with wax paper to rest in the refrigerator for several hours until time for the final preparation.

MELTING CHOCOLATE

If you've ever gone through the tedious, messy process of melting chocolate in a double boiler, you'll thank me for this easy trick. Break up the pre-scribed amount of chocolate into small pieces or buy chocolate bits. Place the pieces in a Pyrex measuring cup and barely cover them with boiling water. Let stand for 5 minutes. Hold the chocolate back with a rubber spatula as you tip the cup to pour out as much water as possible. The chocolate will be soft and ready to use.

SPRINKLING, DRIBBLING, OR DRIZZLING FROM A BOTTLE

Many recipes ask that you sprinkle or drizzle a little oil, vinegar, or wine over food. I learned a simple trick of achieving this right from the bottle. Tilt the bottle, supporting the bottom with your left hand. Place the thumb of your right hand over the opening, leaving just a little free space. Then shake the bottle to let the liquid sprinkle, dribble, or drizzle out in the amounts you determine.

FLAMBÉED FOOD

This definition comes at the end because it's usually the climax of a meal. Add the liquor or liqueur to your food. Light a match to it while you keep your head out of the way. Watch it flame. Swish the pan around. When the fire is out, serve and eat!

III. Eggs, Omelets, Crêpes, and Soufflés

As far as I'm concerned, every single egg that a hen lays is golden. I use jumbo or extra large and try to get them as fresh as possible.

BOILED EGGS

Don't laugh. My husband proved the adage, "He can't even boil an egg!" After putting two eggs in a pan on the stove, he left the room, the water evaporated, and the eggs exploded all over the newly painted ceiling, where I let them hang for a year in revenge.

Get an *egg piercer*. This great little gadget can be purchased at fancy kitchen supply stores. Or you can substitute one of those small push-pins with a nob on the end that are used for a bulletin board, or even a darning needle. Pierce the roundest end of the egg, were there is an air pocket. This tiny hole allows the air to escape so the shell won't crack in boiling water even if the egg has come straight from the refrigerator. After cooking, the egg will peel beautifully. Cover the number of eggs you want with boiling water in a saucepan into which they fit comfortably. If extra-large eggs have come from the refrigerator, set your timer to 5 minutes. If they're at room temperature, 4 minutes will do. After cooking, run them under cold water until they can be handled and give them a crack with a knife to sever the top. Scoop them out of their shells and serve with a dab of butter plus salt and pepper "to taste." To hard-boil eggs, set the timer for 10 minutes. If they boil much longer, the yolks will turn greenish and have a sulphury taste.

FRIED EGGS

For every 2 eggs, place 1 tablespoon butter into a Teflon- or porcelain-lined skillet over medium-low heat. Break the eggs and lower them gently into the skillet. Unless you're rash or the eggs aren't fresh, the yolks won't break. Spoon a little of the butter from the pan over the yolks and when they're as firm as you want, remove them with a spatula or slide them directly from the skillet to a plate. If you like a film over the yolks, put a lid over the pan during the last minute of cooking.

SCRAMBLED EGGS

For one serving break 2 eggs into a bowl and, if you like, add a tablespoon of milk or cream. Beat briefly with a fork until yolks and whites are just blended. Melt

1–2 tablespoons butter

in your lined skillet over medium heat. Add the egg mixture and stir lightly with a fork for a few minutes till it begins to set. When the eggs are as firm as you like them, turn them out of the pan onto a plate and season with salt and pepper.

Variations My two favorite additions are cream cheese or Boursin. After having stirred the eggs in the skillet for a minute, add the cheese in small, crumbled pieces. Continue to cook and stir until the cheese has begun to melt and blended with the eggs. To serve 4 people I use 8 eggs and crumble up a 3-ounce package of cream cheese, but only half that amount of Boursin, since it has a stronger flavor.

OMELETS

The praise received for preparing a classic French omelet far exceeds the effort. Once you get the hang of it, it isn't any more difficult than scrambling eggs. I once watched Rudolph the Omelet King make over a hundred omelets at a party and was inspired to try it myself. (I ran out to buy his famous omelet pan but later discovered that my iron Teflon-lined 8-inch skillet worked better. It needed no salting or special treatment to prevent sticking and could be used for other things without having to save it for omelets only. Since then I've tested a new nonstick [non-chemical] pan spray on both a plain iron skillet and a glazed porcelain one. It's tasteless, and really prevents sticking.)

Guests, serving plates, and forks should be as ready as your utensils and ingredients when you begin the omelets, because they cook for only a minute each. Per serving, into a bowl break

> *3 eggs*

and add

> *1 tablespoon beer*
> *a few dashes of Tabasco sauce*
> *a few gratings of pepper.*

Quickly blend everything together with a fork. (Don't beat the eggs or let them froth.) Over medium-high heat put into your skillet

> *1½ tablespoons butter*
> *or*
> *1 tablespoon butter when using pan spray.*

When the butter has foamed and the foam subsided, turn the egg mixture into the skillet. Make circular swishes with a fork to see that the eggs cover the bottom of the pan. Shake the pan by its handle with one hand and continue to make swirling motions with the fork, lifting the egg mixture slightly with each swirl. In about 30 seconds, tilt the pan up on one side and let the eggs slide down to the other, using the fork to flip them over like an envelope while they're sliding. Slip the omelet upside down onto a plate. It will look like a picture. Once the omelet is folded, the inside will continue to set, so don't be anxious if it still seemed a little moist. Salt to taste.

Variations These additions are made to the eggs after the first few swirls in the skillet, before they've begun to set.

> 2 tablespoons grated Gruyère or Parmesan
> or
> 1 tablespoon chopped herbs: parsley, tarragon, chives, thyme
> or
> 2 tablespoons sliced, sautéed mushrooms
> or
> 2 tablespoons minced ham or smoked beef.

My favorite luncheon or late snack omelet consists of this mixture added *just* before the omelet is folded:

> 2 tablespoons red caviar or black lumpfish caviar
> 2 tablespoons sour cream.

The top of each omelet can be garnished with chopped herbs or grated cheese.

POACHED EGGS

Herbert used to label poached eggs "Uta's Waterloo." Since countless tasty dishes use them as a main ingredient, I simply *had* to conquer this technique.

To produce those beautiful yolks suspended in a smooth sack of white, begin by parboiling the eggs while still in their shells. Use a slotted spoon to lower them, one at a time, into boiling water and slowly count to ten before removing. Have ready a small saucepan with boiling water and 2 teaspoons vinegar. Use a small wooden spoon to rotate the water, stirring faster and faster until there is a deep eddy in the middle. Holding it as close to the water as possible, immediately break the parboiled eggs into the eddy. Turn the heat to low and run the spoon handle around the edge of the pan to maintain the spinning for a second. In 4 minutes, remove the egg with a slotted spoon and proceed with the next egg.

or

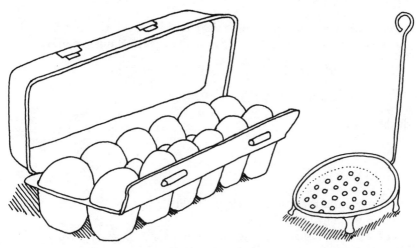

If the preceding method frightens you, get several metal egg poachers from a kitchen supply store or catalogue. They are perforated, oval in shape, and have a long handle by which to take them in and out of water. Set one or more of the poachers into the bottom of the saucepan with the boiling water and vinegar. Break a parboiled egg into each one and turn the heat to low. Poach for 4 minutes.

Poaching Ahead of Time

Many recipes that call for poached eggs are complicated, so it's important to know that they can be prepared many hours ahead of time. As each egg is completed, use the slotted spoon or skimmer to remove it from the pan and slide it directly into a bowl of iced water. This stops the cooking process and washes away the vinegar taste. Refrigerate in cold water till needed. To reheat, bring water to boil in a shallow skillet. Turn off the heat and slide the eggs into the hot water to rest for a minute until heated through. *Finito!*

EGGS BENEDICT

What a dish for a king! Aside from the poaching problem, the trick is to organize the time and assembly.

For each serving you will need:

> *2 eggs, poached*
> *1 English muffin, split in half*
> *2 thin slices of ham, boiled or Virginia*
> *2 tablespoons butter*
> *Hollandaise sauce (page 41)*

First poach the eggs and have them at hand in a bowl of cold water. On the stove set a skillet with water to reheat the eggs at the last minute.

Prepare a smaller skillet with

> *1 tablespoon butter*

in which to heat the ham.

Split the

> *English muffin*

and butter each half. Place it under the unlit broiler. Slice enough ham to cover each muffin half.

Set out the ingredients for blender Hollandaise (page 41). Now you're ready to start cooking on all burners.

Light the broiler to start the muffins.

Melt the butter in the skillet and heat the ham.

Bring the water to a boil in the skillet for the eggs.

When the muffins are golden, place them on individual plates and cover each half with a slice of hot ham. Turn off the broiler and place the muffins on their plates in the oven to keep warm.

Slip the eggs into the hot water in the skillet for a minute. Remove with a slotted skimmer and place one on top of the ham on each muffin.

Make the Hollandaise (page 41), which takes just seconds. Cover each egg with some sauce and serve. They're *fantastique*!

Traditionally, Eggs Benedict are garnished with a thin slice of black truffle, but they are out of the reach of my pocketbook even when readily available. A topping of freshly chopped parsley is lovely.

Variations Instead of ham, try slices of hot smoked beef or a mélange of creamed crabmeat.

A slice of broiled tomato on top of the ham will transform it into a luncheon dish.

Drop a poached egg into a large sautéed mushroom cap instead of on the muffin or onto a slice of coarse white bread that has been sautéed in Clarified Butter (page 46).

Cheese Sauce (page 39) makes a nice topping in place of Hollandaise.

CRÊPES (Serves 4)

Like omelets, many beginning cooks consider crêpes too difficult, but they're *so* easy and *so* good.

The batter should stand in the refrigerator for several hours before use, so I prepare it before my guests rise or even the night before. Into the blender put

> ½ cup cold water
> ½ cup cold milk
> 2 eggs
> 1 cup quick-mix flour
> 2 tablespoons melted butter
> a pinch of salt.

Blend for 1 minute. If any flour sticks to the sides of the blender, push it down with a scraper and blend again. Refrigerate at least 2 hours.

When everyone is almost ready to come to the table, I set out a variety of homemade jam and jelly to allow each person a choice of fillings for the crêpes.

Put a heatproof platter into a 200° oven and as the crêpes are turned out flip them onto the platter to keep hot until they're all done.

In an 8-inch Teflon- or porcelain-lined skillet or in a skillet that has been treated with nonstick spray, heat

> 1 tablespoon butter.

Tilt the pan to coat the bottom. When the butter foam has subsided over medium-high heat, pour in enough batter to equal the circumference of a small grapefruit. Tilt the pan quickly so the batter will thinly coat the bottom of the pan. Cook for a minute or so until the underside is golden, then flip it over with a spatula. Cook a little less than a minute and slide it onto the ovenproof platter. Don't worry that the last side will not look as pretty as the first. Continue making crêpes. You should end up with about a dozen. Add butter to the pan between crêpes if it gets too dry.

If you're serving more than 4 people, the recipe can be doubled. Crêpes can also be made ahead of time in large amounts, covered with plastic wrap, and frozen to be thawed and reheated in the oven just before a future meal.

Luncheon or Late Snack Variations   Place a few tablespoons of one of the following stuffings across the center of each crêpe and roll it up. Place the stuffed crêpes side by side in a buttered shallow baking dish, dot with butter or cover with a white sauce (page 38), and heat through in a preheated 350° oven for 15 minutes.

> Ravioli di Bacci spinach stuffing (page 111)
> Cheese Stuffing for Manicotti (page 106) or Ravioli (page 111)
> Chicken and Mushroom filling for Manicotti (page 108)

LILY'S ORANGE PANCAKES

Lily Lodge Marcus is a beautiful actress, an extraordinary mother, gives concert readings, and makes terrific hot orange pancakes. I dislike the average American pancake that tastes like cotton and fills you up tediously. Consequently, when Lily surprised me one sunny Montauk morning with something that looked similar, my heart sank. But when I took the first bite, I was delighted by this light, fluffy dish, quite unlike its American cousin. It's really more a blinz than a pancake.

Orange Sauce (Serves 12 to 16)

Make the sauce ahead of time. It keeps in the refrigerator for weeks and weeks. I make large amounts so I always have some on hand. Reheat it just before serving and add a teaspoon or more of Grand Marnier as a final fillip! The recipe is sufficient to serve four big pancake eaters for three or four breakfasts. It can easily be cut in half.

Use a vegetable peeler to peel the rind of two oranges. Chop it coarsely and boil it for 5 minutes covered with water and a pinch of baking soda. Wash off and drain the chopped rind and set it to one side.

Squeeze the juice of

> *8 oranges.*

In a large saucepan melt

> *1 stick butter (8 tablespoons).*

Add

> *the orange juice*
> *1 cup confectioner's sugar*
> *the chopped orange rind.*

Bring the sauce to a boil, lower the heat, and simmer for 10 minutes. In a small bowl make a smooth paste of

> *1½ tablespoons cornstarch or arrowroot*
> *3 tablespoons cold water.*

Stir this mixture into the orange sauce, cooking until it thickens slightly. Pour it over the hot pancakes, or let it cool before refrigerating in a sealed jar to reheat when needed.

The Pancakes (Serves 4)

From start to finish they require only a few minutes.

In a bowl blend together

> *1 cup quick-mix flour*
> *1 tablespoon sugar*
> *1 teaspoon salt.*

Briskly fold in

> *1 cup small curd cottage cheese*
> *1 cup sour cream.*

Use a rubber scraper to beat up the ingredients. The batter will still look slightly lumpy because of the cottage cheese.

Fold in

> *4 beaten eggs*

till just blended.

Brush a Teflon griddle or large skillet with a little melted butter and heat it. Spoon the batter onto the griddle, using about ¼ cup for each pancake. About 4 will fit onto a 12-inch griddle and 3 into a 12-inch skillet. Cook over medium-high heat a minute or two on each side until golden. Immediately serve two piled on top of each other and slather with orange sauce. Even dieters can't resist these treats for their Sunday breakfast.

HASKEL AND MARILYN'S BAKED PANCAKE (Serves 2 to 4)

Haskel Frankel was the collaborator on my book *Respect for Acting*. I simply couldn't bear his not being a part of this book. He and his wife gave me the recipe, which is truly worthy of their talents.

Preheat the oven to 400°.

On top of the stove place a 10-inch shallow casserole, preferably Teflon or porcelain lined, or a 9-inch deeper one. Put in

> *4 tablespoons butter (half a stick).*

In a bowl combine

> *½ cup unbleached flour*
> *½ cup milk*
> *1 teaspoon sugar*
> *a pinch of salt*
> *several gratings of nutmeg.*

Fold in

> *2 lightly beaten eggs.*

Melt the butter in the casserole and immediately pour the batter on top of it. *Don't* stir it. Bake it in the oven for about 18 minutes. It should brown lightly and puff up like a balloon, rising above the sides of the shallow casserole. Sprinkle the pancake with

> *2 tablespoons confectioner's sugar*

and return it to the oven for a few minutes. Sprinkle the pancake with

> *1 tablespoon lemon juice.*

This will make it sink, flatten, and turn crispy. Bring it to the table and if you feel it needs it, serve with jam or jelly.

PRESERVING EGG YOLKS AND WHITES

Before proceeding with soufflés I'd like to explain a few things about eggs that may be of interest to kitchen novices.

Many recipes call for either the yolk or the white of an egg. The unused half used to trouble me. Egg whites keep well for several weeks in a tightly sealed container in the refrigerator, and for months in the freezer. To reuse frozen ones, thaw and bring them to room temperature. When measuring the needed amount remember that each large egg white equals one ounce (or eight to a cup). Egg yolks don't freeze well but can be kept in the refrigerator up to a week when carefully covered with a film of water or milk. Cover with plastic wrap.

Obvious uses for the extra whites are in the meringue family. Many sauces call for one or two yolks, and see recipe for Fanny's Mayonnaise (page 42).

SEPARATING, BEATING, AND FOLDING EGGS

Separating the yolk from the whites used to scare me silly. The knowledge that the tiniest fleck of yellow escaping into the white would prevent the white from whipping properly made me even more nervous. It's hard to scoop out intact! If you have qualms, when doing a whole batch, separate the eggs one at a time, always dropping the white into a separate bowl before adding it to the rest. Then you won't ruin the whole amount because of one mistake.

Give the middle of the egg a sharp blow against the edge of a glass or bowl and break it in half. Holding one half in each hand, slip the yolk back and forth between the shell halves, allowing the white to run into a bowl. When the yolk is free of white drop it gently into another bowl. A trick that works for some people is to break the whole egg into the palm of your hand and to separate your fingers slightly to let the white run through into a bowl, leaving the yolk intact in your palm.

Beating whites correctly is important in hundreds of recipes, not just soufflés. The most highly recommended way is to beat them in a copper bowl with a wire whisk. (To save time I use the rotary beater or my Mix-Master.) The principle involves proper aeration of the whites while beating. When using an electric hand rotary beater or the regular rotary beater, keep lifting the beater while you turn the bowl. Always have the whites at room temperature. Add a tiny pinch of salt when the whites have begun to foam and later, when they have stiffened a little, add a pinch of cream of tartar. When they stand in stiff peaks they're finished.

Folding egg whites into a batter is sometimes made to sound more difficult than it is. Usually the batter needs a little lightening up to begin. Simply beat one quarter of the stiff whites into it before folding in the remainder as described on page 18. Remember, it's better to have a few lumps of white than to overfold the batter.

Folding whites into a sauce is easier because it's not *as* important. Use the same motion.

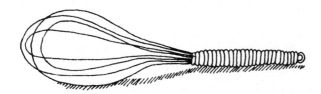

Note: The recipes for all soufflés serve 4 to 6 people. The ingredients for all except the grits soufflé can be cut in half to serve 3 or 4. In that case use a 1½-quart casserole or soufflé dish and reduce the baking time by 5 or 10 minutes.

PLAIN SOUFFLÉ (Serves 4 to 6)

Butter a standard soufflé dish or a deep round casserole. Into the bottom of the dish sprinkle

> 2 *tablespoons bread crumbs*
> > *or*
> 2 *tablespoons grated Parmesan*
> > *or*
> 1 *tablespoon of each.*

Rotate the dish, shake it, and tip it on its side until coated with crumbs. Invert it to knock out excess crumbs and set the dish to one side.

Preheat the oven to 400°.

Now make the basic cream sauce, which is the base for most soufflés.

In a large skillet melt

> 3 *tablespoons butter*

and blend in

> 3 *tablespoons quick-mix flour*

with a wooden spoon. Do it over medium heat, being careful that the butter-flour mixture doesn't brown.

Slowly pour in

> 1 *cup warm milk.*

Stir with a whisk until the sauce is smooth and thick. Remove the skillet from heat.

Separate

> 6 *eggs*

reserving the whites in a large bowl while you blend each yolk one at a time into the sauce. Season the sauce with

> ½ *teaspoon salt*
> *a few gratings of pepper and nutmeg.*

Beat the whites with a pinch of salt until they form stiff peaks, then gently fold them into the sauce. Turn the mixture into the prepared soufflé dish or casserole and place into the preheated oven. Immediately turn down the heat to 375°. Bake for 30 minutes, then stick a cake tester or sharp knife into the center of the soufflé. If it doesn't come out clean, bake another 5 minutes. Serve at once before the soufflé has a chance to sink.

(Fancy wax-paper collars, which are sometimes tied around the top of the dish for extra high rising, are too much trouble for me.)

CHEESE SOUFFLÉ (Serves 4 to 6)

Follow the recipe for the plain soufflé until you separate the eggs. Then to the sauce add

¾ cup coarsely grated Swiss, Gruyère, or Emmenthaler cheese.

Whisk over medium heat until the cheese is blended and begins to melt. Continue the previous recipe by adding the egg yolks and seasoning, then folding in the whites. Bake. Sprinkle

2 tablespoons grated cheese

over the top before serving.

Other Variations Before adding the eggs to the sauce, fold in

1 cup of diced cooked chicken or ham
    or
1 cup of sliced, sautéed mushrooms
    or
1 cup of flaked tuna or crab meat.

If you are using any of these variations try

1 cup hot chicken broth

in place of the milk when making the cream sauce base.

CONNIE'S GRITS SOUFFLÉ (Serves 4 to 6)

Constance Greene introduced me not only to all the secrets and wonders of Montauk, but to this perfect dish so excellent with roast chicken, lamb, pork, or baked fish. If you think you don't like hominy grits, try this soufflé anyway, or substitute corn meal.

Make

> *2 cups of* cooked *Quick Grits*

following the recipe on the box that says "to serve 4."

Into the top of a double boiler put

> *3 tablespoons butter*
> *1 cup milk*
> *1 teaspoon sugar*
> *1 teaspoon salt*
> *a pinch of pepper.*

Bring it just to a boil over direct heat, then stir in the cooked grits till smooth. Set it over a few inches of boiling water and cook for 10 minutes before adding

> *1 cup coarsely grated Swiss or cheddar cheese.*

Continue to stir and cook until the cheese has melted.
Preheat the oven to 350°.
Butter a standard soufflé dish or deep casserole and set it to one side.

In a large bowl beat

> *4 eggs*

till foamy. Carefully add the mixture from the double boiler and gently fold in the beaten eggs. Pour everything into the buttered casserole and bake for 1 hour. Serve at once.

IV. Sauces, Butters, and Dressings

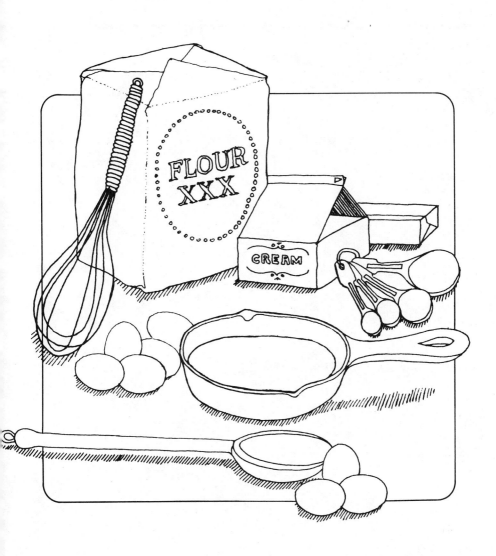

Beautiful velvety sauces can turn plain dishes into gourmet sensations. I used to be put off and confused by fancy names. Béchamel, velouté, suprême, Mornay, Allemande are all the same basic white sauce with additions of cream, cheese, eggs, or herbs. The liquid varies from milk or cream to chicken, beef, or fish broth or wine.

The principle for making these sauces is the same. The base is *roux* (pronounced "roo"), which is a butter-and-flour mixture. When heating the butter don't let it turn brown. Be sure to use the quick-mix flour described on page 10, which blends nicely with the butter, cuts down on cooking time, and never tastes starchy. Use a wooden spoon to blend and cook the butter and flour. Always heat the liquid before adding to the roux. Add egg yolks only after the sauce has been removed from heat or beat them into a little cool liquid before adding to the sauce, so they won't curdle. Use a heavy pan or skillet, preferably Teflon or porcelain lined, to prevent scorching or sticking. If you heed this advice your sauces will always be perfect!

BASIC WHITE SAUCE (Béchamel, velouté)

In a heavy skillet melt

> *2 tablespoons butter*

over medium heat.

Slowly blend in

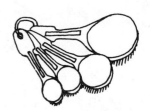

> *2 tablespoons quick-mix flour.*

Cook for a minute or two. Add

> *1½ cups heated milk (or chicken or fish broth or white wine).*

Whisk the mixture until it turns smooth and thickens slightly.

Add

> *salt and white pepper to taste.*

You will have almost 1½ cups of sauce.

RICH WHITE SAUCE (Suprême)

Just before seasoning the finished basic sauce, whisk in

> *½ cup heavy cream*

1 tablespoon at a time. You will have 2 cups of sauce.

WHITE SAUCE WITH EGGS (Allemande)

Let the basic sauce cool for a minute. One at a time beat in

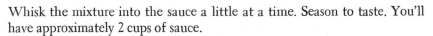

>   *2 egg yolks.*

Reheat the sauce for a minute over low heat.

Or lightly beat

>   *2 egg yolks in*
>   *½ cup of your cool cooking liquid (milk or broth).*

Whisk the mixture into the sauce a little at a time. Season to taste. You'll have approximately 2 cups of sauce.

CHEESE SAUCE (Mornay)

Coarsely grate ½ cup of Swiss, Gruyère, or Emmenthaler cheese. Make the basic sauce and whisk in the cheese a little at a time until it has blended and melted. Season to taste. Makes a scant 2 cups.

CAPER SAUCE

Excellent for poached fish or lamb.
Make the roux and whisk in

>   *1½ cups white wine or fish broth*

instead of milk.
At the last minute fold in

>   *3 tablespoons drained capers.*

MUSTARD SAUCE

Soften

>   *3 tablespoons butter*

and blend with

>   *3 tablespoons Dijon mustard.*

Whisk the mixture into the Basic White Sauce (page 38). Delicious with fish or ham.

Brown Sauces

I have to confess that the classic French brown sauce, requiring many hours of simmering, is too bothersome for me. I take short cuts. When making braised beef or lamb, or potted stuffed pork, I usually have ready-made liquid for a proper brown sauce, and I will explain how to use it in the specific recipes. However, when I need a brown sauce quickly, I make this one.

UTA'S BROWN SAUCE

Using a heavy skillet over medium heat, melt and cook till brown

>   *2 tablespoons butter.*

Blend in and cook

>   *2 tablespoons quick-mix flour.*

Add

>   *1 cup canned condensed beef bouillon.*

Whisk the sauce until it is smooth and has thickened.

Add

>   *1 tablespoon dry vermouth*
>   *a pinch of dried tarragon*
>   *salt and pepper to taste.*

MADEIRA SAUCE

Instead of the vermouth, add

>   *½ cup dry Madeira wine*

to the brown sauce, and eliminate the herbs.

Variations for White and Brown Sauces
1) Start by sautéing a tablespoon or more of minced shallots or onions in 3 tablespoons butter. Add the flour and liquid and finish your sauce. Or add a pressed garlic clove.
2) When the sauce has thickened, whisk in a teaspoon of tomato paste or season with a few dashes of Tabasco or Worcestershire sauce.
3) Try different kinds of dry red wines for the brown sauce.
Once you've begun to improvise, you'll see what fun it can be.

UNCOOKED COLD MUSTARD SAUCE

Blend together

> ½ cup mayonnaise
> ½ cup sour cream
> 2 tablespoons Dijon mustard
> 1 teaspoon lemon juice.

Stir and taste in case you'd like a stronger mustard flavor.

HOLLANDAISE

I've had better luck with the speedy Hollandaise sauce that can be turned out in a blender than with the supposedly finer sauce, tediously whipped up in the top of a double boiler. If your blender has an open top so that liquid added while it's whirling away splatters on the walls, simply put a collar of foil around the top, fastened by a rubber band. Fold the foil toward the center, leaving a hole the size of a lemon through which to dribble liquid; in this case, melted butter.

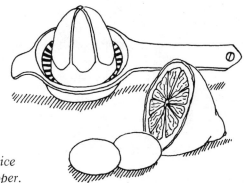

Into the blender put

> 3 egg yolks
> 1 tablespoon lemon juice
> a pinch of salt and pepper.

In a saucepan melt

> 1 stick unsalted butter (8 tablespoons).

Don't let it brown.

Blend the eggs and juice at high speed for a few seconds, then *dribble* in the butter while the blending continues until all the butter except the white lumps and residue at the bottom of the pan has been absorbed. Serve at once.

You will have a scant cup, sufficient for 3 servings of Eggs Benedict (page 27) or 4 servings of a vegetable such as asparagus or broccoli. If you need more, make another batch. Don't simply double the recipe.

DELUXE HOLLANDAISE

When the blender Hollandaise sauce is completed, fold in

> 3 *stiffly beaten egg whites*
>> *or*
>
> ½ *cup stiffly whipped cream.*

When using the sauce for fish or chicken, try substituting

> 2 *tablespoons fish or chicken broth*

for the lemon juice.

BÉARNAISE

Although not as thick as hand-beaten Béarnaise, this sauce is so delicious over eggs, fish, chicken, or filet of beef that I pass it on for your pleasure.

Into a heavy saucepan put

> 1 *tablespoon minced shallots or scallions (white part only)*
> ⅓ *cup dry white wine*
> ¼ *cup white wine vinegar*
> 1 *tablespoon minced fresh tarragon (or* ½ *teaspoon dried)*
> *a pinch of salt*
> *liberal gratings of pepper.*

Boil down this mixture uncovered for about 8 minutes or until it has reduced to a scant 3 tablespoons. Let it cool. A little more will evaporate during the cooling. Now make the Hollandaise sauce in the blender, using the above mixture in place of the lemon juice. Bingo!

FANNY'S MAYONNAISE

I think it's hilarious that I got this excellent recipe from Fanny Warburg, one of the nurses at my doctor's office—so many of my visits there include lectures about avoiding high cholesterol. In any event, it's awfully good. Into the blender put

> 2 *egg yolks*
> 2 *teaspoons sugar*
> 1 *teaspoon salt*
> ¼ *cup white wine vinegar or 2 tablespoons cider vinegar plus*
>> 2 *tablespoons lemon juice.*

If the vinegar is poor, the mayonnaise will be poor. That's also true for the peanut oil. Blend this mixture for about 20 seconds and then *slowly* dribble in

> *1 cup olive oil.*

Toward the end of the dribbling, watch the sauce for thickness. You may not want to use up the oil. If it gets too thick, add a teaspoon of lemon juice.

You will have about 2 cups of mayonnaise, which keeps beautifully in a sealed jar in the refrigerator.

TARTAR SAUCE

Mix together

> *1 cup of Fanny's Mayonnaise (page 42)*
> *2 teaspoons Dijon mustard*
> *1 tablespoon chopped parsley*
> *1 tablespoon minced shallots or scallions*
> *1 chopped sweet pickle or gherkin*
> *1 tablespoon drained capers*
> *a few drops of lemon juice.*

Chill and serve with seafood.

RÉMOULADE

To the Tartar sauce, simply add

> *1 teaspoon anchovy paste.*

Other Variations   Into 1 cup of Fanny's Mayonnaise (page 42) fold ½ cup of stiffly whipped cream. Or fold in your favorite chopped herbs. A few tablespoons of prepared mustard or horseradish added to 1 cup of mayonnaise is nice. Experiment.

TWO GREAT BASIL SAUCES

PESTO

If you have a garden or a window box, grow *lots* of basil. I don't think you can have too much of it once you know what to do with it. A pesto sauce elevates pasta to another planet. Make it in late summer when basil is abundant in great batches, pack it into sterilized jars, seal, and store in the freezer, where it will keep for a year. Give jars to your friends. A tiny little jar at a specialty food store is unbelievably expensive. Try a tablespoon mixed in a salad or a teaspoon on scrambled eggs. Try it on toast. A little stirred into a soup or purée of peas or lentils can be exquisite. Use it as a stuffing for cherry tomatoes (page 265).

Into the blender put

> 1 cup good olive oil
> 3 tablespoons softened butter
> 3 large garlic cloves, peeled and halved
> ½ cup freshly grated Parmesan
> ¼ cup pine nuts or 6 walnuts
> a pinch of salt and
> ½ cup firmly packed fresh basil leaves.

Blend for a few minutes until the sauce is thick and smooth. Pour into jars and seal. Refrigerate or freeze whatever you're not using at once.

PISTOU

Coarsely chop the following herbs until you have

> 1 cup basil
> ¼ cup parsley
> ¼ cup chives
> 3 tablespoons fresh tarragon
> 2 large garlic cloves.

Put the chopped herbs into the blender with

> ⅔ cup good olive oil
> 2 tablespoons lemon juice.

Blend till smooth and set aside. Remove seeds and white veins and cut into thin strips

> 1 large green pepper.

Sauté the strips in a heavy skillet until soft in

> 2 tablespoons olive oil.

In boiling water blanch

> 2 large tomatoes

and slip off their skins.

Squeeze the tomatoes gently to remove as much liquid as possible. Cut them in half and push out the seeds between the membranes. Chop the tomatoes coarsely and add to the peppers in the skillet. Cook and stir for about 5 minutes, until most of the liquid has evaporated. Pour the herb-and-oil mixture from the blender into the skillet and cook and stir for another minute. Add salt and pepper to taste. Done!

Pistou can be used wherever you might use Pesto but I've almost always used up this amount at once over poached chicken or fish. It keeps well in the refrigerator and can be reheated.

CHAUD-FROID SAUCE

The peculiar name probably comes from the fact that the sauce starts out hot and ends up cold. It is out of this world in appearance and taste but you really shouldn't make it unless you can get your hands on fresh tarragon. When the tarragon in my garden puts out its green spikes I wait for the first hot day to make Chaud-froid Sauce for cold poached chicken breasts. It's also beautiful over cold poached fish, in which case substitute fish broth for the chicken broth. Much of the splendor depends on the presentation of the dish, so be sure the chicken or fish is beautifully arranged on a platter before glazing with this sauce.

In a saucepan simmer

> 1 can condensed canned chicken broth with
> 1 thinly sliced carrot
> 1 thinly sliced onion
> ¼ teaspoon thyme.

After 30 minutes add

> 1¼ cup heavy cream
> 2 sprigs fresh tarragon.

Simmer the mixture uncovered for 15 minutes longer to let the liquid reduce a little. Strain it through a sieve. You should have about 2 cups.

Add salt and pepper to taste. In a small bowl sprinkle

> 1 envelope gelatin over
> 3 tablespoons dry vermouth

and let soften for 5 minutes.

Stir the gelatin into the strained sauce and dissolve it completely over low heat. Pour the sauce into a bowl and set the bowl over a dish of cracked ice cubes to start the jelling process. In 20 to 30 minutes, check to see if the sauce has begun to set around the edges of the bowl. If so, remove it from the ice cubes and whisk briskly till smooth. Spoon a thin layer over the bottom of a serving platter. Refrigerate the platter for about 10 minutes until the layer has set firmly. Then arrange the cold chicken breasts attractively on top of it and spoon another thin layer of sauce over the chicken. Refrigerate another 10 minutes or till set and repeat these layers of sauce until it is used up. Leave the bowl of sauce on the counter between layering. If it gets too thick or lumpy, whisk it hard or, if necessary, melt it down again for a few seconds over low heat till smooth.

The final garnish is the crown. Prepare several sprigs of tarragon by dropping them into boiling water for 15 seconds. Remove and refresh the sprigs in ice water for a few seconds, then dry on toweling before arranging them in a design on top of the last layer of Chaud-froid Sauce.

The dish can be prepared in the morning and kept in the refrigerator covered by an inverted bowl or plastic wrap. It may sound like a lot of work, but the result makes it worth while.

This book is peppered with many other sauces belonging to a specific dish. Two special dessert sauces can be found on page 334.

Interesting Butters

CLARIFIED BUTTER

I'm often surprised how many people who cook well don't seem to know what it means to clarify butter. Little white lumps are always found floating on melted butter and clinging to the bottom of the pan. This residue causes butter to burn and smoke at high temperatures and makes the food stick. Many recipes ask that the butter be "clarified" of this residue by the following method:

Melt the butter over low heat for a minute or two. Take the saucepan or skillet to the sink and use a rubber scraper to skim off floating white scum. Tilt the pan to expose the residue at the bottom and scrape it out, or pour the clear butter into another pan, leaving the residue behind.

BROWN OR BLACK BUTTER

Clarify the needed amount of butter. Heat it slowly until it turns brown, or even darker for *beurre noire*.

LEMON BUTTER

Add

>2 teaspoons lemon juice to
>4 tablespoons clarified butter or browned butter.

Stir in

>1 teaspoon chopped parsley (optional).

SNAIL OR CLAM BUTTER

For 2 dozen snails or 3 dozen steamed clams.

Soften

>2 sticks butter (½ pound).

With a fork blend in

>1 tablespoon minced shallots
>2 large peeled garlic cloves, pressed
>1 tablespoon minced parsley
>1 tablespoon minced chervil (or a pinch of dried)
>a pinch of salt
>a few gratings of pepper.

Stuff snail shells as described on page 69.

Melt the mixture and serve as a dip for clams or Poached Shrimp (page 71).

BUTTERED CRUMBS

Into a large skillet pour

>½ cup clarified butter
>1 teaspoon lemon juice.

Stir in

>½ cup dry bread crumbs.

Cook and stir over low heat until the crumbs turn golden. Pour over vegetables.

GRATINS

My interpretation of a dish that has been gratinéed is one covered with a layer of bread crumbs and/or grated cheese, dotted with butter, and placed under the broiler for a minute to form a golden crust.

Dressings

I want to start out with a dressing I use almost exclusively. I vary it with additional ingredients on occasion and use it not only on salads but as a marinade. It can be made in large amounts to be on hand for any occasion. I've ignored the rules that insist that a dressing be made just before using, and keep it bottled in the refrigerator up to two weeks. It does *not* lose flavor or turn stale.

UTA'S FRENCH DRESSING

Into a bowl put

> *2 to 3 cloves pressed garlic*
> *3 tablespoons Dijon mustard*
> *¼ cup white wine or tarragon vinegar*
> *¼ cup fresh lemon juice*
> *½ teaspoon salt*
> *freshly ground pepper*
> *a few gratings of nutmeg.*

Beat the ingredients with a whisk until well blended. Then slowly dribble in

> *1½–2 cups olive oil*

while continuing to whisk. Soon the dressing will start to thicken. Pour it into a bottle and seal. Keep in the refrigerator and shake up vigorously before serving. If it has separated, let it return to room temperature before shaking.

Variations

To

> *1 cup of Uta's French Dressing*

add

> *2–3 tablespoons crumbled Roquefort or blue cheese*
> *or*
> *chopped fresh herbs or a pinch of dried herbs.*

JOHN'S SWEET DRESSING

I'm indebted to the young actor John Lack for this delicious, unusual dressing, which is particularly good on spinach salad (page 262). Like my own dressing, it can be bottled and refrigerated till needed.

Mix together

> ¼ *cup safflower or peanut oil*
> 2 *tablespoons white wine vinegar*
> ¼ *cup ketchup*
> 1 *tablespoon minced or grated onion*
> 2 *tablespoons sugar*
> *a pinch of salt and pepper.*

Shake well.

HORSERADISH DRESSING

This dressing is good on boiled beef or ham, hot or cold.

Stir

> 3 *tablespoons prepared horseradish into*
> 1 *cup sour cream (yoghurt for dieters).*

SWEET OR SOUR CREAM DRESSING

This dressing is lovely in the summer for mushrooms or cold cooked vegetables.

Combine

> ½ *cup heavy sweet cream or sour cream*
> 1 *tablespoon grated onion plus the juice*
> 1 *teaspoon sugar*
> ½ *teaspoon salt*
> ¼ *teaspoon white pepper*
> 1 *tablespoon chopped fresh dill (optional).*

Blend well and chill.

MARY LA'S MUSTARD

Mary Mathews is one of my closest friends. A birthday or Christmas wouldn't be complete without a jar of her sweet homemade mustard. Try it spread over cold meat or poultry in a sandwich, or as a glaze on ham or roast lamb.

Mix

> 1 pound dark brown sugar with
> 1 small 2-ounce can of dry mustard.

In a saucepan heat

> ¼ cup tarragon vinegar

to the boiling point and whisk in the dry sugar and mustard till melted and smooth.

Add

> 2 teaspoons chopped fresh tarragon (a pinch of dried).

Cool it and pour it into several small jars. Seal and store on the pantry shelf. Don't refrigerate or the mustard will turn granular.

MARINADE

For tenderizing and adding exceptional flavors, marinades are an important part of many recipes. I have specified most of them where necessary for poultry, meat, or vegetables. When experimenting with your own, remember that Uta's French Dressing (page 48) works as a marinade all by itself. Additions of wine, chopped herbs, and onions make pleasant variations. A few crushed juniper berries add a wild game flavor. Soy sauce is tasty and helps to tenderize, but use it sparingly because most brands contain monosodium glutamate.

Roast lamb or pork or London broil are delicious after having been marinated overnight in a covered bowl in a mixture of:

> 1 cup beer
> ¼ cup soy sauce
> ½ teaspoon Worcestershire sauce
> 1 tablespoon dry mustard
> 1 teaspoon ground ginger
> 6 tablespoons orange marmalade
> 3 cloves pressed garlic
> ½ teaspoon salt
> ¼ teaspoon ground pepper.

Important: After marinating meat or poultry that is to be browned or roasted, always drain and dry thoroughly.

Unless leftover marinades have been used up in a sauce or during basting, bottle them, seal, and refrigerate, and use again.

JIM'S HERB VINEGARS

For those who love fresh herbs and have a garden in which to grow them, herb vinegars are delicious. They also make marvelous presents. Jim Carruthers is a fine actor and a gourmet cook. He gave me my first mixed-herb vinegar and put me up to the idea.

MIXED-HERB VINEGAR

To

> *1 gallon cider or white wine vinegar*

Add

> *12 pepper corns*
> *sprigs of thyme, tarragon, rosemary, and chervil*
> *1 parsley root*
> *a handful of chopped parsley sprigs.*

Bottle and seal it for several weeks before straining through cheesecloth and dividing among smaller sterilized containers or bottles. Seal again and store till needed. (For sterilizing bottles or jars, see page 339.)

TARRAGON VINEGAR

Crush the leaves of

> *1 dozen tarragon sprigs*

and add them to

> *2 cups warm white wine vinegar*
> *1 peeled garlic clove.*

In 3 days remove the garlic clove and seal tightly.

BASIL VINEGAR

To

> *1 quart warmed white wine or cider vinegar*

Add

> *2 stalks of basil, containing at least 8 leaves on each.*

Seal tightly.

UTA'S HOMEMADE VINEGAR

There are books about distilling your own vinegar. The process seems more complicated than wine making, in my opinion. I use a trick that seems to work just fine.

Into a heavy glass bottle, preferably with a glass stopper that isn't completely air tight, pour

> *¼ cup malt vinegar (known as "the mother").*

Add any leftover wine after parties. I mix all wines, red, white, and rosé, as long as they're dry. After a while, I accumulate enough to almost fill the bottle. This vinegar is highly prized and only trotted out for special recipes or occasions.

V. Hors d'Oeuvre, First Course, Luncheon, or Snack?

Many of the recipes in this chapter can be used on any of the above occasions, so I've decided to put them together and let you choose your own time and place.

Ideally an hors d'oeuvre should whet the appetite for the coming meal. Things like a fondu or large quiche simply whet mine for more of the same.

When I make a spectacular platter of appetizers, I try to see that everyone piles his plate at the outset to avoid continual rising for more. Haven't you ogled a platter across the room and been too shy or lazy to ask for more? I serve buffet suppers only in case of dire necessity because of discomfort and confusion; trying to cut food on a teetering plate in my lap, tipping drinks at my elbow, disoriented conversation across a crowded room seem the antithesis of the intimacy that can be achieved around a table.

If the request for a drink is unusual and I'm not sure how to make it, I ask the guest to do it himself, provided the ingredients are on hand. More and more people seem to prefer an aperitif wine with the hors d'oeuvres so I try to have vermouth, sherry, Cinzano, or Dubonnet on hand. These wines are nice when served plain, on the rocks, or even with a little club soda and a piece of lemon rind. On very special occasions I offer a drink I sampled for the first time in Vienna called Sekt-Orange: freshly squeezed orange juice mixed half and half with chilled champagne. It may sound outlandish but it's *wunderbar*, producing an all-its-own flavor. There's a fine German champagne, much less expensive than a French counterpart, which I don't mind mixing with the juice. Or try adding a frozen cranberry cube to a glass of champagne. I keep a tray ready in the freezer. (Either of these drinks will guarantee eternal friendship when served with a Sunday morning breakfast!)

In an emergency or when I've had little time for preparation, I serve some of the following easy and rather conventional appetizers on a nice assortment of crackers such as rice wafers, English biscuits, Scandinavian rye wafers, sesame or onion crackers, or on very thin rounds of black bread.

> Cream cheese with slices of smoked salmon or herring
> A favorite sausage like German Teewurst
> Hungarian salami
> Goose-liver wurst or a pâté
> Interesting cheese, soft or hard
> Unsalted butter or cream cheese with black or red caviar.

Beluga caviar has never been within my budget. A few times when someone gave me a jar, I hoarded it for myself and my husband. However, there is a perfectly good lumpfish caviar imported from Denmark or Finland which keeps for ages on the pantry shelf unopened and for several weeks in the refrigerator once you've started to use it. Red caviar is more expensive but still possible to serve once in a while for an event.

Small bowls of mixed nuts and Mexican pepita or sunflower seeds can be served when time is short.

Sometimes I cheat and deceive the guests by popping pre-packaged stuffed puff pastry into the oven. Some of the brands are *almost* as good as homemade ones. Frozen tiny wieners wrapped in dough or cheese or shrimp in puff pastry thaw in half an hour and bake in fifteen minutes. They look festive too.

For dieters or health nuts, serve thin strips of raw vegetables such as carrots, green peppers, celery, cucumbers, scallions, etc. Raw cauliflower florets can be attractively mounded in the center of a platter and surrounded with the colorful vegetable strips. Cut up the vegetables in the morning and keep them in a bowl of ice water in the refrigerator till needed.

Dips for chips or raw vegetables have become so commonplace that I draw the line at two. Here they are.

RED CAVIAR AND SOUR CREAM DIP (Serves 6 to 8)

(Substitute yoghurt for sour cream for dieters.)

In a bowl gently blend

> *1 cup sour cream*

with

> *1 tablespoon chopped dill or a pinch of dry dill weed*
> *1 tablespoon grated onion*
> *½ teaspoon lemon juice*
> *1 tablespoon chopped parsley*
> *a pinch of white pepper.*

Fold in

> *4 ounces of red caviar.*

Chill before serving.

UTA'S GUACAMOLE

Peel and pit

> *2 ripe avocados.*

Put the avocados into the blender with

> *1 tablespoon chopped onion*
> *1 or 2 chopped garlic cloves*
> *1 teaspoon olive oil*
> *1 tablespoon lemon juice*
> *salt and pepper to taste*
> *a pinch of chili powder (optional).*

Blend till smooth and chill for several hours. Serve as a dip or spread, or try stuffing cherry tomatoes with 1 teaspoon guacamole in each.

Now it starts to get more interesting. The following hors d'oeuvres can be served separately or in combinations. They're all easy to make.

MARY LA'S PEANUT-BUTTER STICKS (Serves 18)

Mary Mathews of mustard fame gave me a tin of these crunchies for Christmas. As an accompaniment to cocktails they are sensational. Just don't put out too many because the guests will be unable to resist them and will consequently ruin their appetites.

Cut the crusts from

> *1 loaf of thinly sliced "brick-oven-baked" type of bread*

leaving even squares. Place the heels of the loaf plus the removed crusts on one baking sheet. Then cut each slice into 6 to 8 strips and place the strips on a second baking sheet. Bake both for 2 hours at 200°. Place the baked heels and crusts of bread between two sheets of wax paper to make coarse crusts with a rolling pin.

Over simmering water in the top of a double boiler heat

> *1 cup smooth peanut butter with*
> *½ cup peanut oil.*

Stir until it has the consistency of cream.

Place about a dozen baked sticks at a time into the hot peanut butter for 10 to 20 seconds, till they absorb it. Remove with a slotted spoon to drain on toweling for a minute, then roll them in the crumbs. Proceed with the next batch. When completed, they can be served at once or stored in-definitely in a foil-lined tinned box. (If they get limp in a damp climate, they can be reheated on a baking sheet in the oven.)

CAVIAR EGGS (2 halves serve 1 person)

Hard-boil as many eggs as needed. Peel and cut them in half. The edges can be fluted with a paring knife or with a flick of the wrist in one of those gadgets called a tulip egg cutter. Cut a thin slice from the round edge so the half egg will stand upright. Place a dollop of mayonnaise (page 42) in the center of the yolk and top with a scant teaspoon of red or black caviar. Or put black caviar on one half and red on the other.

CAVIAR POTATOES

Whenever I've served this yummy for the first time, the same thing happens. First the guest seems puzzled and wants to know what "that" is. I don't tell. After the first bite, he immediately sends a swift glance to the platter to check how many are left.

Scrub and boil until just tender

> *small new potatoes, red or white skinned.*

Drain and let cool till they can be handled. Retain the flattest side of the potato for standing or slice off a little. Scoop out a hole comprising about ⅓ of the potato and smooth off the skin around the edge of the hole.

Sprinkle the cavity with

> *¼ teaspoon of minced shallot*
> *salt and pepper to taste.*

Then fill the cavity with

> *sour cream*

and smooth off the top.

Place a dollop of

> *red or black caviar over the cream*

and garnish with

> *chopped parsley.*

If you serve them as the only hors d'oeuvre at a cocktail party, 2 or 3 per person should suffice. If you're combining them with other hors d'oeuvres, one will do.

CAVIAR BEETS (Serves 4 to 6)

Drain the juice from

> *1 can of small whole beets.*

Slice a tiny piece from each end so the beet will stand upright. Use a sharp-edged demitasse spoon to scoop out a small cavity. Fill each beet with a mixture of

> *sour cream*
> *a little grated onion.*

Top with a dab of

> *black caviar*

and stick in a toothpick for ease of handling. They look as pretty as they taste.

SMOKED BEEF OR HAM ROULADE (Serves 4 to 6)

Buy prepackaged thinly sliced smoked beef. (The kind the butcher carries has too pungent a flavor for the other ingredients.) Begin by placing

> *1 8-ounce package of cream cheese with*
> *¼ teaspoon lemon juice*

into a bowl in a preheated 200° oven. Immediately turn off the heat. Let the cheese soften in the oven for about 15 minutes until it has almost the consistency of whipped cream. Meanwhile, place one dozen paper-thin slices of beef on a counter, slightly overlapping each other in the shape of a rectangle; 3 rows of 4 slices. Spread the softened cream cheese over the slices in a thin layer.

Slice about

> *5 small sweet pickles (gherkins)*

into ⅛-inch strips and lay them horizontally, evenly spaced, on top of the cheese. Starting at the bottom of the rectangle, roll it carefully upwards to shape a long sausage about 1½ inches thick. Then roll up the sausage in foil, seal the edges, and refrigerate for at least 2 hours. To serve, slice into 1½-inch pieces.

While I'm at it, I usually make two roulades and freeze the second one for another occasion. (If you make my zucchini relish [page 355] drain ¼ cup of it and spread *that* over the cream cheese before rolling up the roulades. It's phenomenal!)

STUFFED CUCUMBERS (Serves 6)

Peel

>*2 fat cucumbers about 8 inches long.*

Cut a small slice from each end. Use an apple corer or the handle of a long spoon to scoop out all the seeds until only the firm flesh of the cucumber remains. Rub inside and out with generous amounts of Kosher salt before setting to drain in a colander over the sink for half an hour. Moisture will *run* out. Then dry them inside and out. (Roll up a piece of toweling to push through the cavity.)

Stuff them with a mixture of

>*1 3-ounce package of softened cream cheese*
>>*(cottage cheese for dieters)*
>
>*2 mashed boneless sardines*
>*2 mashed anchovy filets (optional)*
>*1 tablespoon grated onion*
>*2 slices minced boiled ham*
>*1 tablespoon minced sweet pickle*
>*1 teaspoon Dijon mustard*
>*a pinch of paprika or cayenne.*

Pack the stuffing firmly into the cucumbers and wrap each one separately in a piece of toweling and then wax paper. Refrigerate for at least an hour before cutting into 1½-inch slices to serve.

The stuffing can vary. Try capers with flaked tuna or salmon blended with the cream cheese. Try plain cream or cottage cheese with chopped herbs. On occasion I've stuffed them with unadultered German Teewurst and they were a whopping success.

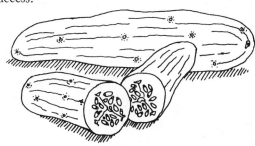

TONY'S OWN PÂTÉ (Serves 6 to 8)

My fabulous dress designer, Tony Altieri, gave me this recipe. It's a gift to you too, and will probably become your own *pâté maison*. It's inexpensive but tastes deluxe. Use small individual molds or one 2-cup mold. A metal bowl can be substituted. Cut the recipe in half for three or four people.

Soften

>1 envelope gelatin in
>2 tablespoons lemon juice

for 5 minutes.

Meanwhile, heat

>1 can condensed beef bouillon.

Add

>the softened gelatin.

Stir over low heat until the gelatin has dissolved completely, then add

>2 tablespoons cognac.

Pour ⅓ of this mixture into the bottom of the mold, or divide the third among the individual molds. Place in the refrigerator to set for about ½ hour.

In a bowl mash together

>1 3-ounce package softened cream cheese
>a 4- or 5-ounce can of inexpensive liver pâté*
>1 tablespoon grated onion.

Pour in the remaining bouillon mixture and blend well. When the gelatin in the mold or molds has set, pour the liver mixture over it and refrigerate at least one hour. Unmold and serve. (Unmolding is explained on page 20.)

---

* These pâtés come in cans or jars. Some are called "Strasbourg type." You obviously won't use the insanely expensive genuine Strasbourg pâté for this dish, but remember this ingredient is the basis of your flavor. Try different ones until you find your favorite. Or try 4 to 5 ounces of soft good goose liverwurst or a German Streich Leberwurst.

MARY LA'S WATER CHESTNUTS WITH BACON

Mary Mathews gave me this crunchy hors d'oeuvre idea. It's become a favorite in our house. Preheat the oven to 225°.

Drain

> *1 can of water chestnuts.*

Using 4 to 6 chestnuts per person, wrap in

> *bacon slices that have been cut into three pieces.*

Stick a toothpick through them to secure the bacon and arrange side by side on the rack over a roasting pan. Place them in the oven for 1 hour, until the bacon has browned and turned crisp. They don't need draining, because the fat will be in the pan beneath the rack. Serve at once, toothpicks and all. Delicious!

MUSHROOMS

If Herbert had his way, he would have a mushroom omelet for breakfast, a mushroom mousse for lunch, and mushrooms for dinner as an hors d'oeuvre, first course, and salad. I've accepted the fact that he's an Austrian mushroom nut.

Buy *firm* mushrooms, the underside of the flesh meeting the stem. When they've begun to unfurl they're aging. No matter what your mother told you, *don't* peel mushrooms. Nip off the tip of the stem with a paring knife and wipe the cap gently with a damp cloth to remove little specks of dirt. If the recipe asks that they be cooked in liquid, they can be washed in cold water.

Let me begin with the easiest of hors d'oeuvres, a delicious morsel that takes no more time than spreading a cracker.

MUSHROOM CAPS A LA PENNIE

Pennie du Pont is a marvelous actress and talk-show hostess, a fine cook, and a true friend. She introduced me to this idea.

Wipe and clean

> *mushroom caps*

and remove the stems to save for another recipe. Fill the caps with softened cream cheese, sprinkle with paprika, chill, and serve!

If you want fancier ones, mash the cream cheese together with minced or deviled ham, grated onion, or minced green peppers. Garnish with chopped parsley or chives.

DUXELLES

You really can't call yourself a cook until you make this mushroom stuffing used in so many recipes, including hors d'oeuvres. Mushroom stems work well together with some whole ones, so the ones from other recipes can be used up. Duxelles freezes and can be stored and then thawed when needed. This recipe can be doubled, if you like.

Wipe clean

> ½ pound mushrooms with stems.

Chop fine and wrap in a strong linen towel. Use elbow grease to twist the towel again and again until no more juice runs out.

In a heavy skillet heat

> 2 tablespoons butter
> 1 tablespoon oil.

Add

> 2 tablespoons minced shallots.

Sauté the shallots for a few minutes before adding the chopped mushrooms to cook for a few minutes over high heat, stirring until the moisture has evaporated. Add

> a pinch of salt, pepper, and nutmeg.

If you don't need it at once, let it cool before storing in the refrigerator or freezer in a tightly sealed jar.

SAUTÉED MUSHROOMS

With a damp cloth wipe

> 1 pound mushrooms.

Slice them evenly, leaving the stems intact. In a large, heavy skillet heat

> 2 tablespoons butter
> 1 tablespoon oil.

Add the mushrooms and stir them to coat with the hot fat. Use fairly high heat and shake the pan to *faire sauté* the mushrooms (make them jump) so they won't stick. Even when they seem to have absorbed the fat, cook, stir, and toss for 4 or 5 minutes.

MARINATED MUSHROOMS

Marinating mushrooms allows me to buy them whenever I see lovely ones, reasonably priced, and prepare when fresh. Once marinated they keep in sealed jars in the refrigerator ready for an hors d'oeuvre or salad. They can be served by themselves or combined with other hors d'oeuvres.

1) Wipe and slice thin medium-sized mushrooms. Small, button-sized mushrooms can be left whole. Put them into a jar and cover with Uta's French Dressing (page 48). Add your choice of chopped herbs; tarragon, parsley, dill, chives, chervil, thyme, etc. Seal and refrigerate a minimum of 12 hours.

2) In a saucepan heat enough of Uta's French Dressing (page 48) to cover the amount of washed and sliced mushrooms you want. Add the mushrooms and simmer for 5 minutes. Allow to cool before placing them with the dressing into sealed jars. Refrigerate a minimum of 2 hours.

3) Wash and slice

> 1 pound medium-sized mushrooms (leave button-sized ones
>   whole).

Drop them into a sauce pan with

> ½ lemon.

Squeeze the lemon into the water and drop in the rind. Simmer for 5 minutes. Let the mushrooms cool in the liquid before draining and removing the lemon. Pat them gently dry with toweling. Fold them into a sauce of

> ½ cup heavy cream
> ¼ cup sour cream
> 1 tablespoon grated onion
> 2 teaspoons sugar
> ¼ teaspoon white pepper.

Refrigerate in a bowl covered with plastic wrap for at least 2 hours.

MUSHROOMS DIVINE (Serves 4)

Once this dish was called *Champignons sous Clôche,* or mushrooms under a bell. It was cooked and served covered by a glass bell. It's so elegant that I honor it by serving it as a separate first course to get undivided attention.

Buy at least

>*12 large mushrooms about 2 inches in diameter.*

Remove the stems and wipe the caps carefully so they won't break. Chop the stems.

In a large skillet heat

>*2 tablespoons butter*
>*1 tablespoon oil.*

Add

>*the chopped stems*
>*2 tablespoons minced shallots*
>*1 tablespoon chopped parsley.*

Sauté the mixture over medium heat for about 5 minutes before removing it to a plate, using a slotted spoon. To the skillet add

>*2 tablespoons butter.*

Cook the mushroom caps, cavity side down, for 2 minutes over low heat. Turn off the heat while you invert them to fill each cavity with the reserve chopped mixture. Sprinkle with a little salt and grated pepper and baste with the butter in the pan. Cover with a tight lid or foil and cook over low heat no more than 5 minutes. Remove the cover and sprinkle the mushrooms with

>*2 tablespoons brandy (flambé, if you like, page 22).*

Serve immediately on pretty plates and swoon with delight. If you want further glamour, remove the crusts from slices of coarse bread, 1 slice per person. Sauté the bread in clarified butter (page 46) on each side and place the mushroom caps on the bread.

MUSHROOM MOUSSE (Serves 6)

Another mushroom joy, which can be molded in a 4-cup mold or metal bowl but looks prettiest in a 9-inch ring mold, and is relatively simple to make. The center of the ring mold can be filled with new peas, cooked cauliflower, or broccoli florets that have been tossed in butter and garnished with chopped parsley. Your guests will know it's party time when you serve it as a first course, side dish, or even as the main course of a luncheon.

Preheat the oven to 325°.

Butter the mold lavishly so the mousse won't stick.

Mince

> *1 pound wiped mushrooms.*

Make a roux of

> *2 tablespoons heated butter*
> *2 tablespoons quick-mix flour.*

Cook and stir the mixture in a heavy skillet over medium-high heat and add the mushrooms. Stir to coat them with the flour mixture and cook for another few minutes. Turn off the heat and allow the mushrooms to cool while you beat

> *4 eggs*
> *a pinch of salt*
> *a pinch of paprika.*

Stir this mixture into the mushrooms in the skillet. In another bowl whip until stiff

> *1 cup heavy cream.*

In still another bowl whip till stiff

> *3 egg whites.*

Fold the whipped cream into the *cooled* mushroom mixture, then gently fold in the beaten egg whites. Pour the mixture into the buttered mold and smooth off the top. Cover the mold with a piece of buttered wax paper that has been cut out to fit. Set the mold into a pan of shallow water and put the whole thing into the hot oven to bake for 1 hour. Test with a cake tester to see if it comes out clean. Use pot holders when putting a serving plate across the top of the mold and turn both upside down. If it doesn't unmold easily, tap the mold lightly around the sides with a knife until the mousse slides out. Hurrah!

PEGGY'S MUSHROOM STRUDEL (Serves 6 to 8)

Recently a group of students gave me a luncheon. This phenomenal feast began with Peggy Sturman's hors d'oeuvre, Mushroom Strudel. Strudel dough, or fillo leaves as the Greeks call it, did not seem in the range of my capabilities, although I knew that some people from the "old country" still made it. Now I learned it was available in packages at specialty food stores and in most Greek and German markets. The first time I tried this recipe I was quaking, but Peggy was right. It's easy. And such fun!

Let me begin with the mushroom stuffing, which entails no new techniques and should be made first in any event.

The Stuffing

Wipe

> *1 pound mushrooms and chop fine.*

Mince

> *2 tablespoons shallots.*

In a large skillet heat

> *6 tablespoons butter.*

Over low heat, sauté the shallots in the butter for a few minutes and then add the mushrooms. Turn the heat up. Stir and cook for several minutes. Then add

> *2 tablespoons Madeira*
> *1 tablespoon chopped tarragon (or a pinch of dried)*
> *1 teaspoon salt*
> *a few gratings of pepper.*

Continue to cook and stir until the liquid from the mushrooms has almost evaporated and the mixture is a little mushy. Let it cool before folding in

> *½ cup sour cream.*

Preheat oven to 375°.

Set the stuffing aside while you prepare the strudel dough.

Handling and Stuffing Strudel or Fillo Leaves

The paper-thin leaves inside the box are wrapped in plastic and should be refrigerated until ready to use. There are dozens of leaves in each box, about 12 by 16 inches each. You will only need a few for each recipe.

In a saucepan melt

> *1 stick butter (8 tablespoons).*

Brush a baking sheet with a little of the butter. Set the butter to one side and have ready the softest pastry brush, sable, or even better one made of goose feathers. (Mine is imported from Hungary and was ordered from a kitchen catalogue.)

Set out

>1 cup dry white bread crumbs.

Lightly dampen a towel and spread it, wrinkle free, on the counter. If it's too moist the leaves will stick. Now get set for an adventurous game.

Tenderly remove

>6 leaves of strudel (or fillo).

Return the remainder to their plastic bag and put them back in the refrigerator. Keep the leaves you're using covered with plastic until each one is stuffed so they won't dry out.

Spread one leaf on the damp towel, being careful not to tear it, and brush it liberally with melted butter. Use a light touch with your soft brush or goose feathers. Sprinkle ⅙ of the crumbs across the surface of the buttered leaf. Spread another leaf evenly over the first, brush with butter, and sprinkle with crumbs. With a spoon place ⅓ of the stuffing at one end of the shorter side of the leaves, about ½ inch in from the edge. Shape it like a thin sausage. Now comes the fun.

Take the two corners of the towel near the mushroom filling in each hand and lift the towel slightly to let the strudel roll down and around the stuffing like a jelly roll. If necessary, keep raising the towel with gentle flicks to keep the strudel rolling. When completed, drape the other end of the towel across one end of the baking sheet and lift again to roll the strudel in place on the greased baking sheet.

Make two more strudel in the same way and roll them onto the baking sheet without touching each other. Use the remaining butter to brush the tops of the strudel.

Up to this point I usually prepare the strudel in the morning. The whole baking sheet can be covered with plastic wrap and refrigerated until baking time. They can also be frozen for as long as you like, thawed, and brought to room temperature before baking or baked at once for 15 to 20 minutes, until crisp and golden. Slice them carefully with a sharp knife into 2- to 3-inch serving pieces and serve hot. You'll never be forgotten for serving this wonder.

OTHER STRUDEL STUFFINGS

Once you have the hang of working with these leaves, you'll want to try other stuffings, such as the Apfel Strudel (page 306) or baklava, which is printed right on the box. Try the Manicotti Lotsa Cheese stuffing on page 106, or the Ravioli di Bacci stuffing on page 111.

Feta Stuffing

Preheat oven to 375°.

This makes five strudel.

In a large bowl combine:

> ½ *pound crumbled feta cheese*
> ½ *pound ricotta cheese*
> ½ *cup yoghurt*
> 2 *eggs*
> 4 *tablespoons minced parsley.*

Blend the mixture well. Have ready

> 10 *strudel or fillo leaves.*

Brush 2 leaves with butter and sprinkle with crumbs as described on page 67. Use ⅕ of the stuffing for each strudel and roll up as before. Brush the tops with melted butter and bake for 20 minutes.

OEUFS EN GELÉE (Jellied Eggs)

In Paris, when I was very young, I used to taste the romantic atmosphere of France, including the food. The first time I sampled delicately poached eggs suspended in jellied broth I felt like a real Parisienne. Now whenever I prepare them, I begin to hum "La Vie en Rose." As a first course for lunch or dinner on a hot summer day they're unmatched.

Poach

> 1 *egg (page 26)*

per serving and set aside in cold water.

Into the bottom of small glass bowls or individual molds pour

> ½ *inch of canned jellied madrilène*
> or
> ½ *inch canned beef broth with gelatin.*

Refrigerate until the jelly has set, about ½ hour.

If you have fresh tarragon add it now in the following way. Place a few sprigs in boiling water for 20 seconds, remove, and refresh in ice water before patting dry with toweling. Arrange a few leaves prettily over the first layer of jelly in the molds before placing the egg on them so they will show through when inverted. When served in bowls, save the decoration of leaves till the end to float on top.

Carefully spoon one poached egg into the molds or bowls over the jelly and cover completely with more of the madrilène or beef broth. Add

1 teaspoon dry vermouth

to each egg and refrigerate till set. To unmold see page 20.

Note: It may be necessary to trim the egg whites a bit to fit small molds. Do it neatly to keep the prettiest shape.

SNAILS IN SHELLS OR MUSHROOM CAPS

My passion for snails turned my daughter Letty into an addict before she was six years old. Waiters would gaze in wonder when with a piping voice she demanded "Escargots Provençal, please!"

Fresh snails clinging to their shells with a powerful muscle are not only hard to find but difficult to dislodge. I buy them in cans already out of their shells. They've been simmered in wine and only need to be drained before their final cooking. Empty shells can be purchased together with the canned snails. When you have the amount you need, they can be washed in soapy water and cleaned with a bottle brush, rinsed, and drained to be used again and again. If you become a snail buff, you'll want snail plates made of tin or ovenproof earthenware. They have small indentations to keep the snail shells upright so the butter won't run out. You'll need oyster forks to prod the cooked snails from their shells, and you may even want a set of snail tongs to hold the hot shells. I think the tongs are a luxury.

As a first course 6 snails per person are sufficient. As the main course of a luncheon or supper party, a dozen are appropriate. To prepare them, drain the snails and push each one into a shell letting the little "tongue" peek out. Then stuff each one with

1 teaspoon prepared snail butter (page 47).

Preheat oven to 425°.

Place the stuffed shells on the indentations of the snail plates. Set the plates on a baking sheet that has a rim so the butter won't drip into the oven and bake for 10 to 15 minutes until they're heated through and the butter is bubbling. Serve at once.

To serve snails in mushroom caps, you need no special equipment.

Preheat oven to 425°.

Use lovely

> *medium-sized mushrooms, 3 per person.*

Wipe the caps with a damp cloth and carefully remove the stems. Sauté the caps on each side gently for 2 minutes in a large skillet with

> *2 tablespoons butter*
> *1 tablespoon oil.*

Into each mushroom cavity set two snails and top with

> *1½ teaspoons snail butter (page 47).*

Place the filled caps side by side on an ovenproof platter or in a shallow casserole. Cover loosely with foil and bake for 10 minutes. Serve at once on rounds of sautéed toast or simply on pretty plates.

STEAMED CLAMS (4 dozen for 4 people)

My favorites are hard-shelled little neck clams, not the long-necked "steamers." To rid them completely of grit, sand, and their own leavings, put them in a sink half full of water with

> *½ cup coarse salt*
> *½ cup corn meal.*

This briny solution makes them spit out their waste. Leave them in the sink for a few hours and then scrub under cold water.

Put less than one inch of water into a large pot and bring it to a boil. Add the clams and cover the pot. Turn the heat to medium. In 5 minutes the clams should open. Remove them with a slotted spoon or skimmer and divide among individual bowls. Serve with melted snail butter (page 47) and lemon wedges.

OYSTERS ON THE HALF SHELL

This isn't a recipe, just a tip about something I only learned a few years ago. I thought raw oysters could be eaten only at expensive restaurants. I passed by the oysters at the market lying on ice in their impossible-to-open shells. Then I was told the market would open them, clean them, and pack them on shaved ice so that I could bring them home a few hours before dinner to arrange at the last minute on plates with lemon wedges and a few spoons of horseradish looking fit for kings—which they are! I serve them once a year for my own wedding anniversary.

POACHED SHRIMP

I'd like to settle for frozen or canned shrimp, but only the fresh ones will do. Two jumbo shrimp per person are plenty as an hors d'oeuvre. Treat yourself when you can afford to.

Cleaning shrimp is just as easy before or after cooking. Poaching them in the shell is supposed to add flavor, but I can't tell the difference. To remove the shell, first pull off the legs. Remove the top shell, saving the tail till last. Remove the remaining shell gently to retain as much of the tail as possible. With a sharp pointed knife make a slit down the back of the shrimp and use the point of the knife to lift out the vein and any roe that may be present. Occasionally the shrimp are so clean they have no vein.

Bring a pot of water to boil with

> *1 teaspoon vinegar or lemon juice.*

Drop the shrimp gently into the water a few at a time. Lower the heat and let the shrimp poach about 3 minutes. Drain at once. If you haven't yet removed the shells and cleaned them, let them cool before doing so.

Sprinkle with lemon juice and refrigerate till needed. Serve with

> *Red Caviar and Sour Cream Dip (page 55)*
> *or*
> *Tartar Sauce (page 43)*
> *or*
> *Rémoulade (page 43)*
> *or make*

THE BEST SEAFOOD DIP

Blend together

> *½ cup currant or beachplum jelly*
> *½ cup chili sauce*
> *2–3 tablespoons prepared horseradish.*

MARINATED SHRIMP

Poach the shrimp as described above. While still warm, cover with

Uta's French Dressing (page 48)

and stir in your choice of chopped fresh herbs such as dill, parsley, tarragon, rosemary, or chervil, plus

one tablespoon grated onion.

Cover and refrigerate 12 hours.

COLD SHRIMP AVOCADO (Serves 6)

Clean and poach

1 pound medium-sized shrimp.

Toss them in

½ cup Uta's French Dressing (page 48).

Add

1 small onion, thinly sliced
1 small celery stalk, diced
2 tablespoons drained capers
a pinch of ground thyme
a pinch of cayenne
salt and pepper to taste.

Chill for several hours. Just before serving on lettuce leaves, add

a diced avocado.

Note: Hot shrimp recipes can be found under Shrimp, page 118.

PROSCIUTTO WITH MELON OR PEARS

Such a beautiful hors d'oeuvre, and sinfully easy to prepare. Good ingredients are important. A fatty, oversalted prosciutto won't do. Make sure it's lean and thinly sliced. I often substitute a smoked rolled loin of pork from Germany called Lachs Schinken, sliced transparently thin, or Westphalian smoked ham. They're expensive but worth it. I prefer Spanish or Danish melon but honeydew or canteloupe are fine.

Cut the melon in half to scoop out seeds and pulp. Remove the rind and cut the flesh into small uniform wedges approximately 1 inch thick and

2 inches long. Sprinkle with a few drops of lemon juice and wrap a thin slice of whichever ham you've chosen around each wedge. Secure the ham with a toothpick and arrange on a platter.

When using pears, see that they are ripe but firm. Peel and remove the core. Slice into wedges and dip in a little water and lemon juice so they won't discolor. Pat dry with toweling before wrapping with ham.

ARTICHOKES

Let your grocer help you pick out the best. They should be firm and uniformly green. If they have darkened leaves with brown edges, leave them for someone else. If you're not using them the same day, wash, dry, and store in a plastic bag in the refrigerator, where they'll keep for several days. Choose a pot large enough for the artichokes to move freely in water. Fill three quarters with water and add

> 1 tablespoon vinegar or lemon juice
> 1 tablespoon salt.

Bring it to a boil. Meanwhile, cut the stems from the artichokes so they can stand on end. Place the artichokes on their sides and use a sharp knife to cut about 1 inch from the tips. Use kitchen shears to cut the spikey tip from the remaining leaves. Immediately rub all cut ends with half a lemon so they won't discolor.

One by one lower the artichokes into the boiling water. Place the lid over a third of the pot to catch steam and prevent the artichokes from bouncing above the water while boiling. Depending on size, they will be cooked in 20 to 35 minutes. With a two-tined fork pierce the bottoms to test for crunchy tenderness. Drain upside down in a colander or dish drain. When they can be handled, give them a *gentle* squeeze to let excess moisture run out. Before serving warm or cold set them on a platter or individual plates and gently spread the leaves until you can reach in to pull out the small translucent spiney leaves in the center. Discard them and use a sharp-edged spoon to scoop out the hairy, tendrils comprising the "choke" until the top of the heart is exposed and smooth.

As a first course try pouring

> *3 tablespoons Uta's French Dressing (page 48)*

into the cavity of each artichoke. Each leaf can be dipped into the center before eating and when you get to the heart it will be pleasantly soaked in dressing. Or try the same procedure using

> *Hollandaise Sauce (page 41)*
> *or*
> *Lemon Butter (page 47).*

Stuffing Variations   Blend flaked tuna, crab meat, or salmon with sautéed mushrooms and mayonnaise. Stuff the artichokes ½ to ¾ full. Or use

> *Diced cooked chicken with mushrooms and mayonnaise*
> *or*
> *Marinated shrimp*
> *or*
> *Poached shrimp with Hollandaise*

The very look of the artichokes makes you know a party is in progress!

MARGARET'S ROAST PEPPERS

Margaret Stark is a wonderful painter and an extraordinary cook who can throw together a six-course dinner for ten people after having painted all day! Her way of doing peppers is like a festive game.

The purpose of roasting peppers is to blister and blacken the skins until they can be easily peeled, exposing bright green skin, never allowing the peppers to get soft or mushy. They're often roasted in the oven or under the broiler, but Margaret sets 2 or 3 peppers at a time directly over the burner on top of the stove. (They can also be done on the licking flames of a fireplace or over hot coals on a barbecue.) Watch them closely and turn them with tongs or long-handled spoons until evenly blistered and blackened on all sides. Hold them under running water to wash and wipe off the skins. The black ash on the stove wipes away quickly. Cut the peppers in half to remove seeds and slice out the bitter white veins. Cut into serving pieces and drizzle with

> *olive oil.*

Sprinkle with

> *salt, pepper, and a few drops of lemon juice.*

Cover with plastic wrap and keep at room temperature till needed, to be served with crackers or thin slices of pumpernickle.

They are truly special when sliced and arranged "artistically" in designs. Roast 1 red bell pepper and 2 green ones. After cleaning, cut petals from the red pepper and stems and leaves from the green ones. Arrange on a white platter to make poinsettias for Christmas, tulips for spring, roses for summer, spiked asters for autumn; or just go hog wild to make abstract designs. Finish with the oil, lemon juice, salt, and pepper.

Cheesy Balls, Bombes, Tarts, and Fondu

Man cannot live on bread alone. But what about cheese? I can go on a cheese binge the way same people eat fudge. Is there anything better than ripe Brie slathered on French bread accompanied by a glass of wine? Some of the following recipes are too rich for an appetizer but perfect for lunch or an after-theater party. A quiche or fondu makes a marvelous meatless evening meal.

LIPTAUER (Serves 8)

This is not a truly "cheesy" dip, but it's my husband's favorite, an Austrian specialty for which there are as many recipes as cooks in Vienna.

Into the blender put

> 8 ounces cottage cheese (1 cup)
> 3 ounces softened cream cheese (a small package)
> 1 stick softened butter (8 tablespoons)
> ½ cup sour cream
> 1 tablespoon paprika
> 1 teaspoon dry mustard
> 1 tablespoon grated onion
> salt and pepper to taste.

Blend till smooth. Fold in

> 1 tablespoon drained capers

and mound the cheese on a plate. Swirl the outside into a fluted design with the handle of a spoon or a rubber spatula and garnish with

> sprinklings of paprika
> 2 tablespoons chopped chives or parsley.

Refrigerate a minimum of 2 hours. Serve as a dip for raw vegetables or spread on thin slices of pumpernickle.

CHEESE CROUSTADES

Little toasted cups filled with melted cheese, topped with tomato and basil, make my mouth water just to think of them. The cups are fun and easy to make and keep for ages in plastic bags in refrigerator or freezer. So make more than needed.

Preheat oven to 400°.

Use

> one loaf coarse "brick-oven-baked" type of bread, sliced.

Cut 3-inch rounds from the center of each slice with a wide-mouthed old-fashioned glass or a biscuit cutter. (Put leftover crusts in a paper bag for a day or so to make bread crumbs in the blender.) Generously butter the cups of a muffin tin and lightly press in the bread rounds. Then drizzle a little olive oil over the bread in the cups and bake for 10 minutes or until the edges of bread start to brown. Tip the pan upside down and the croustades will fall out. Make the next batch.

Serve 2 to a customer. For a dozen croustades use

> ½–¾ cup coarsely grated cheese (Swiss or cheddar or both).

Fill the croustades almost to the top with the grated cheese and cover each one with

> 1 tablespoon tomato topping*
> a dab of Pesto sauce (page 43)
>   or
> a few chopped basil leaves (a pinch of dried)
> salt and pepper to taste.

When using fresh or dry basil instead of Pesto, dot with butter and bake the croustades spaced an inch apart on a baking sheet for 10 minutes. Serve at once.

---

* To make the tomato topping, blanch two tomatoes in boiling water for 10 seconds and slip off the skins, squeeze to remove juice and seeds, chop them, and place a spoonful over the croustade. Or use canned tomato sauce. The kind including small hunks of tomato is the best.

CHEESE BOMBES (Serves 4)

Fabulous and filling, use them for lunch or an after-theater bite. One per person is plenty.

Begin with

> 20 *crackers—buttery or sesame crackers are best.*

To make the crumbs, place the crackers between 2 sheets of wax paper and crush them with a rolling pin.

Using two bowls, separate

> *4 eggs.*

Beat the whites till stiff and whisk the yolks till foamy. Coarsely grate

> *2 cups cheese, Swiss, cheddar, American, or a combination.*

Put the cheese in a bowl and stir it lightly together with

> *2 tablespoons quick-mix flour*
> *½ teaspoon salt*
> *a pinch of cayenne.*

Fold the beaten whites into the cheese mixture.

Divide the mixture into 4 even parts and form loosely into balls. They will be gooey and not well rounded. That's all right. Dip them into the beaten yolks one at a time, using your hands to coat them well and scoop them out again. If this seems too messy, try brushing them with a pastry brush or use two wooden spoons. Roll each ball in cracker crumbs on the wax paper. Make sure they're encrusted but don't worry about the shape. Place on a plate in the refrigerator and cover them with an inverted bowl for a minimum of 2 hours. Save the remaining crumbs and yolks for later.

When your company arrives, pour 3 inches of cooking oil into a small iron casserole and, using your thermometer, heat to 350°. While it's heating, reshape the balls. Now it will be easy. Roll them once more in the remaining yolks and then in the cracker crumbs and lower gently into the hot fat. Fry for about 5 minutes until they're puffy and golden. Remove with a slotted spoon and drain on toweling. Serve at once.

(If deep-frying is new to you, read about it on page 16.)

TONY'S GREEK CHEESE BALLS (Serves 8)

My wonderful dress designer, Tony Altieri, is an improviser in the kitchen, and loves short cuts as much as I do. These cheese balls, showy and delicious, can be whipped up in the morning and finished in a few minutes just before serving. The recipe can be cut in half for 4 people.

In a large bowl beat

> *4 whole eggs.*

Stir in

> *¾ cup farmer's cheese*
> *3 ounces of softened cream cheese (one package).*

Add

> *a pinch of baking powder.*

Blend. The mixture will be slightly lumpy. Refrigerate for at least 4 hours.

When the guests have arrived, in a large heavy skillet heat

> *1 inch of vegetable oil.*

Use your deep-fry thermometer and wait till the oil reaches 385°.

Spread a sheet of wax paper on the counter and sprinkle it with

> *2–3 tablespoons quick-mix flour.*

Spoon pancakes about 2 to 3 inches in diameter onto the flour on the paper and dust the tops with flour. Lower the pancakes into the hot fat a few at a time. Cook a minute or so until golden on the under side before turning them to cook on the other side. Remove with a slotted spoon and drain on toweling. Serve at once. They can be garnished with chopped parsley.

SUISSE TOAST (Serves 6 to 8)

For brunch, lunch, or a late snack it can be served in large amounts but as an hors d'oeuvre, go easy.

Clarify

> *1 stick of butter (page 46).*

Remove the crusts from

> *12 thin slices of coarse "brick-oven-baked" type bread.*

Cut each slice in half diagonally. Then sauté the bread a few slices at a time in a large skillet using the clarified butter, about 3 tablespoons per batch. In a bowl mix

> ½ pound Swiss or Gruyère cheese, coarsely grated
> 2 lightly beaten eggs
> ½ cup whipped heavy cream.

Season the mixture with

> salt, pepper, and grated nutmeg to taste.

Then spread it equally on the toast and arrange the slices on a baking sheet. Put them about 6 inches away from the broiler until the cheese melts. Serve at once and eat with relish!

MOZZARELLA IN CAROZZA (Serves 6)

Mozzarella in a carriage. I can just see it riding around in the Borghese Gardens. This is another dish too rich to eat before a meal, but I certainly ate it a lot *between* meals when we were in Rome.

Use traditional Italian bread but get the roundest loaves possible, because the skinny loaves won't work. Cut half-inch slices and use a biscuit cutter or wide-mouthed glass to make rounds about 3 inches in diameter. You'll need 4 rounds per person, or 24 rounds.

Slice

> 12 pieces of mozzarella ¼ inch thick.

Make sure the cheese is smaller in circumference than the bread rounds. Place a slice of mozzarella between every two rounds of bread, sandwich style, and set aside.

In a bowl beat together

> 3 large eggs
> 3 tablespoons milk.

In another bowl pour

> 1 cup milk.

On wax paper spread

> 1 cup dry bread crumbs.

In an iron casserole heat

> 3 inches peanut or vegetable oil to 375°.

Dip each "sandwich" into the bowl of milk and press the edges together securely so the cheese won't escape. Coat both sides with bread crumbs and finally dip and turn them in the egg mixture. Lower gently into the hot oil. Fry a few at a time till golden. Drain on paper towels and serve at once plain or with Anchovy Sauce (below). *Fantastico!*

ANCHOVY SAUCE

In a saucepan melt

> 1 stick butter

and stir in

> 2 tablespoons chopped anchovy filets
> 1 tablespoon chopped parsley
> 2 teaspoons drained capers
> 2 teaspoons lemon juice.

Heat almost to the boiling point. Serve in a pitcher to let the guests pour it on their Carozze.

CAROLE'S QUICHE (Serves 4)

I *love* quiche but used to dread the required pie crust. First I settled for a prepackaged frozen pie crust from the supermarket. Then I learned to make the easy Cream Cheese Crust on page 295 and finally the proper Pie Crust on page 296. (Use the prepackaged crust *only* if you're a real beginner.)

Carole Ann Lewis was my acting student until she branched out brilliantly into the field of modern dance. When she taught me to make this marvel I puffed up with pride as high as the quiche.

Line a 9-inch pie plate with one of the suggested crusts above. Pinch the edge of the crust upward before fluting to raise it slightly. Prick it with a fork along the bottom and sides and set aside.

Preheat the oven to 375°.

Sauté till crisp

> 4 slices lean bacon.

Drain it and crumble over the bottom of the pie shell.

Seed and devein

> 1 green pepper

and chop it coarsely. Sprinkle into the shell.

Coarsely grate

> 1 cup Swiss or Gruyère cheese

and spread loosely over the bacon and green pepper. In a bowl beat together

> 2 whole eggs plus one egg yolk
> 1½ cups half-and-half
> a pinch of salt
> a few gratings of pepper and nutmeg.

Pour the mixture over the cheese into the pie crust. Then dot with

> 2 tablespoons butter.

Bake in the hot oven until the quiche is puffy and golden, 25 to 30 minutes.

MINIATURE QUICHES (Serves 4 to 8)

Formidable with a French pronunciation is a good description for these hors d'oeuvres. Serve 1 or 2 per person. Don't be alarmed by the softness of the crust; it will bake into perfect little shells.

Blend together

> 1 stick softened butter
> 1½ ounces softened cream cheese.

Work in

> ½ cup flour.

Work the dough into a soft mass and divide equally into 8 small balls. Place the balls into the cups of a muffin tin and form thin crusts by smearing them over the bottoms and sides of each cup with your two middle fingers. Make sure there are no holes. Refrigerate the dough for at least 2 hours.

Preheat the oven to 350°.

Across the bottom of each little crust spread about

> ½–1 teaspoon Duxelles (page 62)
> ½–1 teaspoon minced ham or smoked beef.

Then divide among the cups

> ¾ cup grated cheese, Swiss or Gruyère.

Beat together

> 3 eggs
> ⅔ cup milk
> salt, pepper, and nutmeg to taste.

Pour the egg mixture into each cup almost to the brim, allowing it to seep through the grated cheese. Dot each cup with a few dabs of butter and set the muffin tin on a baking dish to catch overflowing butter. Place in the hot oven and bake for 25 minutes, until the little quiches have puffed and turned golden. Let them cool for 10 minutes before lifting out with a pointed knife. Serve and sigh with delight.

CHEESE FONDU

In late autumn with the first nippy frost I begin to dream of cheese fondu. A meal in itself, it can be served for lunch or an informal supper with a salad and a bottle of wine. You need long-handled forks and an alcohol burner or hot plate. Start with a heavy casserole or chafing dish. Rub the dish with

> *2 halved garlic cloves.*

Leave the garlic in the dish and add

> *2 cups dry white wine*
> *1 teaspoon lemon juice.*

Heat the wine on the stove until it starts to shiver and produce tiny bubbles. Remove the garlic. Meanwhile mix together

> *4 cups coarsely grated Swiss cheese (½ pound Emmenthaler and*
>   *½ pound Gruyère is best)*
> *4 tablespoons quick-mix flour.*

Add the cheese mixture to the hot wine a little at a time, using a whisk to stir until the cheese melts and turns gooey. Season with

> *salt, grated pepper, and nutmeg to taste.*

Cut up 2 long and skinny French breads into 1-inch cubes, making sure to leave a little crust on each cube. Serve the bread in a large bowl.

Everyone will be spearing hunks of bread, dipping them into melted cheese over and across each other and vying for more. They will dribble and giggle and make a mess so don't use your best table cloth. Have extra paper napkins on hand. Set the fondu on a burner or hot plate in the middle of the table, placing chairs closely together so no one has to reach too far. At the last minute, into the bubbling cheese stir

> *2 tablespoons kirschwasser.*

Pile in and be happy!

VI. Soup Tricks

Honesty is the best policy so I will start right out by admitting that I do not spend time on those classic stocks, the base for great soup, that simmer five and six hours with beef and veal and chicken and marrow bones and knuckle bones and vegetables and seasonings, that are reduced, degreased, destrained, and as far as I'm concerned distraught. They just aren't for me or my life style.

Sometimes I cheat. The lowest I ever sank was when I blatantly lied about the delicious lobster bisque we were devouring. When asked for my fabulous recipe, I answered blithely that it was complicated and I'd provide it when we both had more time. My husband reddened with shame because he had bought it in a can and watched while I jazzed it up with a little sherry and whipped cream. I later made a full confession.

My shelves are stocked (no pun intended) with cans of condensed beef bouillon and condensed chicken broth. These cans can be fortified with other ingredients for beautiful and unusual flavor. I do, however, make real stock from the Boiled Beef (page 182) and Pot au Feu (page 184). The broth from these dishes can be reduced, fortified and enhanced with other ingredients. Plain Poached Chicken (page 141) guarantees delicious chicken broth served as is or used as a base for sauces or other soups.

The famous stock pots that keep so well in underheated European kitchens will spoil and turn sour in America, but I've learned some useful tricks. Whenever I have a reserve broth from fish, meat, or poultry, I strain it and bottle it and keep it in the refrigerator. The fat that rises and congeals at the top is a protective layer. If I want to keep the broth more than a week, I remove the fat and pour the liquid into ice trays, then store the frozen cubes in plastic bags.

A clear soup cleanses the palate after an hors d'oeuvre and readies it for the main meal. Let me begin with the simplest.

BASIC BEEF CONSOMMÉ (Serves 4 to 6)

Into a saucepan put

> 2½ *cans condensed beef bouillon (a can contains 10¾ ounces)*
> ½ *cup water*
> 1 *large scrubbed, chopped carrot*
> 1 *small chopped onion*
> 1 *tablespoon chopped celery stalk*
> 3 *parsley sprigs*
> *a pinch of thyme*
> ¼ *cup dry red or white wine or 2 tablespoons dry vermouth.*

Simmer over medium-low heat for ½ hour. Strain, and check for seasoning.

> *or*

Reduce to 1 quart the broth from any of the

> *Boiled Beef recipes (pages 182–87)*
> > *or*
> *Pot au Feu (page 184).*

Degrease and strain the reduced broth. Reheat and check for additional seasoning.

Note: To make unclouded, crystal clear consommé pour 1 quart of cool beef broth into a sauce pan and add 2 raw egg whites. Place it over low heat and whisk it briskly until it starts to simmer. Allow it to simmer *gently* for 10 minutes and then strain it through several thicknesses of cheesecloth. To serve, reheat with an optional addition of 2 tablespoons dry wine or madeira. To make jellied consommé, dissolve 2 teaspoons gelatin in 2 tablespoons boiling water and stir it into the broth. Refrigerate till set.

CONSOMMÉ WITH EGG

Add a poached egg to each bowl of consommé just before serving.

CONSOMMÉ WITH VERMICELLI

Add 1 cup of uncooked vermicelli to the consommé and cook 5 minutes longer.

VEGETABLE CONSOMMÉ

Scrape and dice

> *2 large carrots.*

Simmer, covered for 20 minutes in

> *½ cup water with*
> *1 tablespoon butter*
> *1 teaspoon sugar*
> *a pinch of salt.*

Meanwhile, in a separate pot in 1 quart salted water boil uncovered for 5 minutes

> *1 cup fresh shelled peas.*

Drain the vegetables and add them at once to the hot consommé.

CONSOMMÉ WITH AVOCADO

Peel and dice

> *1 chilled avocado.*

Add to the soup just before serving.
The contrast of hot soup and cold avocado is very special.

Garnishes   Any of the consommés can be sprinkled with

> *chopped parsley*
> *chopped chives*
> *chopped watercress or*
> *grated Parmesan.*

ONION SOUP (Serves 6)

Thinly slice

> *2 large onions (to equal 2 cups).*

In a large skillet heat

> *2 tablespoons butter*
> *1 tablespoon oil.*

Add the sliced onions, cover, and cook for 15 minutes over low heat. Stir in

> ½ teaspoon salt
> a pinch of sugar.

Cook uncovered for ½ hour until the onions turn a nice brown color.

Sprinkle with

> 2 tablespoons quick-mix flour.

Cook and stir 3 minutes.

Remove the mixture to a large heavy casserole and stir in

> 1½ quarts Basic Beef Consommé (page 85)
> 2 additional tablespoons dry red wine.

Simmer over low heat for another 30 minutes. Stir occasionally, skimming off scum.

Make

> 6 rounds of toasted French bread.

Place the bread rounds in individual serving bowls and pour the soup over them.

Serve with a separate bowl of

> ½ cup grated Parmesan or Swiss cheese.

Each person can sprinkle on as much cheese as he likes. Party time!

BASIC CHICKEN CONSOMMÉ (Serves 6)

Into a large saucepan put

> 2½ cans condensed chicken broth (10¾ ounces per can)
> ½ cup water
> ¼ cup dry white wine or 2 tablespoons dry vermouth
> 2 scrubbed, chopped carrots
> 1 small chopped onion
> a sprig of fresh tarragon or a pinch of dried
> a few parsley stems (leaves discolor the light broth).

Simmer for 30 minutes, skimming off foam or scum.

Strain through several layers of cheesecloth and add

> salt and white pepper to taste.
>
> or

Reduce the broth from Poached Chicken (page 141) to 1½ quarts.

Chill and degrease it. Reheat and strain through several layers of cheese-cloth. Taste for additional seasoning.

or

Boil down Chicken Stock (page 139) to reduce by one-third. Strain, de-grease, and check for additional seasoning.

MADRILÈNE

To the basic chicken consommé add

> 1 cup tomato juice
> 1 teaspoon lemon juice.

STRACCIATELLA

Like so many Roman foods, this soup is comforting.

Reheat the basic chicken consommé to a simmer. In a separate bowl bowl lightly beat

> 2 eggs.

Whisk in

> 2 tablespoons grated Parmesan
> 2 tablespoons minced parsley
> a pinch of salt
> a few gratings of nutmeg.

Then whisk the egg mixture into the simmering soup for a few minutes. The egg will form little flakes. Serve at once.

AVGOLEMONO (Chicken Soup with Egg and Lemon)

This unusual Greek soup is just as good cold in summer as hot in winter.

Slowly simmer for 15 minutes

> 1½ quarts basic chicken consommé with
> ¼ cup raw rice (optional).

In a large bowl beat

> 3 eggs.

Whisk in

> ¼ cup lemon juice.

Gradually whisk

> 2 cups hot broth

into the egg-and-lemon mixture.

Then add the rest of the broth, whisking until it thickens slightly. Serve at once with floating thin slices of lemon.

To serve cold, pour the Avgolemono into a pretty bowl and chill for several hours before adding the thin lemon slices. If it has jelled after chilling, whisk it briefly for a few minutes till smooth and creamy. Add the lemon slices.

THICK SOUPS AND PURÉES

On a cold winter's night a main meal of split pea or lentil soup with sausages, served with homemade bread, a big salad, and mugs of Pilsner or Hofbrau beer or a large bottle of red wine will make you feel like a contented peasant—deluxe! Either soup is a delicious first course served in *small* bowls with a few croutons if the rest of the meal is not heavy.

LENTIL SOUP AND SPLIT PEA SOUP

Everyone who makes these soups gets dogmatic about their own recipes. I've been given dozens of them and all were simply slight variations of the directions printed right on the package of dry lentils or split peas. Begin by following the instructions on the box and then, when you feel inclined, experiment with your own substitutions or additions. Try using only half the specified amount of milk and making up the difference with chicken or beef broth. Add a few tablespoons of dry vermouth or sherry. Add other vegetables such as diced carrots, slivers of garlic, celery leaves, or chopped celery stalks. You really can't fail with these hearty soups.

When I want to make a whole meal of either soup, I add sausages.

> Skinless frankfurters
> Knockwurst
> Bockwurst
> Link or Deerfoot sausages, etc.

Use them singly or in combinations. Cut into bite-sized hunks and brown them lightly on all sides in hot vegetable oil. Add to the soup for the last 10 minutes of cooking.

You can also add

> ¼–½ *cup Pistou or Pesto (pages 43–44).*

If any soup is left over, on the next day add a little liquid to thin it out and reheat for lunch. You won't be sick of it!

CRÔUTES OR CROUTONS

To make *crôutes* for thick soups, cut French bread into 1-inch slices and bake on a baking sheet in a preheated 325° oven for 20 minutes or until dry and browned. Baste with a little olive oil and bake 10 minutes longer.

Follow the same procedure for croutons, cutting the French bread into one-inch cubes.

SEAFOOD BISQUES OR CREAMED FISH SOUPS

As I confessed at the beginning of the chapter, I use them straight from fancy brand canned varieties, adding a few tablespoons white wine or dry vermouth, cream or sour cream. They can be garnished with chopped herbs or lemon wedges or whatever suits your fancy.

VEGETABLE SOUP WITH BASIL SAUCE (Serves 6 to 8)

A glorious hearty soup—hale, too! It should precede a very light meal or be served as the main course of a luncheon or supper.

You must have on hand

> ½ *cup of Pesto (page 43)*
> *or*
> ½ *cup Pistou (page 44).*

Into a kettle put

> 3 *quarts boiling water*
> 2 *cups diced carrots*
> 2 *cups diced, peeled potatoes*
> 2 *cups diced onions*
> 1 *tablespoon coarse salt.*

Simmer 35 minutes and add

>2 *cans drained kidney beans*
>2 *cups fresh string beans, cut into 1-inch pieces*
>1 *slice stale white bread, crumbled*
>*a pinch of thyme*
>*a pinch of pepper.*

Simmer another 20 minutes. In a bowl whisk together

>½ *cup Pesto or Pistou with*
>1 *cup of the hot soup.*

Slowly whisk this mixture into the rest of the soup. Serve in bowls with

>*crôutes (page 90)*
>>*or*
>*a loaf of French bread.*

It's a meatless feast.

HOT POTATO AND LEEK SOUP OR COLD VICHYSSOISE
(Serves 4 to 6)

This soup blows my "bisque theory" because it's infinitely superior to the canned varieties. If you've had only cold vichyssoise, you may not realize what a wonderful hot winter soup it is. It's not difficult to make provided you can get fresh leeks that aren't priced out of reason.

Coarsely chop

>3 *leeks (white parts only; save the greens for other seasoning)*
>1 *onion.*

Sauté the vegetables for a few minutes in a heavy casserole in

>2 *tablespoons butter.*

Add

>4 *medium-sized peeled, sliced potatoes*
>2 *cans condensed chicken broth*
>1 *cup water.*

Cover the casserole and simmer 20 minutes until the potatoes are tender.

Put the vegetables into the blender in two batches to purée quickly.

Just before serving, heat the soup again with an addition of

>*1½ cups heavy cream.*

Top with chopped chives.

If you cool it and then refrigerate for several hours, it automatically becomes vichyssoise, which should also be topped with chopped chives. Add a dollop of sour cream in each bowl if you like.

ZUCCHINI SOUP (Serves 6)

I invented this only a few years ago when the zucchini were taking over my garden.

Peel, then slice zucchini lengthwise. Scoop out seeds and pulp before chopping coarsely. You need

>*3 cups chopped zucchini.*

Put the vegetable into a kettle with

>*3 cans condensed chicken broth*
>*1 cup water.*

In a skillet over low heat sauté

>*1 chopped onion in*
>*4 tablespoons butter.*

In 5 to 10 minutes, when the onions are soft, add them with their butter to the soup kettle plus

>*3 parsley sprigs*
>*a few celery leaves*
>*a pinch of thyme*
>*salt and pepper to taste.*

Cover the kettle and simmer for 20 minutes. Then use a fork to fish out parsley and celery leaves. Put the soup into the blender in two batches and purée till smooth. Reheat and serve, or reheat with

>*1 cup heavy cream or 1 cup sour cream.*

You can serve it cold after several hours of refrigeration. Mix with cream or sour cream or with just a dab of sour cream floating in each bowl.

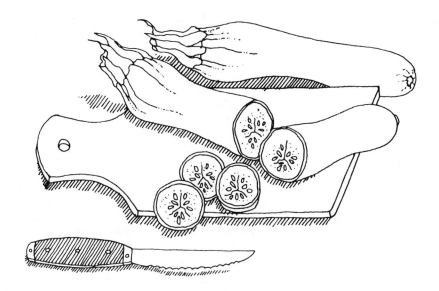

BROCCOLI SOUP (Serves 6)

Follow the recipe for Zucchini Soup, substituting

> *3 cups pared and chopped broccoli*

for the zucchini.

CUCUMBER SOUP (Serves 4)

The cucumbers in my garden, like the zucchini, grow to gargantuan size, probably because they're next to the compost heap. Unless you too have giants, you'll need about 3 medium-sized cucumbers, so that after peeling, scooping out seeds and chopping you'll have

> *2½–3 cups chopped cucumbers.*

Simmer for 15 minutes in a covered saucepan with

> *1 small chopped onion in*
> *1 cup water.*

Purée this mixture in the blender until smooth.

In a large saucepan heat

> *1½ cans condensed chicken broth.*

In a bowl mix till smooth

> ½ can condensed chicken broth
> 3 tablespoons quick-mix flour.

Whisk this mixture into the hot broth in the saucepan. Then add the

> cucumber and onion mixture with
> a pinch of salt and white pepper.

Simmer and whisk till the soup thickens slightly. Whisk in

> 1 cup sour cream (yoghurt for dieters).

Serve at once garnished with chopped fresh dill or ½ teaspoon dill seeds.

   To serve cold, refrigerate for several hours. Whisk again and garnish with dill.

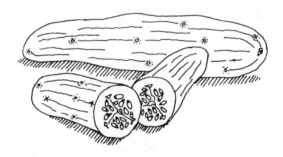

WATERCRESS SOUP (Serves 6)

This soup is tangy—terrific.

Wash and coarsely chop

> 3 bunches watercress.

Reserve a few leaves for the garnish. Then chop

> 8 scallions, white parts only.

Cook the scallions in a saucepan for 10 minutes over low heat in

> 2 tablespoons butter.

Add the

> chopped watercress
> ½ teaspoon salt.

Cover the pan and cook over low heat for 5 minutes until the leaves are soft. Sprinkle in

2 tablespoons quick-mix flour.

Cook for another 10 minutes, stirring occasionally. Then slowly stir in

1 quart Basic Chicken Consommé (page 87).

Simmer 5 minutes longer, then purée in the blender in two batches. Reheat the soup. In a bowl beat

2 eggs in
1 cup cream.

Dribble the egg mixture into the hot soup, whisking all the time. Serve at once and garnish with the reserve watercress leaves.

To serve cold, chill for several hours before garnishing.

ICED AVOCADO SOUP (Serves 4 to 6)

This is the last, not the least, of my favorite *cooked* soups.

Peel and halve

2 ripe avocados.

Put them in the blender with 1 teaspoon lemon juice and purée till smooth.

Pour the purée into the top section of a double boiler with

2 cans condensed chicken broth.

Heat the mixture over boiling water *just* till it starts to bubble. Then add

1 cup cream
a pinch of chili powder
salt and white pepper to taste.

Stir over heat till blended and set aside to cool. Refrigerate a minimum of 2 hours. Serve with thin floating slices of avocado.

UNCOOKED COLD BLENDER OR WHISKED SOUPS

In summer I serve at least two cold soups every weekend. Any of the last five soups can be prepared days ahead of time, refrigerated, covered tightly, whisked up again, and garnished at the last minute. They are delightful for luncheons, snacks or before a light dinner.

MITCH'S GAZPACHO (Serves 4)

A small volume could probably be filled just with recipes for this cold Spanish vegetable soup. I've tried dozens of them and am fully convinced that Mitch's is the best. Mitchell Erickson is multitalented—an actor, a casting director, a fine cook, and an angel. He taught me this best of gazpachos many years ago. The only person ever to turn up his nose at it was Boris Aronson, the famous scenic designer. My husband once suggested I call this book *Don't Serve Gazpacho to Boris*.

In the blender break up

> ½ *a stale roll or 1 slice stale bread.*

Cover with

> *1 cup tomato juice*

and blend till smooth.

To the mixture add

> ½ *peeled cucumber*
> *2 chopped shallots or scallions*
> *1 peeled, halved garlic clove*
> ½ *green pepper, deveined, seeded, and chopped*
> *3 tablespoons olive oil*
> *2 tablespoons tarragon vinegar*
> *1 teaspoon salt*
> *several gratings of pepper and nutmeg.*

Cover again with

> *2–3 cups tomato juice.*

The blender should be as full as possible without causing an overflow while blending. Blend till smooth. Chill for at least 2 hours before serving. It may separate sightly, so give it a final whirr in the blender before pouring into bowls.

Garnish with chopped chives or dill, thinly sliced cukes, or lemon wedges.

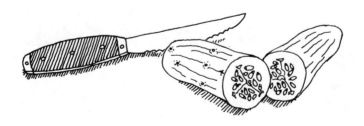

BORSCHT GAZPACHO (Serves 4)

In our family we're not borscht lovers, but this cold beet soup is an exception. Not even Boris Aronson would turn it down.

In the blender combine

> 1 8½-ounce can of beets plus juice
> 1 can condensed beef bouillon
> 1 small chopped onion
> 1 tablespoon lemon juice
> 1 tablespoon tarragon vinegar
> 1 cup sour cream
> salt and pepper to taste.

Blend till smooth and chill at least 2 hours. Whisk up again before serving. Garnished with chopped chives and lemon wedges.

GREEN GAZPACHO (Serves 4)

Hal Holden's recipes will dot this book. He's a perfectionist on stage, in the garden, and in the kitchen. As a matter of fact, he's a perfect *friend*. His recipe for green gazpacho brings the entire garden into the soup.

Into the blender pour

> ¼ cup condensed canned chicken broth
> 1 cup chopped watercress leaves
> 1 cucumber, peeled, deseeded, and chopped
> 1 green pepper, deveined, seeded, and chopped
> 3 tablespoons chopped dill
> 2 tablespoons chopped shallots or onion.

Blend this mixture thoroughly before adding

> 1¾ cans condensed chicken broth
> ½ cup mayonnaise
> ½ cup sour cream
> 2 tablespoons white wine vinegar
> 2 teaspoons sugar
> salt and white pepper to taste.

Blend till smooth and chill a minimum of 2 hours. Whisk up again before serving.

JELLIED CUCUMBER SOUP (Serves 4 to 6)

Beat and whisk this wonderful soup, but don't put it in the blender.
Peel

> 2 medium-sized cucumbers.

Remove the seeds and coarsely grate the flesh. Put into a bowl with

> 1 small grated onion
> ½ cup fresh mint leaves, minced
> ¼ cup lemon juice.

Whisk the mixture briskly until quite smooth. Then add

> 2 cans jellied Madrilène
>   or
> 2 cans jellied chicken broth.

Whisk again until smooth. Taste for additional seasoning and divide equally among glass bowls. Refrigerate overnight until completely set.

Garnish with fresh mint leaves.

CHILLED YOGHURT SOUP (Serves 4)

This has been called "'the last of the red-hot, iced, uncooked soups from Uta's kitchen."

In a large bowl whisk together

> 2 cups plain yoghurt
> 1 can condensed chicken broth
> 2 cucumbers, peeled, seeded, and grated
> ¼ cup minced radishes
> 1 tablespoon white wine vinegar
> 1 tablespoon olive oil
> 2 tablespoons fresh mint leaves
> 1 teaspoon sugar
> a pinch of salt and white pepper.

Pour into 4 pretty bowls to chill. Garnish with sliced radish and mint leaves.

VII. Pasta! Oh, Pasta!

In Rome one day I decided to do as the Romans do and have a plate of fettuccine for lunch. I learned then that pasta, to me a synonym for something rubbery encased in sticky tomato sauce, could be delicate, gentle, subtle, even comforting. I had another plate for dinner and soon I was eating it three times a day. From fettuccine, usually enhanced only by butter, a little cream, and grated Parmesan, I went on to other pasta, stuffed with ricotta or other delicious cheese, with spinach or with diced chicken or turkey breast. Soon I was able to distinguish between freshly made pasta and pasta made the day before. After such a discovery how can one even consider the commercial brands that stand for months on the grocer's shelf? When I returned to the States, I was determined to master pasta in my own kitchen.

I tried every available pasta recipe and followed the instructions to the letter. Making the dough gave me no trouble, but rolling it to the proper thinness and cutting the noodles correctly seemed impossible. Then one day I discovered the pasta machine. In no time I could roll out perfect fettuccine.

The machines are expensive (about $50), but they're a lifetime investment. There are many kinds but their methods for making pasta are similar. Mine screws to the table with a clamp and has a removable handle that fits into three different slots. The first slot turns two rollers that knead and flatten the dough. On the opposite side of this slot is a knob with different settings to control the thickness of the dough, the last setting turning out a sheet of dough almost paper thin. The second slot on the machine turns the blades that cut the noodles or fettuccine and the last slot cuts vermicelli, those little wormlike noodles so good in a bowl of broth, among other things. When making something like manicotti, ravioli, or lasagna, I simply roll out flattened sheets of dough and cut the squares or rectangles

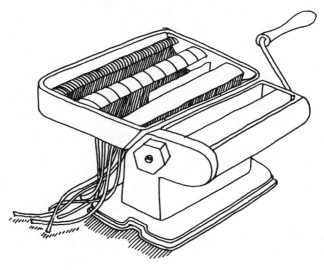

with a pizza cutter. If you become really adept and enthusiastic you might even learn to make tortellini or farfalle.

PASTA DOUGH (Serves 4 to 6)

The machines are accompanied by instructions and recipes but I want to share the things I've learned which are left unexplained.

Except for the green noodles on page 104, the ingredients for all my pasta are identical. Only the thickness of the dough and its cutting varies.

Golden semolina flour, from the best part of durum wheat, is used almost excusively for pasta in Italy. It's not easily come by and must be *finely* milled. Someone once gave me the coarser kind and the dough wouldn't hold together. Otherwise use unbleached flour to make marvelous dough. The recipe can be doubled, tripled, or cut in half and nothing changes except the time it takes to roll out and cut.

Into a bowl put

> 2 *scant cups unbleached flour (or fine semolina).*

Make a well and break in

> 2 *extra-large or jumbo eggs.*

Add

> 2 *tablespoons olive oil*
> 1 *teaspoon salt.*

Blend the mixture with a fork until it begins to stick together. Work it with your fingers; if it feels dry or too crumbly, run your hands under tap water before working the dough into a ball. If it seems too moist or sticky, work in a little more flour. In other words, more flour if it's sticky or a few drops of water if it's dry. Turn the ball of dough onto a lightly floured board and knead it like bread, pushing down and away with the heel of your hand, pulling together with bent fingers, turning the ball over and repeating the process again and again. Because of the machine, it's only necessary to knead for a few minutes, until the dough is fairly smooth. Roll the dough into a sausage about 2 inches in diameter and cover with an inverted bowl while you set up the machine. Traditionally the dough should now rest for an hour. I don't take the time, but immediately cut it into inch-thick slices and flatten them with the heel of my hand. The slices are then run through the front rollers, in the following manner:

1) Run each slice through the widest setting 4 times. If the strip of dough gets too narrow, turn it sideways the next time through the roller. If it gets some holes or ragged edges, fold it over on itself and run through the rollers again.

2) Run the dough through the middle setting, a piece at a time. During the rolling, as flour is absorbed, if the dough gets sticky, dust lightly with flour.

3) Run the strips of dough just once through the thinnest or next to thinnest setting. When completed they will be approximately 1 foot long, 5 to 6 inches wide, and very thin.

FETTUCCINE (Serves 4)

It takes about 20 minutes from the time I start the dough until I bring the platter of steaming fettuccine to the table. In the beginning it took much longer because I hadn't grasped the order of assembly.

In the kitchen set out a large platter and place on it

> *8 tablespoons unsalted butter cut into pieces.*

Have ready

> *½ cup grated Parmesan*
> *2 tablespoons chopped flat Italian parsley*
> *3 tablespoons cream.*

Noodles must have plenty of room to swirl in boiling water. Fill a large pot with

> *4–6 quarts water*
> *2 tablespoons salt*
> *1 tablespoon oil.*

While the water is coming to a boil on the stove, make the basic Pasta Dough (page 101), ending by running the very thin strips through the fettuccine cutter one by one. (I feed the strip into the cutter with the left hand and turn the handle with the right until it's halfway through. Then I switch hands, turning the handle with the left and gently catching the emerging noodles in the right.) Drop the noodles straight into the pot of boiling water as they come from the cutter. Guests love to watch this part because it's like a magic act. It's then they believe they're getting home-made pasta. When all the noodles have begun to bubble briskly, separate the strands with the handle of a wooden spoon. Then leave them alone to boil for about 5 minutes.

Meanwhile, put the platter with the butter into a 200° oven to warm up.

Empty the noodles into a colander in the sink. *Never* "wash off the starch." Holding the colander firmly in both hands, bounce the fettuccine briskly up and down until no more moisture is visible. Dump them at once on the butter on the platter and sprinkle with the 3 tablespoons cream. Toss the

> *½ cup grated Parmesan*
> *minced parsley*

on top. Bring the steaming platter to the table. Cheers will ring out and continue as you blend everything together, using two forks (wooden salad forks are best). The blending must be done quickly, turning and lifting the noodles until butter, cream, cheese, and parsley have coated the strands completely. Develop these motions into a flourishing routine.

Pile individual plates or bowls high with fettuccine and let each guest mill out his own pepper and sprinkle on more cheese.

Some people serve the pasta in a chafing dish, melting the butter at the table, but I believe it's just as festive my way.

Note: You may have noticed that I omitted an orthodox step of noodle making. After cutting, the strands are almost always dried before cooking. To do this the fettuccine are spread on sheets of wax paper or draped over the back of a chair for at least 30 minutes. They shouldn't touch each other or they'll stick together. I did it for years. Now I believe the only advantage is that the pasta can be prepared ahead of time, but I'm convinced the enthusiasm for "Uta's Fettuccine" results from cooking it the minute it's made. I'll fight the experts on this point, but try it both ways to decide for yourself. You may have to stretch the cooking time to 7 or 8 minutes if the noodles have been dried.

One afternoon in Montauk some students dropped in and I decided to treat them to pasta. They'd never sampled my wares and were waiting and ready in the dining room. When the pasta was assembled on the huge platter in the kitchen, I shouted, "Hey kids, get a load of *this*!" The platter had just come from the oven and forgetting to use pot holders, I lifted it with a flourish and shrieked, throwing the hot platter high into the air as the noodles flew around the room and over my head and shoulders. The students still aren't sure the whole thing wasn't an act.

Variations   I usually serve fettuccine the Roman way, as a first course, followed by broiled chicken, a roast, or scallopine. To embellish them for a main course, add

> *sautéed mushrooms*
> *diced, cooked chicken*
> *diced Virginia ham*
> *new peas*

or a combination of these things.

Most sauces disguise the flavor of pasta to such an extent that I wonder why people don't simply use the stuff from a box. I make two exceptions.

> *Pesto Sauce (page 43)*
> *or*
> *Pistou (page 44).*

However, *chaq'un à son gôut!* Try your favorites.

PASTA VERDE (Green Noodles) (Serves 4 to 6)

Green pasta, made by adding cooked spinach to the dough just before kneading and rolling out, is a special treat. In order to get the right texture and avoid a dough that looks like lumpy green tweed or is wet and soggy, I've devised the following steps.

Set a large pot on the stove with

> 4–6 quarts water
> 2 tablespoons salt
> 1 tablespoon oil.

Don't heat it yet, but place a sieve across the top lined with several thicknesses of cheesecloth.

Completely thaw

> 1 10-ounce package of chopped spinach.

Cook it in a skillet over medium-low heat for a few minutes with no additional liquid. Put it into the blender with whatever moisture has accumulated in the skillet and blend for several minutes till the mixture is smooth. You will have to stop the blender to push down the spinach over and over in order to achieve this. Scrape the spinach from the blender into the lined sieve over the pot of water. Press down hard on the spinach with the back of a spoon. The spinach water and a little of the purée will drip into the cooking water. When the spinach itself is as dry as possible, twist it again in the cheesecloth and put it, cheesecloth and all, into several layers of toweling to absorb still more moisture. You should be left with

> 5 tablespoons dry spinach.

To serve 4 to 6 people make the dough as described on page 101, using:

> 2 scant cups unbleached flour
> 1 jumbo or two small eggs
> 1 tablespoon oil
> 1 teaspoon salt.

When the dough has been mixed together with a fork, incorporate the

> 5 tablespoons spinach

and knead it into the dough for at least 5 minutes, working in a little more flour if necessary. When it is smooth and not at all sticky, run it through the rollers as for the fettuccine or any of the following recipes.

MANICOTTI (Serves 4 to 6)

After fettuccine, manicotti is my favorite pasta. The stuffings are exquisite, the sauces sublime; but let me begin with the dough.

Follow the procedure for basic Pasta Dough (page 101) but cut the ingredients by half, using:

1 scant *cup unbleached flour*
1 *extra large egg*
1 *tablespoon oil*
½ *teaspoon salt.*

When the dough has been mixed, kneaded, and run through the rollers until you have several long, wide sheets of thin dough, lay the sheets out on a lightly floured board and cut them into approximately 3-inch squares, using a wheel cutter. Gather the leavings and snippets of dough and work them into a ball. Flatten with the heel of your hand, run through the rollers again to make one or more extra sheets of dough, and cut more squares. You will have about 24 squares.

Cook about 10 squares at a time in the large pot of salted water with the oil for 5 or 6 minutes. Remove the squares to a colander with a slotted spoon and run them under cold water for a second so they can be handled. Place them on a cloth towel, turning them once so both sides will be dry. (Don't use paper toweling because the manicotti will stick.) Cook the next batch of squares, drain, and dry until all are completed. Have ready one of the stuffings that follow.

Preheat oven to 400°.

Near one end of each square place about 1½ to 2 tablespoons stuffing shaped like a little sausage and roll it up in the dough.

Oil a shallow baking dish (9 by 12 by 2 inches is a nice size). Place the stuffed manicotti side by side in a layer across the bottom. If need be, criss-cross a second layer over the first.

If you make this pasta in the morning, you can now cover the dish with wax paper and refrigerate till needed. Otherwise make the sauce at once and pour what you need to cover the manicotti, reserving extra sauce for serving. Bake for 15 minutes.

STUFFING FOR MANICOTTI LOTSA CHEESE (Serves 6)

The stuffing can be made the night before using and refrigerated to firm it up so it will be easier to handle.

In a bowl combine

> 1 cup freshly grated Parmesan cheese
> ½ cup diced mozzarella
> 1 cup ricotta (substitute cottage cheese if necessary)
> 4–6 chopped walnuts (optional)
> 2 tablespoons chopped parsley
> 2 lightly beaten eggs
> grated pepper and nutmeg
> a pinch of salt.

Blend the mixture thoroughly. (Refrigerate if you want.) Spread

> 1½–2 tablespoons stuffing

sausage fashion across the end of each manicotti square and roll it up.

Note: This stuffing works well rolled in Crêpes (page 28) to be baked in the same manner as manicotti.

SAUCE FOR MANICOTTI LOTSA CHEESE
(With or without mushrooms) (Serves 6)

Preheat the oven to 400°.

In a saucepan over low heat sauté

> 4 tablespoons minced shallots in
> 1 stick butter (8 tablespoons)
> ½ pound coarsely chopped mushrooms (optional).

Stir and simmer over low heat for 10 minutes.

Over the mixture, one at a time sprinkle

> 6 tablespoons quick-mix flour.

Blend it in with a wooden spoon. Then slowly add

> 4 cups warm half-and-half.

Stir until the sauce begins to thicken. A little at a time, add

> 1 cup coarsely grated Swiss or Gruyère cheese
> ¾ cup grated Parmesan
> 1 teaspoon salt.

Continue stirring over low heat until the sauce is satiny smooth.

Cover the manicotti generously with some of the sauce and grate a little pepper over it. Bake for 15 minutes. Serve the remaining sauce in a pitcher at the table so the guests can slosh more over their portions.

Note: Any leftover sauce or stuffing can be frozen in tightly sealed jars. It keeps for ages and reheats well.

STUFFING FOR MANICOTTI BELLAVISTA (Serves 6)

I gave this dish its name because you even begin to *see* beautiful things while eating it. It can serve as the main course of your dinner. The stuffing takes time so I usually make it in the morning. While I'm at it, I often double the recipe and freeze half for another meal, another day.

Poach one

> *3–3½ pound chicken (page 141).*

Remove the meat from the bones and discard the skin. On a large board chop the meat finely.

Wipe and chop

> *1 pound mushrooms.*

In a large, heavy skillet melt

> *2 tablespoons butter*
> *1 tablespoon oil.*

Cook the mushrooms in the fat over medium heat, stirring and separating until they have given off some of their moisture. Sprinkle the mushrooms with

> *2 tablespoons quick-mix flour.*

Blend and cook for several minutes. Add the cooked, chopped chicken and blend the mixture. Turn off the heat. In a saucepan make a small amount of white sauce: Melt

> *1 tablespoon butter*

and blend in

> *1 tablespoon quick-mix flour.*

Cook and stir for a minute. Add

> *½ cup warm milk*
> *a pinch of salt and white pepper.*

Stir until smooth and thickened. Pour the sauce into the mushroom-chicken mixture and blend.

After the manicotti squares have been cooked and dried on a towel, place about

1½–2 tablespoons stuffing, shaped like a sausage

across one end of each square and roll it up. Place the stuffed manicotti side by side in one or two layers into an oiled, shallow baking dish.

At this point the dish can be covered with wax paper and refrigerated till needed. If you still have stuffing, seal it in a jar and freeze it.

SAUCE FOR MANICOTTI BELLAVISTA

The amounts for this sauce may seem huge, but it's so *delicioso* that I've seldom seen any left over.

Preheat the oven to 375°.

In a large skillet heat

6 tablespoons butter.

Blend in and cook for 2 minutes

4 tablespoons quick-mix flour.

Slowly dribble in

3½ cups warm half-and-half.

Stir and let the sauce come to a boil. Lower the heat and simmer for several minutes until the sauce thickens and turns smooth.

In a bowl lightly beat

2 egg yolks in
½ cup half-and-half.

Whisk the mixture into the sauce and cook for another minute. Season with

1 teaspoon salt
¼ teaspoon white pepper.

Pour about half the sauce over the manicotti in the baking dish, making sure they're well covered. Sprinkle with

4 tablespoons grated Parmesan

and dot with

2 tablespoons butter.

Bake for 15 minutes or until the sauce begins to bubble. Reheat the remaining sauce and whisk again till smooth. Serve in a pitcher with the manicotti.

RAVIOLI (Serves 6)

In Italy the little jackets of pasta called *ravioli* were once used to encase leftovers: chopped beef, lamb, veal, chicken, and all kinds of vegetables mixed with binders and placed into little ravioli packages. If the idea appeals to you, once you get the hang of it you can invent your own stuffings. The Toscana and Bacci stuffings on page 111 don't use leftovers, but they're my favorites.

Follow the procedure for making Pasta Dough (page 101), but use

> 1 scant *cup flour*
> 1 *jumbo egg*
> 1 *tablespoon oil*
> ½ *teaspoon salt.*

When the dough has been kneaded and rolled into a sausage 2 inches thick, cut it into wider slices (1½ to 2 inches each) so the strips will be as wide as possible and much longer than those used for fettuccine or manicotti after being rolled through the various settings. Aim for thin strips of dough about 5 inches wide and 24 inches long. Lay them out on a lightly floured board and cut them in half, lengthwise. Each half should be at least 2 inches wide.

Have the filling ready. Put 1 heaping teaspoon of stuffing every 2 inches down one halved strip. If the dough has begun to dry, dip a pastry brush into warm water and moisten it around the edges and in between the little heaps of filling. Now, *lightly* place the other half of the sheet on top of the filled one. Use your index finger to press the dough together around the edges and between each spoonful of filling, making sure the dough is stuck firmly together so the ravioli won't come apart in the cooking. With a pastry wheel, straighten out the edges and cut the ravioli into neat little squares between fillings. Let them rest on a kitchen towel or on lightly dusted-with-flour wax paper. When they're all made, they can be refrigerated between sheets of wax paper until time to cook. Or they can be cooked at once.

In a large kettle bring to boil

> 4 *quarts water*
> 1 *tablespoon oil*
> 2 *teaspoons salt.*

Turn down the heat so the water simmers. Slide in about 10 ravioli and cook for 10 minutes. If you crowd too many into the pot, they'll get gummy. Test for tenderness by nibbling a corner without biting into the filling. If it needs further cooking, drop it back into the pot for another minute or so.

To keep the ravioli warm while you cook the remaining batches, heat the oven to 200°. Put a pan in the oven large enough to hold a metal colander. As each batch is completed, remove with a slotted skimmer and slide it into the colander in the oven to drain and stay hot.

You will have about three dozen ravioli. Place about 2 tablespoons butter into the bottom of individual serving bowls and divide the ravioli among them by *gently* sliding them out of the colander.

Serve with a pitcher of melted butter, a bowl of grated Parmesan, a pepper mill, and a dish of chopped parsley to let each person doll up his own ravioli.

RAVIOLI FILLINGS

The Manicotti Lotsa Cheese recipe on page 106 is excellent. So is this variation on it.

RAVIOLI TOSCANA

In a bowl combine

> 1 cup ricotta cheese
> 1 cup coarsely grated Swiss, Gruyère, or Emmenthaler
> ½ cup diced mozzarella
> 1 beaten egg
> ½ cup cream
> salt, pepper, and nutmeg to taste.

Blend well and refrigerate for at least 1 hour before using.

Note: This stuffing is also delicious rolled up in Crêpes (page 28) and baked like the Manicotti Lotsa Cheese.

RAVIOLI DI BACCI

Thaw

> 1 10-ounce package frozen chopped spinach.

Cook it in a heavy skillet over low heat without any additional water until just hot. Remove it to a fine sieve and squeeze out every drop of moisture with the back of a spoon. Into the blender put

> 2 large eggs
> 1 cup ricotta (cottage cheese if need be)
> the dry cooked spinach.

Blend till smooth. Little by little, while blending, add

> 6 tablespoons grated Parmesan
> 4 tablespoons quick-mix flour
> 1 teaspoon salt
> a few gratings of pepper and nutmeg.

Blend till smooth and refrigerate a minimum of 1 hour. Use a scant table-spoon of this filling for each ravioli. Any amount left over will freeze well.

RAVIOLI SAUCES

I prefer ravioli topped just with melted butter and grated Parmesan. If you want sauces, try the White Sauce (page 38) or the Cheese Sauce (page 39). Both sauces for Manicotti (pages 107 and 109) work beautifully.

BACCI DI CARUSO (Serves 6)

Herbert and I discovered these mouth-melting wonders, otherwise known as the Kisses of Caruso or Green Gnocchi, on the Via Appia in Rome at a restaurant incongruously called Escargot. I began experimenting and came up with something special.

Prepare the ingredients for Ravioli di Bacci (page 111) in exactly the same way. Transfer the mixture from the blender to a bowl and refrigerate *uncovered* for at least 2 hours, until quite firm.

In a large kettle bring to a boil

> 4 quarts water
> 1 teaspoon salt
> 1 tablespoon oil.

Lower the heat until the water makes only an occasional little air bubble, as for poaching. From the cold spinach mixture spoon out large plum-sized Bacci and push them from the spoon gently into the water. Continue until the batter is used up. They will sink to the bottom. *Don't* cover the pot. In 3 to 5 minutes the kisses should float upward. If they don't, gently loosen them from the bottom one by one with the edge of a wooden spoon. Let them float another 3 to 5 minutes and remove them with a slotted skimmer, a few at a time. Without shaking them, allow the water to run from the spoon before sliding into warm individual bowls.

Serve with a small pitcher of melted butter and a dish of grated Parmesan. They will be a dream come true!

VIII. Seafood

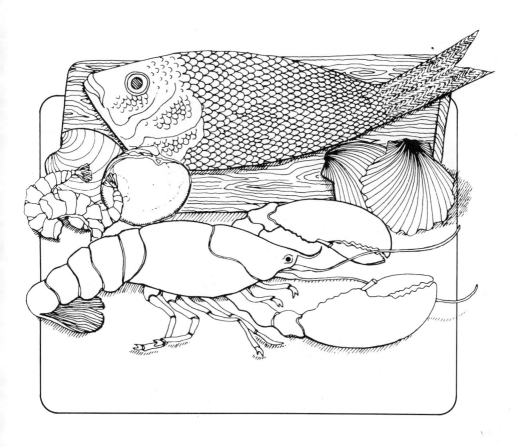

The Italians call it "frutta del mare," or fruit of the sea. I love it. After I began living in Montauk, my appreciation for it increased. This "resort" was once a simple fishing village, and the established families are still hard at work bringing up food from the briny depths.

The annual "blessing of the fleet" is an event not to be missed. We stand on the dock among singing choir boys, acolytes swinging incense, nuns, and priests ready to bless each boat as it sails by, festooned with garlands of flowers and paper streamers. An occasional boat draped in black is a grim reminder that a fisherman died at sea.

As with fruit and vegetables, the seasonal anticipation of each fish or shellfish doubles the pleasure. Throughout the year I can watch the fishing boats from the windows of my house and I speculate about the kinds of fish or the abundance of the catch. I wonder when the fishermen sleep as I see their lights speckling the ocean on a black night. Sometimes they are indistinguishable from the stars. On a wild sea in January or February, I shiver to see the boats toss and flounder among the churning waves, and try to imagine what the men are going through in their yellow slickers, stalking their quarry like a bunch of Ahabs.

The fun of trips to the marinas in the late afternoon to watch the fishing boats bring in a day's haul has never abated. The gulls swoop over the ships in hot pursuit shrieking out their delight and avarice. Whether it's a gray, misty day or crystal, sharp blue and shining, storming with clouds and gusts, or even drizzling with rain, it's always beautiful. Although fishermen seem to have a rocklike temperament, the activity around each landing slip becomes more and more feverish as the boats unload.

If I can't get to the docks in Montauk for my seafood, I have a large selection of extraordinary fish markets available in New York City—from Fulton Street and Greenwich Village to the upper east side.

Since my life is on the Eastern Seaboard, I'm only going to deal with the seafood available to me and the kind I prepare most often, although there are so many delicious sweet-water fish. I still remember the Wisconsin lake trout, bass, and white fish from my childhood.

On page 70 I've already discussed clams and oysters. Poached and Marinated Shrimp are on page 72. Snails, often referred to as shellfish, are on page 69. But I haven't yet discussed one of my favorite seafoods, the scallop.

Scallops

The small, delicate bay scallops are preferred, but when they're scarce or too expensive, I settle for the larger sea scallop and use them for the same recipes, each one cut into three pieces. Years ago they were sold in a sandier condition, but they still need thorough washing to remove traces of grit or sand. Then they should be drained and dried thoroughly on toweling.

MARGARET'S SIMPLEST TASTY SCALLOPS (Serves 3 to 4)

Margaret Stark, my beautiful painter friend, showed me this simplest of all ways to serve scallops.

Wash and dry

> 1 pound bay scallops (or sliced sea scallops).

In a skillet large enough to cook the scallops in a single layer, melt

> 4 tablespoons butter.

Sauté the scallops in the butter over medium-high heat for 3 or 4 minutes, stirring and turning until they turn pale gold. Serve at once sprinkled with a little salt, pepper, and lemon juice. Garnish with chopped parsley.

If you want to add wine, follow the above recipe and when the scallops are golden, remove to a serving plate, using a slotted spoon. To the remaining butter in the skillet, add

> ½ cup good dry wine.

Stir over heat for 30 seconds and add

> the juice of half a lemon.

Stir again. Believe it or not, the sauce will thicken slightly. Spoon it over the scallops and serve *tout de suite*.

SCALLOPS IN WINE WITH MUSHROOMS
(Coquilles St. Jacques) (Serves 4 to 6)

This is a light, elegant first course. I serve it in scallop shells, but small glass plates look festive too.

Wash and drain dry

> 1 pound bay scallops (or sea scallops cut in thirds).

Wash and slice

> ½ *pound mushrooms.*

In a large, heavy skillet with a lid, simmer a combination of

> 1 *cup dry white wine*
> 2 *tablespoons minced shallots or scallions (whites only)*
> 1 *bay leaf*
> *a pinch of salt and pepper.*

Cook over low heat for 5 minutes before adding the mushrooms and scallops. Cover and simmer another 5 minutes. Remove the scallops and mushrooms from the liquid with a slotted skimmer and set to one side. Discard the bay leaf.

Boil down the liquid uncovered to one cupful. Pour it into a measuring cup.

In the skillet melt

> 3 *tablespoons butter.*

Blend in

> 3 *tablespoons quick-mix flour.*

Use a wooden spoon to stir and cook over low heat a few minutes before whisking in the cup of liquid. Add

> 1 *cup warm cream.*

Stir and cook until the sauce thickens. Remove from heat.

In a bowl beat

> 2 *egg yolks with*
> ¼ *cup cream.*

Slowly whisk this mixture into the sauce. Return to medium heat, bring to a boil, and whisk another 30 seconds. Season to taste with

> *salt*
> *white pepper*
> *a little lemon juice.*

Add the scallops and mushrooms to the sauce and fold them in well.

Butter 6 scallop shells or one shallow baking dish and divide the scallops among them. Sprinkle with

> ½ *cup coarsely grated Gruyère or Swiss cheese.*

Dot with

> 2 *tablespoons butter.*

Serve them at once after placing them under the broiler for a minute until the top turns golden.

SCALLOPS PROVENÇALE (Serves 6)
(With herbs, garlic, cheese, and wine.)

I used to consider this hearty but elegant main course an economy dinner. Now, with soaring prices, I serve it for special events. The recipe can also be cut in half to be served in shells as a first course. It's always a treat.

Mince

> *1 large onion to equal ¾ cup*
> *4 shallots or scallions (white part only)*
> *2 large garlic cloves.*

Sauté the vegetables in

> *3 tablespoons butter*

in a heavy skillet over medium-low heat for 10 minutes until they're soft but not brown. Set them to one side.

Wash, drain, and dry

> *2½ pounds bay scallops (or sliced sea scallops).*

Sprinkle them lightly with salt and pepper before placing them a handful at a time into a brown paper bag with

> *½ cup quick-mix flour.*

Hold the bag shut and shake to bounce the scallops around until well coated with flour, then lift them out and shake to allow excess flour to escape between your fingers. Sauté in four or five batches in a large skillet in

> *2 tablespoons butter*
> *1 tablespoon oil.*

Stir and turn the scallops until they are golden on all sides. Remove them to a plate and begin the next batch, adding a little more butter and oil to the skillet if needed. Leave the last batch in the skillet and return the rest of the scallops to it. Add the onion, shallot, and garlic mixture and over everything pour

> *1 cup dry white wine*

and add

> *a pinch of thyme*
> *1 bay leaf.*

Stir with a wooden spoon for a few seconds to blend and scrape the bottom of the skillet to deglaze it. Then cover with a lid and simmer 5 minutes. Remove the lid and fish out the bay leaf. Pour the mixture into a shallow oiled baking dish and sprinkle with

> ½ cup coarsely grated Swiss or Gruyère cheese.

Dot with

> 2 tablespoons butter.

If serving at once, run the dish under the broiler till the cheese melts. If you've refrigerated it during the day, reheat in a 350° oven for 15 minutes before running under the broiler.

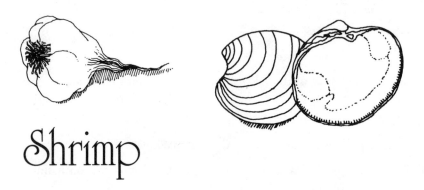

Shrimp

Poached Shrimp, which I usually serve cold, is on page 71. Marinated Shrimp is on page 72. They can be served with a sauce, blended into salads, or combined with other food such as artichokes. I have only two other favorite ways of preparing this jewel of the sea. Be sure to try the next recipe which uses a terrific batter (also used for chicken or veal scallops). It's light, puffy, and golden and gives the food real zing.

UTA'S FLUFFY BATTER (Serves 4 to 6 as a hors d'oeuvre, 2 to 3 as an entrée)

Make in the morning, because lengthy refrigeration improves it.

In a bowl combine

> ¼ cup flour
> ½ teaspoon curry
> a few gratings of nutmeg
> a pinch of salt.

In another bowl lightly beat

> 1 egg yolk with
> 3 tablespoons beer (milk is a fair substitute).

Save the egg white for later. Add the egg mixture to the flour mixture and stir till smooth. Cover and refrigerate. Just before needed, beat the egg white till stiff and fold it into the batter.

BATTERED SHRIMP (Serves 4)

Peel

> 1 pound raw shrimp.

Be careful not to yank off the tails. With a sharp pointed knife slit open the backs and lift out vein and roe. Wash the shrimp under cold running water and dry thoroughly. This much can be done an hour before cooking. Then, in a large skillet heat to 375°

> 1 inch vegetable or peanut oil.

Use your thermometer. (Read about deep-frying on page 16.) Meanwhile, beat the egg white as described above and fold into the batter. Hold a shrimp by the tail and swoosh it in the batter till coated. Lower it into the hot fat. Continue dunking each shrimp in the batter and adding it to the fat. Turn the shrimp once and in a minute or two it will be a puffy golden poem. Remove with a slotted spoon and drain on toweling. Serve as is or accompanied by

> Hollandaise Sauce (page 41)
> or
> Tartar Sauce (page 43).

GOURMET'S SHRIMP DELIGHT (Serves 4)

After the initial cleaning, slicing, and chopping, this dish takes about 10 minutes to prepare (although your guests will think you spent all day on it).

Peel, devein, wash, and dry thoroughly

> *1½ pounds shrimp.*

Wipe and slice

> *½ pound mushrooms.*

In a large skillet over medium heat sauté till soft

> *1 small chopped onion in*
> *4 tablespoons butter.*

Raise the heat a little and add the shrimp. Cook and stir 4 or 5 minutes until firm. Remove the shrimp and onion to a warm plate with a slotted spoon. To the skillet add

> *1 tablespoon butter*
> *the sliced mushrooms.*

Sauté them briskly over higher heat until they turn lightly brown. Sprinkle with

> *1 tablespoon quick-mix flour.*

Cook and stir another minute or so. Turn down the heat and quickly return the shrimp and onion to the pan. Pour in

> *1 cup sour cream.*

Blend, stir, and cook for a few minutes until the cream is heated. Season with

> *salt and white pepper to taste*

and serve.

> (*Optional:* Stir in a diced avocado at the last minute.)

BOILED LOBSTER

I'm a passionate animal lover, and a dilemma sets in when you are also a passionate lover of cooked lobster. Somewhere between these two states of passion a moment of murder must be dealt with. I've devised a method that allows the smallest amount of anguish for both me and the lobster. The only visual confrontation with the live lobsters is at the dock, when the salesman fishes them from the tank for inspection. The size of tails and claws is important because they're the best part. I usually select a

pound-and-a-half lobster per person.

After they've been put into a thick brown paper bag, I make sure to keep the bag tightly closed and when I get home I put it straight into the refrigerator where I know the creatures are nicely numbed by the cold. Don't refrigerate them longer than a few hours. When the time is ripe, I fill my huge lobster pot (page 4) about ¾ full of water and add

a handful of sea salt or coarse salt.

(I used to drag up a bucket of water from the sea along with handsful of kelp and other seaweed to season the water. It's a waste of time.)

When the water is boiling briskly the moment of truth is at hand. I handle it this way: take the paper bag from the refrigerator with one hand, holding the lid of the pot poised in the other. Aim the bag upside down over the pot. Turn your back to the stove and shake the lobsters out into the pot. Keep your eyes shut while you bang the lid down, and be comforted by the knowledge that death was instantaneous. In any event, don't dwell on it.

Ignore all the old fishermen's recipes that recommend starting the lobster in cold water and allowing them to come slowly to a boil. It will ensure a loud, banging, lingering death.

Let the water return to a boil. If it starts to boil over, slip the lid a little to one side. In 15 minutes you will have gorgeous, tender, cooked lobster. Remove them from the water with tongs or two big spoons and drain them in the sink. Use pot holders to hold them first by the head and then by the tail to let water run out. Place them, one at a time, on a

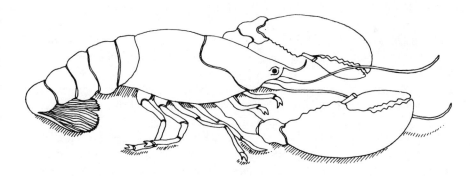

large cutting board and use a sharp knife to make a slit down the underside of the tail. Spread the tail slightly apart. Hold upside down to let more water run out. Serve at once.

Set the table to include a large bowl for empty shells. If you don't have lobster-crackers, use nutcrackers. Set out tiny oyster forks to help pick little pieces of meat from the shells. Prepare

> Lemon Butter (page 47)

and serve it in individual bowls for dunking. Put a bowl of

> Fanny's Mayonnaise (page 42)

in the center of the table for anyone who prefers it and pile in.

Fish

COOKING METHODS

The cliché about a fish being delicate is true. It has to be handled tenderly, with patience, and usually it should be cooked slowly over low heat.

Fish recipes fall into four different categories. Once these are clear, it is easy to proceed with variations.

1) Gentle cooking or sautéing in butter and oil over low heat.
2) Breaded or floured fish fried in butter and oil.
3) Fish poached or steamed in wine and fish broth.
4) Baked fish.

Variations in the recipes lie in the choice of butters, seasoning, poaching liquids, and sauces.

TYPES OF FISH

Categories for North or Middle Atlantic fish are confusing. For instance, what we call "sole" is a catch-all name for flounder, fluke, yellow-tail, gray sole, and lemon sole. They are all delicate, filet well, and can be served in many ways. Fluke is fattier than flounder, yellow-tail is tangier, lemon sole has a subtler flavor, and gray sole is the most expensive. I'm not sure why.

Bass, striped bass, and bluefish, all typical catches on the Eastern Seaboard, are larger, as a rule, and richer. They can be fileted, but I often leave them whole for poaching. Halibut falls between these and the larger fattier fish such as tuna, swordfish, and salmon. The tiny fish such as smelts, baby flounder, or baby blues are too small to filet. I prefer them breaded and fried whole. I'm not crazy about cod so I've omitted it.

AMOUNTS NEEDED

On the average you will need a scant ½ pound of fish per person. Sometimes you will need large amounts of poaching liquid or fish *fumet* to cover the entire fish, and other times you'll need only a little for steaming. For sautéing, use at least 2 tablespoons of butter per half pound of fish. Sauces are generously prescribed but the leftovers preserve well.

CLEANING AND PREPARING FISH

Fishermen or fishmongers fileting a fish are as beautiful to watch as fine sculptors or woodcarvers at work. When attempting it myself, my clumsiness makes me wildly impatient and I end up blaming it on the razor-sharp knives. So I leave it to the experts. At the dock or at the market, I ask them to do the fileting for me. If I want to cook a whole fish, I ask them to scale the fish and remove the entrails. To make a fish fumet, I ask for the skeletons, heads, and tails that other customers have left behind. When I get the fish home, I wash and dry it. Unless I'm planning to cook it the same day, I always freeze it, wrapped in wax paper or plastic.

Sautéed Fish Filets

Use filets of fish weighing under 2 pounds, such as small bluefish or bass and any of the sole family, flounder, fluke or yellow-tails, lemon or gray sole.

AU NATUREL (Serves 4)

The simplest way of preparing filets takes only a few minutes, and may possibly be the best way.

With salt and pepper sprinkle

>   *1½–2 pounds clean fish filets.*

In a large heavy skillet melt

>   *4–5 tablespoons butter.*

When the butter has foamed and the foam subsided, turn the heat to low and add the filets, cooking gently for 2 or 3 minutes on each side. When turning them over, use a flipper gently so they won't break apart. When the fish is firm and easily pierced with a toothpick, it's done. Remove to a platter and pour the butter from the pan over it. Season with a few drops of lemon juice, sprinkle with chopped parsley, *et voila!*

IN BROWN OR BLACK BUTTER (Serves 4)

Follow the preceding recipe, *except* that you will begin with

> 6 tablespoons Brown or Black Butter *(page 46)*

Dust the filets with a little quick-mix flour and cook in the prepared butter over low heat. When the cooked fish has been moved to the platter, to the butter in the skillet add

> ¼ *cup slivered almonds*

and sauté them for a minute until light brown. Pour the butter and almonds over the fish. Garnish with chopped parsley and lemon wedges.

BATTERED TINY FISH

Prepare smelts or baby flounder or blues exactly as for breading except that you will dip them first into just a little flour and then into the Fluffy Batter (page 118) and deep-fry them like Battered Shrimp (page 119).

BREADED SMELTS, BABY FLOUNDER, OR BABY BLUES
(Serves 4)

These small fish should be no more than 4 inches long and 1 inch thick. One pound will serve 4 people. When they're this size or smaller they don't usually need to be scaled or degutted, but if you prefer it, ask them to do it for you at the market. You also have the option of leaving on heads and tails. I do.

Follow the breading technique described on page 21, first sprinkling the fish with salt and pepper, then dusting with flour, coating with beaten egg, and finally rolling in bread crumbs. At this stage they can be covered with wax paper and refrigerated for several hours. Or they can be sautéed at once in

> 3 or 4 tablespoons butter
> 1 tablespoon oil.

Turn the fish after 2 minutes or so over medium-high heat. When they are golden on both sides, remove to a platter and garnish with lemon wedges and chopped parsley or chopped dill.

BREADED FISH FILETS

Cleaned and dried fish filets are breaded and cooked exactly like the preceding smelts or other small fish.

BATTERED FISH FILETS WITH ZUCCHINI (Serves 6)

In the morning make Uta's Fluffy Batter (page 118) and double the amount. Refrigerate it. Save the egg whites.

Make a marinade for the fish by combining

> ½ cup olive oil
> ⅓ cup lemon juice
> 1 teaspoon salt
> a pinch of white pepper.

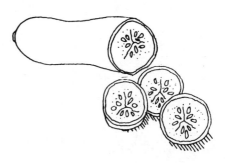

Into 1-inch pieces cut up

> 1½ pound flounder filets.

Add them to the marinade, making sure they're well coated. Cover and refrigerate.

An hour or so before dinner, peel

> 6 small zucchini.

Cut them into strips about 2 inches long and ½ inch wide. Place the strips in a colander and sprinkle with

> 2 tablespoons coarse salt.

Let them drain for 45 minutes. Pat them dry and set aside while you beat up the egg white and complete the batter (page 118).

In a heavy skillet heat to 375°

> 1 inch of vegetable or peanut oil.

Meanwhile, remove the slices of fish from the marinade and dry thoroughly with toweling. Dust lightly with flour and dunk, piece by piece, first into the batter and then into the hot oil. Don't crowd the pan. Do it in batches. The oil will be deep enough so you won't have to turn the fish. When it is finished, removed from the oil and drained on toweling, keep it hot on a platter in a 200° oven while you repeat the process with the zucchini strips. Dust them with flower, dip into the batter until coated, and then lower them into the oil in batches until completed. Season to taste with salt and pepper and serve at once with lemon wedges. It's pretty terrific.

Poached Fish Filets

You'll find these delicate dishes most often in France and Austria. Now you can have them on your own table.

IN WHITE WINE (Serves 6)

Preheat the oven to 350°.

Wash and dry

> 2½ *pounds fish filets.*

Sprinkle lightly with salt and pepper.

Mince

> 3 *tablespoons shallots.*

Spread them over the bottom of a shallow buttered baking dish (one that can take direct heat). Place the filets on top of the shallots overlapping each other. Dot with

> 2 *tablespoons butter.*

Cover the fish with

> ¾ *cup dry white wine.*

If needed, add a little water.

Cut out a piece of wax paper the exact size of the rim of the baking dish and smear it on one side with butter. Place the paper over the fish, butter side down. Let the liquid come to a simmer on top of the stove before placing the dish into the middle of the hot oven. Bake for 10 minutes and give the fish the toothpick test. When easily pierced, it's done. If it isn't, bake another few minutes.

Turn off the oven and remove the dish. Draw the cooking liquid from the dish with a bulb baster or gently pour it off into a bowl, without disturbing the fish. Replace the wax paper on the fish and put the dish back into oven, leaving the door ajar to keep the fish warm without further cooking while you prepare the sauce.

The Sauce

Use the poaching liquid, supplemented as needed with wine, cream, or eggs, to make one of the White Sauces on page 38. An addition of capers is always sprightly. Pour the sauce over the fish in the baking dish and serve at once.

POACHED FISH IN WHITE WINE WITH MUSHROOMS
(Serves 6)

Follow the preceding recipe for poached fish filet. Just before pouring the wine over the fish, stop to add

    ½ pound sliced mushrooms

that have been sautéed for a few minutes in

    2 tablespoons butter.

Spread the mushrooms over the fish, then add the wine. Continue with the given recipe.

GRATINÉED, SAUCED POACHED FISH

If you enjoy a lightly browned gratinée after the sauce has been poured over the cooked fish, sprinkle

> *¼–½ cup grated cheese*

over the sauce. Coarsely grated Swiss, Emmenthaler, or Gruyère or finely grated Parmesan are all very nice. Dot the cheese with butter and run the dish under the broiler to brown for a few minutes. Serve at once.

CHEATER'S SOLE FLORENTINE (Serves 6)

As you probably know, the term "Florentine" when applied to cooking means food served on a bed of spinach. I always think I'm cheating when I use food I haven't cooked from scratch, but I really like the packaged frozen creamed spinach when combined with other ingredients.

Preheat the oven to 350°.

Poach and drain

> *2 pounds filet of sole (page 126).*

Set to one side while you follow the directions on the package for cooking

> *2 10-ounce packages frozen creamed spinach*

or make creamed spinach (page 262).

Butter a large, shallow baking dish and spread the spinach over the bottom. Arrange the filets on top of the spinach, slightly overlapping each other.
Make White Sauce with Egg (page 39) and pour it over the fish.

Sprinkle the sauce with

> *¼–½ cup coarsely grated Swiss cheese*

and dot with

> *2 tablespoons butter.*

Bake until all the ingredients have been heated through, about 20 minutes.

COLD FLOUNDER IN VODKA SAUCE
(To be served with cocktails or as a first course.)

Select the smallest flounder still large enough to filet. You'll need

> *2 small sole or flounder filets per person.*

Roll up each filet and tie it with kitchen twine. Place side by side in a heavy pan and cover them completely with

> *Fish Fumet (page 130)*
> *or*
> *half white wine, half water.*

Cover the pan and poach the fish for less than 10 minutes over very low heat. Pierce with a toothpick to see if it's done. Drain and chill in a covered bowl in the refrigerator for at least 4 hours.

The sauce should refrigerate the same length of time, so make it the minute you've finished the fish. In a bowl combine

> *½ cup sour cream*
> *½ cup mayonnaise*
> *3 teaspoons Dijon mustard*
> *1 teaspoon lemon juice*
> *1 pressed garlic clove*
> *1 tablespoon grated onion*
> *a pinch of salt and white pepper.*

Stir the ingredients thoroughly and then stir in

> *4 tablespoons Russian vodka.*

Finally fold in

> *1 small jar red caviar.*

Cover with plastic wrap and refrigerate at least 6 hours.

At serving time, cut the strings from the filets and arrange them on a platter or on individual plates and slather them with the sauce.

COLD FLOUNDER IN AVOCADOS

Prepare rolled flounder or sole filets and poach them as described in the preceding recipe. After refrigeration, cut the strings and arrange them in avocado halves that have been rubbed with lemon juice. Place 1 or 2 filets in each half, depending on the size of the avocado, and douse each one with

> *3–4 tablespoons Uta's French Dressing (page 48).*

They can be embellished even further by surrounding with a few cold poached shrimp.

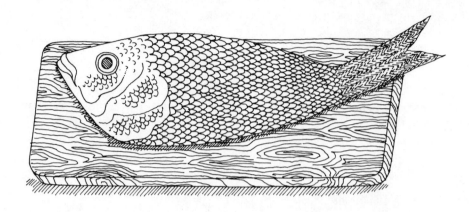

POACHED WHOLE FISH (Serves 6-8)

Serving a three-to-six-pound whole fish on a platter cloaked in a pale, fluffy sauce always makes me feel grand, civilized, old world. I've acquired a fish poacher; a long rectangular pot fitted with a rack that can be lifted out by handles. The fish rests on the rack and is easily lifted out when finished, to be slipped onto a platter without trouble or breakage. Before I owned the poacher, I used a large roasting pan, lowering the fish into it and lifting it out again by the long ends of string and cheese cloth in which the fish was wrapped. It works almost as well. I'll describe both methods in detail a little further on.

My idea of perfection would be a whole salmon from Nova Scotia or Scotland. But I'll settle for a whole poached bass or bluefish. Unless the fish is too big for the pot, leave the head and tail intact. Have the fish scaled and the entrails removed at the market. Ask the fishmonger to sell you a pound of fish heads and tails at bargain prices or even give them to you as a present to make your poaching liquid.

As soon as you get home, wash the fish and the leavings and refrigerate them until you're ready to begin. Start by making the broth or fumet. The surplus freezes well. It also jells when cold and can be used for aspics.

Fish Fumet (The Poaching Liquid)

Into a kettle put

> 1 pound fresh, washed fish scraps. (Heads, tails, skeletons and skin. Most fish will do. Don't use mackerel—it's too fishy.)

To the scraps add

> *1 large sliced onion*
> *2 large sliced carrots*
> *a few celery leaves*
> *a few parsley stems (leaves darken the broth)*
> *the rind of half a lemon*
> *5 peppercorns*
> *1 teaspoon salt*
> *1 cup dry white wine*
> *1½ cups water.*

Simmer the broth uncovered for ½ hour, no longer. Strain through a sieve and a few layers of cheesecloth. Let it cool before using for poaching.

Cooking the Fish in a Poacher

Oil the rack of the pot before placing the fish on it so it won't stick. Place the scaled, cleaned fish on the rack, leaving head and tail intact unless it's too long for the pot. If it is, chop off head and tail and freeze them for another fumet. Pour the poaching liquid over the fish. It won't cover the fish. It may just cover the bottom of the rack, so cut out several large layers of cheesecloth, wet thoroughly with broth, and drape over the fish to keep it very moist during the cooking. Put the lid on the pot and bring the liquid to a simmer before lowering the heat to maintain just the slightest little bubbles.

Poach the fish for ½ hour, or 5 minutes to the pound. A toothpick should easily penetrate to the bone when it's done. Lift the rack from the pan, using pot holders. Remove the cheescloth and slide the fish gently onto a warmed platter. Place it into the oven at the lowest possible temperature to keep warm while you make the sauce (see below).

Poaching the Fish in a Roasting Pan

Follow the above procedure, *except* that you wrap the entire fish in several layers of cheesecloth. Tie the cloth with string at both ends of the fish, leaving long tails that can easily be reached to lift out the fish at the end of the cooking time. Oil the bottom of the roasting pan before placing the fish in it. If the pan has no cover, mix a little of the poaching liquid with water and dunk a clean kitchen towel into it till sopping wet. Place the towel over the fish and baste during the poaching to keep moist at all times. When the fish is done, remove the lid or towel and lift out the wrapped fish by the long ends of string and cloth. Place it on a warmed platter before cutting off the cheesecloth. Tenderly pull it out from under the fish. Keep warm in a low oven, as low as it will go.

The Sauce

You can choose any of the White Sauces (pages 38–39), but double the amounts. They go well with the fish, using the poaching liquid as a base. I like this variation the best.

In a heavy skillet blend

> *4 tablespoons quick-mix flour*
> *4 tablespoons melted butter.*

Cook over low heat for several minutes. Slowly add

> *3 cups hot, strained poaching liquid or fumet.*

Let the mixture come to a boil over low heat and whisk it until it starts to thicken.

In a bowl lightly beat

> *3 egg yolks*
> *1 cup cream.*

Dribble this mixture into the sauce and continue to whisk over low heat for a minute.

Capers are traditionally omitted from sauces that use milk or cream. I enjoy them anyway, so try adding

> *3 tablespoons drained capers*

folded into the sauce.

Serving the Poached Fish

Take the platter of fish from the oven and tilt it to let accumulated moisture run off. Use the point of a knife to loosen a corner of fish skin and peel it from the top of the fish. At this stage I usually mask the fish with sauce. However, if you're courageous and want to debone the fish first, slide a knife along the top of the spine to lift the top half of fish from the bone with two spatulas or flippers and place it gently beside the bottom half. Use the knife to lift out the spine and large center bones. You can now replace the top of the fish over the bottom, or you can leave the two halves open. Wipe the edge of the platter with toweling before pouring the sauce over the fish. It's beautiful no matter how you slice it!

BARBECUED WHOLE FISH

I can't resist adding this recipe for barbecue-owners. All the wonders of my life seem to come together when I prepare fish in this way; the sea, the garden, the terrace, the entire land and seascape.

I bring home a large scaled fish, entrails removed, head and tail intact, and wash and refrigerate it before getting the coals ready on the barbecue. Just before cooking time, I stroll through the garden to cut stalks of fresh fennel, parsley, dill, and tarragon. Sometimes I add a stalk of mint. The grill gets thoroughly brushed with oil before being set over the glowing coals. Then I place the sheaves of herbs across the grill, quickly brush the fish with light sesame oil, and lay it on top of the steaming, fragrant herbs. In 5 to 10 minutes, depending on the size of the fish, I lower the heavy lid of the barbecue and cook it for another 10 minutes. (If your barbecue has no lid, turn the fish as carefully as possible with two spatulas, trying not to break it.) When it's firm and easily pierced with a toothpick, I lift it gently from the herbs and serve it at once with lemon butter or lemon wedges, and I thank the Lord for the bounties of life.

BAKED FISH (Serves 6)

Use clarified butter (page 46) to avoid smoking or burning while baking. Although the sole family can be prepared in this way, I usually bake the fattier fish. Swordfish or halibut are nice.

Preheat the oven to 325°.

Oil a large, shallow baking dish and put in

> 3 pounds whole, cleaned fish
> or
> 3 pounds fish steak in one or more pieces.

Rub the fish with

> 4 tablespoons clarified butter.

Bake for 30 minutes, basting every 5 minutes with more clarified butter. Pierce with a toothpick. When easily pierced, remove the fish to a warm platter. Sprinkle with

> salt and pepper.

Garnish with chopped parsley and lemon wedges and serve. It can also be served with one of the White Sauces (pages 38–39).

COVERED BAKED FISH (Serves 4)

Use

> 2 pounds of fish pieces cut in 2-to-3-inch squares.

Preheat the oven to 350°.

Rub the pieces with

> *clarified butter*

and sprinkle lightly with

> *salt, pepper, and nutmeg.*

Place the pieces into an oiled baking dish or casserole that has a lid. Cover and bake 10 minutes. Remove the lid to add

> *2 tablespoons dry white wine.*

Cover and bake 10 minutes longer. Give it the toothpick test. Serve on a warm platter and cover with the sauce from the baking dish.

Sprinkle with a few

> *drained capers and*
> *chopped dill or parsley.*

Surround with

> *lemon wedges.*

FISH FILETS BAKED IN SOUR CREAM (Serves 4 to 6)

Preheat oven to 350°.

Oil a shallow baking dish. Wash

> *2 pounds fish filets.*

Place the filets in overlapping layers into the dish, seasoning each layer with

> *2 teaspoons lemon juice*
> *salt and white pepper.*

Cover the fish with

> *1½ cups sour cream.*

Bake for 25 minutes or until easily pierced with a toothpick. Garnish with chopped dill or parsley and serve at once.

COLD SALMON MOUSSE (Serves 4 to 6)

For grand dinners I occasionally make this recipe for a first course. It's also a lovely summer luncheon dish.

In a small bowl soften

> *1 envelope gelatin in*
> *2 tablespoons vermouth.*

Meanwhile, in a saucepan over low heat cook

> *1½ tablespoons minced shallots in*
> *2 tablespoons butter.*

When the shallots are soft add

> *1 cup fish fumet (page 130), or chicken broth, in a pinch.*

When the liquid is hot, add

> *the gelatin in wine.*

Simmer over low heat and stir until the gelatin is completely dissolved. Pour the contents of the pan into the blender. After having removed bones and skin from

> *1 8-ounce can of salmon*

add it to the blender and purée till smooth. Fold in

> *1½ tablespoons brandy*
> *salt, pepper, and nutmeg to taste.*

When the mixture is completely cool, fold in

> *½ cup heavy cream, whipped.*

Lightly oil a 2-to-3-cup mold or metal bowl and pour in the salmon mixture. Refrigerate for 4 to 5 hours. Just before serving, put scalding water into a larger bowl and dip in the mold just to the brim for a second. Shake the mold gently to see if the mousse has loosened. Put a plate over the top and invert the whole thing. Lift the mousse from the mold and serve at once.

SEA SQUAB (Blow Fish)

My son-in-law, Brandy, used to catch this strange-looking fish with regularity and then throw it away. One day he learned that the tails were delicious, and after a little research discovered they were otherwise known as "sea squab." When the fish is first caught, it really blows up as if in a rage. The head is so ugly I won't dwell on it.

Remove and discard everything except the tail. The tails are small and you'll need

> *3 or 4 tails per serving.*

They can be ·

1) deep-fried in batter like the shrimp (page 119)
2) sautéed like fileted fish (page 123)
3) breaded like smelts (page 124) or
4) poached like filets (page 126).

FROGS' LEGS (Serves 6)

Frogs' legs have the taste of very special fish and the texture of chicken breast. Ask the butcher to skin them for you.

All the recipes suggested for the sea squab are applicable to frogs' legs. But I have one more recipe for frogs' legs or sea squab that is a fitting end to this chapter.

Sprinkle

> *2½ pounds frogs' legs (or sea squab) with*
> *2 tablespoons brandy.*

Cover with plastic wrap and refrigerate for 3 to 4 hours.

Mince

> *2 tablespoons shallots*
> *2 tablespoons onion*
> *2 tablespoons garlic.*

Sauté this mixture in a skillet over low heat for 5 minutes in

> *5 tablespoons butter.*

Dry the frogs' legs or sea squab thoroughly with toweling (reserving the marinade) and dust them lightly with a quick-mix flour.

Turn the heat under the skillet to medium high and sauté the frogs' legs in the vegetable mixture and butter until they are golden on all sides. Remove them to drain on towels. To remaining butter in skillet add

> *the brandy marinade.*

Stir and cook for a minute.

Place the frogs' legs on a platter and pour the sauce from the skillet over them. Sprinkle with lemon juice and chopped parsley and serve at once. *Très bons!*

IX. Poultry

At the beginning of my first marriage, when Christmas Eve rolled around I decided to carry on the family tradition by serving roast goose. I was in my teens and it hadn't occurred to me yet that cooking might present some problems. As I look back on the ensuing disaster, I can only imagine that I must not have owned a cookbook or, if so, that I couldn't have read it very thoroughly. I remember I didn't have a roasting pan and used the broiler tray that came with the stove. Confidently I salted the goose and stuffed it with fresh and dried fruit and nuts, because I had a vague recollection that my mother had done "something like that." I also recalled that the fruit was moist, so I doused it with brandy and put the whole thing in the oven. My young husband and I were running around in matching pajamas and robes, setting the table and finishing the Christmas decorations. The guests were to be my brother Holger, who was arriving early to help us with dinner, my father, and the famous director Guthrie McClintic. At one point I stopped to check on the goose. Grease was spouting from it like a fountain and the pan was about to overflow. I yelled for help. My husband tilted the pan to let the grease run out into the pot I held under it. When the same procedure had to be followed twenty minutes later, I decided the goose was sick. The third time we drained the grease, we tipped the pan too far. The goose slithered out and landed in the middle of the kitchen floor while bubbling fat spattered our hands, feet, and faces. Our shrieks were heard for blocks, our tears flowed, and despair set in. We simply gave up, shut the kitchen door, and tried to forget about the goose still lying on the floor. As we nursed the wounds of our bodies and souls, my brother walked in. He roared with laughter, picked up the goose, put it back in the pan, wiped out and relit the oven, and finished the roasting. He even cleaned up the pools of fat on the floor. He put unguentine on our burns, wiped our tears, helped us with the rest of the meal and also devised a hot cordial from the extra fruit stuffing by adding brandy, wine, and spices. The dinner was a smashing success and since then, every Christmas Eve I've served a *proper* roast goose (page 171).

We eat more and more poultry because of rising meat prices. When I think of the many recipes, the varieties of the poultry itself, size, texture, and taste, it's foolish to think of it as second best. We enjoy everything in the chicken family, from the tiniest broiler to the largest capon. We love duck and goose and once in a while a small fat turkey.

Chicken Facts

The size of the chicken is usually related to its age, the smallest being the youngest. I was once so dumb I thought the labels dictated the kind of preparation; a broiler was broiled, a fryer fried, a roaster roasted, and a hen boiled. It didn't occur to me that a fat broiler or fryer could be roasted. I was right, however, that an old hen could *only* be boiled; for fricassee, salads, or minced stuffings.

Unless I'm doing one of the many chicken breast recipes, I buy the chicken whole, and if it needs to be cut up, I do it myself at the last moment. It may be an old wive's tale, but I'm convinced the chicken loses flavor if it's cut up long before cooking. I couldn't do without my poultry shears. Although I know how to bone a chicken breast, I take advantage of the butcher's skill and let him do it for me the same day I'm going to cook it. If you want to learn how, ask him to let you watch. He'll probably be flattered.

CHICKEN STOCK

"Waste not, want not!" I turn green at the sight of someone throwing out unwanted chicken "waste." Everything is usable. Every other recipe seems to call for stock or chicken broth. I use it in such quantities that even though I make my own I still need to supplement it with canned broth. I have a "stock pile" in the freezer which I allow to accumulate until I have a proper amount of hearts, gizzards, necks, wing tips, backbones (if the chicken has been cut up), and skin. I save the liver in a separate package for special use, or if I want it for a snack, I sauté it on the spot to mash deliciously on a piece of toast. The fat attached to the skin just inside the cavity can be frozen and "rendered" (page 17) when needed to make a marvelous base for frying and sautéing other food. (A recipe for rendered goose fat, the gem of poultry fats, is on page 172.)

The amount of chicken pieces used in relation to the amount of liquid is not crucial because the stock will eventually be combined with other ingredients. Here's an approximate recipe. Into a kettle with

> *2 quarts water*

put

> *1 pound washed chicken pieces; hearts, gizzards, wing tips, necks,*
>   *backbones, and skin*
> *1 diced celery stalk*
> *a dozen parsley stems (leaves darken the stock)*
> *1 small chopped onion*
> *1 small chopped carrot*
> *2 peppercorns*
> *a pinch of salt.*

Add pinches of your favorite herbs as desired. Simmer the stock covered for about 1½ hours. Strain through cheesecloth or a fine sieve and keep in sealed containers in the refrigerator. The fat that rises and hardens on the top is a protective covering, so don't remove it until the stock is needed. If you freeze it, leave room for expansion at the top of the container.

POULTRY CARCASS STOCK

The stock made from the carcass of a chicken, duck, turkey, or goose may very well be the best of all.

Place the pieces of a broken up carcass and all left over poultry bones into a kettle with

> *1 cup coarsely chopped onion*
> *1 cup coarsely chopped carrots*
> *1 chopped celery stalk, plus leaves*
> *1 coarsely chopped parsnip*
> *a few parsley sprigs and stems*
> *1 garlic clove, cut up*
> *a pinch of thyme*
> *½ teaspoon salt*
> *a few peppercorns*
> *6–8 cups water, depending on the size of the carcass.*

Cover and bring to a boil. Skim off the scum. Reduce the heat and simmer, tightly covered, for two hours. Strain through a fine sieve or cheesecloth.

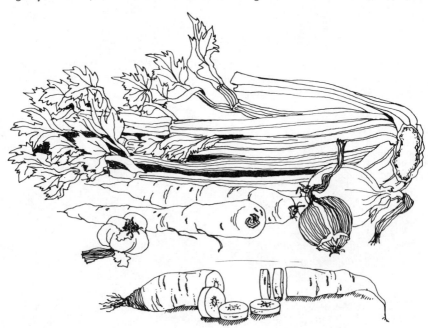

PLAIN POACHED CHICKEN (Serves 4)

Chicken poached in wine (page 150) is more elegant than this recipe, but I often need cooked chicken for salad or chopped stuffing. Then I prepare it in such an easy way that even Herbert can make it for himself when I'm not home. Any size chicken will do.

The large fat hens no longer seem readily available, but use one if you can. Otherwise wash a

> *3½–4-pound chicken.*

Put it in a kettle and cover it three quarters with boiling water, leaving the breast exposed. Add

> *a few sliced carrots*
> *1 chopped celery stalk with leaves*
> *1 large quartered onion*
> *a few parsley stems*
> *2 peppercorns*
> *1 teaspoon salt*
> *a pinch of tarragon and thyme*
> *the heart and gizzard.*

Cut out two layers of cheesecloth, moisten it in the water, and place over the breast. Cover the pot, bring the water back to a boil, then lower the heat to keep the liquid barely simmering for about 2 hours. Jiggle a drumstick; if it moves in its socket, the chicken is done. Remove it from the kettle and serve with a white sauce or with mayonnaise. Or dice it or slice it for salads or stuffings.

Strain the broth and follow the same procedure for refrigerating or freezing the preceding Chicken Stock.

TRUSSING A BIRD

The method to be described is identical for any poultry you cook whole, whether you're planning to roast it, stuff it, braise it, or poach it in wine. Some people make a fuss about it, but it's not difficult and you'll end up with a compact bird that has no protruding limbs to overcook, burn, or char.

I use small skewers and kitchen string. It can also be done with a trussing needle and heavy-duty thread. Take your choice and sew in the same manner that I skewer and tie.

When roasting a chicken or browning it before braising or poaching, wipe the chicken with a damp sponge rather than washing it. Then dry thoroughly with toweling. It won't respond properly to these methods if it's

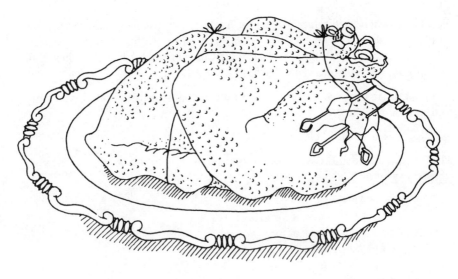

wet or damp. Anything that goes into the cavity, whether it's stuffing or just a piece of lemon, should be placed inside before trussing.

First, fold back the wing tips under the wings. They'll stay in place. Pull the neck skin across the neck opening between the wings and secure it to the backbone with a skewer (or sew it in place). Tie a piece of string around the front end of the chicken to hold the wings snugly against the body. Remove the loose fat from the skin inside the cavity between the legs and save it for rendering. Stick three or four small skewers across the open cavity, evenly spaced, and criss-cross them with string the way you would lace up a boot. Cross the legs over the closed cavity and tie them together. Take another piece of string to tie around the lower half of the chicken, holding the legs tucked snugly against the body. All done!

ROAST CHICKEN

From a tiny squab chicken to a capon, any chicken can be roasted. Only the cooking times varies. Figure ½ pound per person.

>   40 minutes for a small squab chicken weighing one pound
>   50 minutes for a 1½-pound broiler
>   60 minutes for a 2-pound chicken
>   1 hour and 20 minutes for a 3-pound chicken
>   1 hour and 45 minutes for a 5-pound chicken
>   For larger capons, figure 15 minutes per pound.

Preheat the oven to 450°. (It will be turned to 350° later.)

Remove giblets and fat from the cavity. Damp wipe and then dry the chicken.

Rub inside and out with

> *a quartered lemon or lime.*

Use your hands to rub inside and out with

> *2–3 tablespoons softened butter.*

Into the cavity sprinkle

> *a pinch of tarragon or thyme.*

I never salt the chicken until after it's been cooked because I believe it toughens the meat. Three stuffings are on pages 144–45. If you are using one, add it at this point.

Truss the chicken, following instructions on page 141.

Place the chicken in a shallow roasting pan and set it in the middle of the hot oven for 10 minutes, then lower the heat to 350°.

In a small saucepan melt

> *2 tablespoons butter*
> *1 tablespoon oil.*

Have it ready with a pastry brush to baste the chicken every 10 minutes or so. I used to be lazy about this, but it guarantees a juicy, evenly browned chicken.

When the roasting time is over, jiggle the drumstick. If it moves in the socket, it's done. Or stick a pointed knife into the fat part of the drumstick. If the juice running out is yellow with no touch of pink, the chicken is done.

Season the chicken with sea salt and grated pepper as soon as it comes out of the oven after it's received its last swipe of butter with the pastry brush.

Additional Options and Notes for Roast Chicken

When roasting tiny chickens or Rock Cornish game hens, do two or three at a time. After roasting, split them in half to serve one half per person.

If you want to avoid basting while the chicken is in the oven, dip a large napkin or several layers of cheesecloth into melted butter and place over the breast and thighs. Remove for the last 15 minutes in the oven to allow browning.

or

Cover the breast and thighs with a few pieces of blanched bacon (simmered in water for 10 minutes and drained). Never use foil or "browning bags." The chicken will be steaming, not roasting.

If the chicken should stay hot while making gravy or other food, put it into the oven on a platter, keeping the door ajar and the heat turned off. Don't reheat roast chicken. It will dry out.

Gravy

If you want gravy, take it into consideration before starting the chicken. Strew the bottom of the pan with

>   *1 thinly sliced onion*
>   *2 thinly sliced carrots.*

Place the trussed chicken on top of the vegetables. When the chicken has been removed from the pan and is resting in the warm oven, skim as much fat from the pan juices as possible. Add

>   *1 tablespoon chopped shallots or scallions.*

Sauté them in the pan for a few minutes on top of the stove and then pour in

>   *1 cup chicken or beef broth.*

Cook and stir over high heat until the liquid has reduced by half. Strain it. If you like, blend in

>   *⅓ cup cream.*

Reheat and add

>   *salt and pepper to taste.*

THREE STUFFINGS

If stuffing is left over, freeze it in sealed containers for another time. *Never stuff a chicken until the last minute. Both chicken and stuffing may contaminate if you do it ahead of time, even when refrigerated.*

MUSHROOM STUFFING

Make the Duxelles on (page 62) and double the recipe.

>   *Optional:* If you saved chicken livers, sauté for 3 or 4 minutes

>   *4 chicken livers in*
>   *2 tablespoons butter.*

Mince and add to the Duxelles.

Add

> 2 tablespoons softened cream cheese
> 1 tablespoon softened butter
> 1 tablespoon chopped parsley
> salt and pepper to taste.

Stuff the chicken loosely with this mixture. The stuffing will swell a little during the cooking. Truss the chicken and proceed with the roasting, adding about 15 minutes to the cooking time.

SPINACH STUFFING

Make the stuffing for Ravioli di Bacci (page 111). Loosely stuff the chicken with it, truss, and roast.

When the stuffing has been removed from the chicken for serving, baste it with pan juices or melted butter.

KASHA STUFFING

Make Kasha (page 242). You can cook it with or without the mushroom and onions. Simmer it about 5 minutes less than usually required so it will still be moist when being stuffed into the chicken. Truss and roast the chicken and add 15 minutes to the roasting time. Leftover Kasha can be refrigerated and reheated for another meal or snack.

BROILED CHICKEN (Serves 4)

Every time I watched Julia Child on television I learned something new. She once announced a program about broiling chickens and I flicked on the set with little enthusiasm, thinking there was nothing I didn't know about that subject. In a few minutes she had demonstrated a way of cutting a whole chicken and flattening it to create a uniform height so nothing protruded to burn or cook unevenly.

Wipe

> a 2½–3-pound chicken
> or
> 2 1–2-pound chickens.

Use poultry shears to cut out the backbone. Starting at either side of the protruding neck nob, cut straight down through the back and up again on the other side of the tail. Save the bone for your "stock pile." Open up the chicken and place it on a board, breast side up. With the flat side of a cleaver or the heel of your hand, give the breast a hard whack to flatten it and break the bone. Turn the wing tips back and tuck them securely under the wings. Loosen the leg joints slightly and tuck the legs snugly against the breast.

Preheat the broiler.

Rub the chicken on both sides with

>*2 tablespoons softened butter*
>*1 teaspoon oil.*

Butter the broiling pan or, better still, a shallow baking dish just large enough to hold the flattened chicken comfortably. Arrange the chicken in the pan or dish breast side down, making sure the cavity lies as flat as possible. Place it under the broiler. After five minutes, lower the heat to 475°. Always leave the broiler door ajar!

Meanwhile, in a saucepan melt

>*2 tablespoons butter*
>*1 tablespoon olive oil.*

Use a pastry brush to baste the chicken every 5 minutes. After 15 minutes for small chickens or 20 minutes for a larger one, turn the chicken breast side up. Use tongs or wooden spoons to rearrange the thighs, making sure they're tucked against the flattened breast. See that the wings are flat against the bottom of the pan. Continue broiling and basting every 5 minutes for another 15 to 20 minutes. Baste for the last time after removing from the oven and sprinkle the chicken in the pan with the juice of a lemon and a tablespoon of coarse salt or sea salt and grated pepper. De-grease the pan a *little* and pour the lemony drippings over the chicken.

Chickens en Casserole

A chicken can be roasted in a casserole with or without a cover, or it can be braised or poached. The flavor of the cooking liquids will be absorbed by the fowl to enhance it further. Don't use anything much smaller than a three-pound fryer or roasting chicken, but the following recipes should suffice even for a medium-sized capon if you add a little more butter or liquid, as the case may be.

CHICKEN WITH TARRAGON (Serves 4)

Preheat the oven to 325°.

Rub

> *a 3-pound chicken*

inside and out with

> *2 tablespoons softened butter.*

Sprinkle the chicken with

> *a little grated pepper.*

Into the cavity place

> *a few sprigs of fresh tarragon (or a pinch of dried).*

Truss the chicken (page 141).

In a large, heavy skillet melt

> *2 tablespoons butter*
> *1 tablespoon oil.*

Brown the chicken in the fat over medium-high heat. Use two wooden spoons to turn it so the skin won't break. It will take about 15 minutes to brown evenly on all sides. Meanwhile, in a heavy casserole that has a lid and into which the chicken will fit comfortably, over low heat cook

> *1 thinly sliced onion*
> *2 thinly sliced carrots in*
> *2 tablespoons butter.*

In 10 minutes, add

> *4 sprigs of fresh tarragon (½ teaspoon dried).*

Place the browned chicken, breast side up, on top of the vegetables and baste with any remaining butter in the skillet. If the butter has burned, remove it from the skillet; if it's been used up, melt

> *2 tablespoons butter*

and baste the chicken with it. Sprinkle the chicken and vegetables with sea salt or coarse salt. Cover the casserole first with a layer of foil and then with the lid. Roast for approximately 1 hour and 15 minutes. Jiggle the drumstick and if it moves in the socket, the chicken is done. Put the chicken on an ovenproof platter, remove the skewers and trussing strings, and return it to the oven with the heat turned off and the door ajar to keep warm while you make the sauce.

The Sauce

To the vegetables and juice in the casserole add

> *2 cups chicken stock or 1½ cans condensed broth.*

Simmer for several minutes. Let rest for a minute and skim off as much fat as possible.

In a small bowl mix

> *1 tablespoon cornstarch*
> *2 tablespoons Madeira wine.*

Blend till smooth and stir the mixture into the broth. Simmer and stir for a few minutes longer, until the sauce starts to thicken. Taste for additional seasoning. Strain through a fine sieve and serve in a pitcher, or pour directly over the chicken.

Note: Chickens en Casserole are *not* delicious when overcooked, so watch them carefully and always test to see that they're done after the minimum cooking time.

COQ AU VIN ROUGE (Serves 4)
(Chicken Poached in Red Wine)

I part company with most cooks in the preparation of this famous standby, because I prefer the whole chicken to chicken that has been cut into pieces.

Wipe and dry

> *a 3-pound chicken.*

Rub inside and out with softened butter and truss it (page 141).

In a heavy casserole into which the chicken will fit nicely, over low heat sauté

> *6 slices lean, blanched bacon (simmered in water 10 minutes) in*
> *2 tablespoons butter.*

Remove the bacon and set aside.

In the fat in the casserole, brown the chicken over medium-high heat using two wooden spoons to turn it and brown it properly on all sides. It will take about 15 minutes. Make sure the fat doesn't burn. Remove all but 1 tablespoon of fat with a bulb baster. Add the bacon to the chicken and cover the casserole tightly. Turn the heat low and allow the chicken to simmer for about 15 minutes. Remove the cover and pour

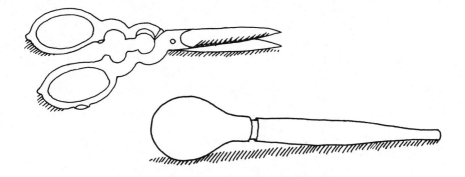

> *3 tablespoons brandy*

over the chicken.

Light a match to flame the brandy, being sure to keep your head back. Spoon the flaming juice over the chicken until the flames have died out. To the pot add

> *1 cup beef or chicken stock or canned condensed broth*
> *2 cups dry red wine.*

The liquid should just cover the chicken, so use less or add more accordingly. Add

> *2 pressed garlic cloves*
> *2 teaspoons tomato paste*
> *½ teaspoon thyme*
> *1 bay leaf.*

Simmer the chicken over low heat for about 45 minutes. If the drumstick moves when slightly jiggled, the chicken is done. Put the chicken on a platter, remove the skewers and trussing string, and place it in a 200° oven to keep hot. To the liquid in the pot add

> *salt and pepper to taste.*

Let it settle for a minute before skimming off as much fat as possible. Bring to a brisk boil uncovered and let it reduce to about 2½ cups. In a small bowl mix

> *1 tablespoon cornstarch*
> *2 tablespoons cold water.*

Stir the mixture till smooth and whisk it into the sauce. Replace the chicken in the casserole with the sauce and bring the whole pot to the table or arrange it on the platter and pour the sauce over it. Garnish with

> *a few parsley sprigs.*

COQ AU VIN BLANC (Serves 4)
(Chicken Poached in White Wine)

Wipe and dry

> *a 3½–4-pound chicken.*

Rub inside and out with

> *2 tablespoons softened butter.*

In the cavity put

> *sprigs of fresh tarragon (or a pinch of dried).*

Truss the chicken (page 141).

Preheat the oven to 325°.

In a heavy casserole over low heat sauté for 10 minutes

> *1 large onion, thinly sliced*
> *2 large carrots, thinly sliced in*
> *2 tablespoons butter.*

Place the trussed chicken on top of the vegetables breast side up and over it pour

> *1½ cups dry white wine*
> *1–2 cups chicken broth.*

The liquid should come about halfway up the sides of the chicken. Add

> 6 *parsley stems (leaves darken the broth)*
> *a few tarragon sprigs (or a pinch of dried)*
> *1 teaspoon salt*
> *the heart, liver, and neck of the chicken.*

Dip several thicknesses of cheesecloth into the liquid in the pot and drape it over the breast and thighs to keep them moist. Place a lid on the casserole and put it into the preheated oven for 1½ hours. Lightly jiggle a drumstick. If it moves in the socket, it's done.

Gently take the chicken from the pot with two wooden spoons and allow it to drain in a colander. Remove skewers and trussing strings and tip it to let the liquid drain from the cavity.

The Sauce

Strain the juices from the casserole through a fine sieve into a bowl. Press down on the vegetables to extract all flavor. Wipe the casserole with toweling and replace the chicken in it with a little of the strained juice. Put the casserole back in the oven with the heat turned off and the door ajar.

Skim as much fat from the strained juice as you can. In a large saucepan melt

> *4 tablespoons butter.*

Blend in

> *6 tablespoons quick-mix flour.*

Cook and stir for a few minutes and then add

> *2½ cups of the strained juice.*

Simmer and stir until the sauce begins to thicken. Then stir in

> *½ cup heavy cream.*

Simmer and stir until the sauce will coat a wooden spoon. Season to taste with

> *salt, white pepper, and a little lemon juice.*

Lift the chicken gently out of the casserole and place it on a hot platter. Mask it with the sauce and decorate with parsley, watercress, or fresh tarragon. Pour the remaining sauce into a pitcher and serve separately.

Note: This chicken is also fabulous served cold with a Chaud-froid Sauce (page 45), using the liquid as a base.

GAME HENS EN CASSEROLE (Serves 6)

A hearty, satisfying dish for a chilly autumn evening, it's relatively inexpensive. It can be made in the morning and reheated for 20 minutes just before serving.

Buy

> *3 Rock Cornish game hens.*

Let them reach room temperature before cutting in half with a large, sharp knife. Damp wipe and then dry them thoroughly. Rub on both sides with softened butter and set aside.

Choose a casserole large enough to hold the 6 hen halves comfortably propped up side by side. In the casserole melt

> *4 tablespoons butter*
> *1 tablespoon oil.*

In the butter sauté

> *2 slices of bacon till crisp.*

Reserve the bacon. Pour off and discard half the fat.

Sprinkle the hen halves with pepper and brown them on both sides in the fat in the casserole. It will take about 15 minutes to do them all, two or three at a time, over medium-high heat, being careful not to let the fat burn. Remove the hens with a slotted spoon and let rest on a plate. In the fat in the casserole for 10 minutes gently cook

> *4 tablespoons minced shallots*
> *1 thinly sliced onion*
> *1 thinly sliced carrot.*

Remove the vegetables with a slotted spoon. Into the remaining fat blend, stir and cook

> *4 tablespoons quick-mix flour.*

After a few minutes add

> *2 cups dry white wine*
> *2 cups chicken broth or canned condensed broth.*

Cook and whisk the sauce until it comes to a boil and starts to thicken. Turn down the heat and stir in

> *½ teaspoon thyme*
> *6 or 7 chopped basil leaves (or a pinch of dried)*
> *½ teaspoon chervil (or fresh sprigs if you can get them).*

When the sauce has simmered for a few minutes, add the cooked vegetables and place the hen halves side by side at an angle. If the sauce doesn't cover the birds, spoon some from the casserole to moisten the uncovered part. Cover tightly and simmer for 40 minutes till done.

Meanwhile, after the hens have begun simmering, wipe and slice

> *1 pound mushrooms.*

Sauté them 5 minutes in

> *4 tablespoons butter.*

When the hens are done, remove them to a plate with a slotted spoon. Strain the sauce through a sieve into a bowl, pressing down hard on the vegetables to extract flavor. Add salt to taste. Wipe out the casserole and pour back the strained sauce. Bring it almost to a boil and replace the hens. Place the cooked bacon strips over the hens and sprinkle the sautéed mushrooms on top. Simmer for a minute or two to heat through before bringing the whole beautiful dish to the table.

Chicken Pieces

I used to have lovely recipes only for boned chicken breasts because I preferred them to wings, legs, and thighs, but I was in a dilemma because chicken breasts when purchased separately cost much more per pound than buying the whole chicken. I've finally found some tempting recipes that let me use up everything without a sense of compromise. Ask the butcher to bone the breasts (and, ideally, cook those the same day). Then ask him to cut the rest of the chicken into small pieces. When you get home, freeze the backbone, neck, wing tips, and innards for the "stock pile." Wrap the pieces of legs, wings, thighs, and backs separately to freeze until you want to make one of the following recipes. You may enjoy them so much you'll want to include the breast, in which case simply quarter the unboned breast.

BACKHENDL, OR CHICKEN À LA SACHER (Serves 4)

Once Herbert took me to Vienna. It was the only time a visit to Europe *surpassed* my dreams. He introduced me to the haunts of his youth, among them the Café Sacher. I finally tasted their famous Backhendl (literally, baked chick, but actually chicken pieces fried in an airy batter). After seeing and tasting it I finally worked out a recipe.

Begin in the morning by making Uta's Fluffy Batter (page 118). Let it rest in the refrigerator and add the beaten white just before you start cooking.

You will need at least

> 3 *small chicken pieces per person.*

(For more than 12 chicken pieces, double the batter recipe.)

Sprinkle the chicken pieces with salt and pepper and dust them lightly with quick-mix flour. In a heavy casserole heat to 360°

> 2–3 *inches peanut or vegetable oil*

using your thermometer. While it's heating, beat the egg white and fold into the batter.

Dip the chicken pieces one at a time into the batter to coat thoroughly and then slide them into the hot fat. Let them fry 5 to 10 minutes until they fluff up and turn golden. Turn them once if they aren't covered by the fat. Do them in batches. Don't crowd the pan. Remove them with a slotted spoon and drain on toweling. Keep them hot on a platter in a 200° oven until all the pieces are cooked.

Serve at once with chopped parsley and lemon wedges.

CHICKEN PAPRIKA (Serves 4)

For this Hungarian classic, be sure to use first-class, mild, imported paprika. It can make a real difference.

Wipe and dry

> 12–16 *small chicken pieces.*

Sprinkle with a little salt.

In a heavy, deep skillet or casserole with a lid heat

> 2 *tablespoons butter*
> 1 *tablespoon oil.*

When the foam has subsided, add the chicken pieces a few at a time in order not to crowd the pan. Sauté in batches on each side over medium heat until golden brown. Add butter between batches as needed. Remove to a plate. Check the butter in the skillet. You should have

2 tablespoons butter.

Add

2 cloves pressed garlic
1 cup thinly *sliced onions.*

Turn the heat to medium low and cook the vegetables for 10 minutes until they're soft, stirring occasionally. Add

2 tablespoons imported paprika.

Stir it into the pan to coat the onions. Add

1 cup chicken broth or canned condensed broth.

Bring the broth to a boil, stirring occasionally. Add the browned chicken pieces and return to a boil before turning the heat way down. Cover skillet or casserole snugly and simmer for 15 minutes. Meanwhile, in a bowl blend till smooth

2 tablespoons quick-mix flour
1½ cups sour cream.

Use a slotted spoon to remove the chicken and onion from the casserole and keep warm on a platter in a 200° oven.

Stir the sour-cream mixture into the liquid in the casserole and whisk until it starts to thicken after 5 to 10 minutes over low heat. Return the chicken and onions to the sauce and simmer for 1 minute before serving.

EXOTIC CHICKEN PIECES (Serves 4)

One week before you plan to cook this dish, prepare the lemon oil. It's a cinch. Simply stud

1 lemon with
12 whole cloves.

Press the point of the cloves into the rind evenly all around the lemon.

Place the lemon in a small bowl and cover with

½ cup olive oil.

Seal the bowl with plastic wrap and refrigerate for a week.

An hour or less before your dinner, wipe and dry

> *12–16 small chicken pieces.*

Sprinkle with a little salt and pepper and dust lightly with quick-mix flour.

Remove the lemon from the oil, discard the cloves, and thinly slice the lemon. Chop

> *2 large onions.*

In a skillet heat

> *4 tablespoons lemon oil.*

Cook the onions in the oil over medium-low heat for 10 minutes, until soft. Remove them from the skillet with a slotted spoon and set aside. Turn up the heat and brown a few chicken pieces at a time, adding more oil as needed. When they're all done, return them to the skillet plus the onions and the lemon slices. Add

> *½ cup chicken stock or canned condensed broth.*

Cover the skillet and simmer for 15 minutes.

Add

> *a handful of raisins*
> *a handful of chopped walnuts.*

Simmer uncovered for a few more minutes and serve at once.

HERBI'S FRIED CHICKEN (Serves 4)

As with fish or veal, Herbert often longs for chicken with *Brösel,* in other words bread crumbs. I know he can't be alone in his longings.

Wipe and dry

> *12–16 small chicken pieces.*

Follow the breading technique (page 21) by sprinkling the pieces with salt and pepper before coating them first with flour, then with beaten egg, and finally with bread crumbs. (If you wish, this much can be done ahead of time. Cover the pieces with wax paper and refrigerate until cooking time.)

Sauté the breaded chicken pieces in a heavy skillet over medium-high heat in

>*4 tablespoons butter*
>*1 tablespoon oil.*

Fry until golden brown. Do them in batches so you don't crowd the pan, and add butter as needed. Keep them hot in a 200° oven until they're all finished. Serve with lemon wedges and chopped parsley. My husband likes to dip them in

>*Fanny's Mayonnaise (page 42)*
>*or*
>*Cold Mustard Sauce (page 41).*

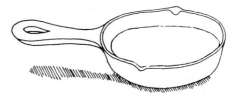

Boned Chicken Breasts or Suprêmes

Each chicken has one breast. Each *half* of a breast, skinned and boned, is called a suprême.

Since I do a raggedy job, I ask the butcher to bone the breast. To skin it, push a finger between flesh and skin and pull. It slides right off. A little bit of cartilage remains, holding the two halves together. Cut this off when separating the halves.

Serve one suprême to a customer, and use the breasts of

>*2½–3-pound chickens*

for a properly plump portion.

SAUTÉED SUPRÊMES (Serves 4)

Prepare

>*4 suprêmes.*

Sprinkle them on both sides with a little white pepper and roll lightly in

>3 tablespoons quick-mix flour.

Shake off the excess. Clarify

>1 stick butter (page 46).

Into a large skillet pour

>6 tablespoons of the clarified butter.

Cook it over medium heat until it turns light brown. Add the suprêmes and let them cook 4 or 5 minutes on each side. Remove the chicken from the skillet and add the remaining 2 tablespoons butter to the pan.

Heat for a minute and add

>2 tablespoons chopped parsley
>1 tablespoon lemon juice
>½ teaspoon salt.

Stir, then sprinkle the seasoned butter over the suprêmes and serve.

SUPRÊMES POACHED IN BUTTER (Serves 4)

Preheat the oven to 400°.

Sprinkle

>4 suprêmes (above) with
>2 teaspoons lemon juice
>a little white pepper.

Choose a shallow casserole with a lid. Invert the dish on a sheet of wax paper and outline the edge on the paper with a pencil. Cut out the paper and butter one side. Heat in the casserole

>4 tablespoons butter.

When the butter foam has subsided, roll the suprêmes in the butter till well coated. Place the buttered paper over the dish and then put on the lid. Place the chicken in the preheated oven for 10 minutes. Press down on the chicken with a wooden spoon. When it's firm and a little bouncy, it's done. Don't overcook.

The Sauce

With a slotted spoon remove the suprêmes to a platter and keep hot in the oven with the heat turned off and the door ajar. To the butter and juice in the casserole add

¼ *cup chicken broth*
3 *tablespoons dry vermouth.*

Boil down the liquid until it gets a little gooey. Then whisk in

1 *cup warm heavy cream.*

Boil down again until it thickens slightly. Salt to taste and stir in a little

minced parsley.

Pour the sauce over the chicken and serve at once.

SUPRÊMES IN CHAUD-FROID (Serves 6)

When you want to put on airs for a few people on a hot summer night, serve them this delicacy and they'll never forget you.

Prepare 6 Suprêmes Poached in Butter (preceding recipe), omitting the sauce. Set the cooked suprêmes on a platter and let them cool.

Make Chaud-froid Sauce (page 45). I spent a lot of time on it with this particular recipe in mind. Follow the instructions to the end and you'll have an haute cuisine meal to impress even the haughtiest.

CUBED CHICKEN BREASTS CHINOISE (Serves 4)

Cut into 1-inch cubes

2 *whole chicken breasts boned and skinned.*

Marinate for a few hours in

¼ *cup soy sauce*
3 *tablespoons dry vermouth*
1 *teaspoon ground ginger*
a few grains of cayenne pepper.

When you're almost ready for dinner, dry the chicken well. Reserve the marinade. In a large skillet heat

2 *tablespoons vegetable oil.*

Add the chicken cubes and stir over medium-high heat until golden on all sides. Into the bowl with the reserve marinade stir

4 *tablespoons currant or beachplum jelly*
2 *tablespoons strained peaches (baby-food peaches are fine).*

Add this mixture to the chicken in the skillet. Simmer and stir for about five minutes until the sauce thickens slightly. Serve at once. Bliss!

HERBERT'S FAVORITE CHICKEN BREASTS
WITH AVOCADO (Serves 4)

Not only Herbert but everyone falls silent when this dish is savored. Thoughts turn inward. An occasional "Ahhh" escapes from someone's lips. The consensus is that it's a sexy dish. Preparation is simple and speedy.

Ahead of time, cut

> 2 whole chicken breasts, skinned and boned

into 1-inch cubes and place them in a bowl to rest at room temperature sprinkled with

> 1 tablespoon lemon juice.

Cover the bowl.

Wipe and slice

> ½ pound mushrooms.

Mince

> 2 tablespoons shallots.

Peel and pit

> 1 large avocado.

Cube the avocado and place in a bowl, sprinkling it with lemon juice so it won't discolor. Seal with plastic wrap and keep in the refrigerator until needed.

Just before dinner, dry the chicken cubes with toweling. In a large deep skillet or shallow casserole heat

> 3 tablespoons butter.

When the foam has subsided, cook the chicken over medium-high heat for a few minutes, stirring and turning until it's firm and white. Remove it with a slotted spoon. In the skillet sauté

> the minced shallots

using more butter if necessary.

Add

> the sliced mushrooms.

Cook and stir until the mushrooms are light brown. Then add

> 2 tablespoons brandy.

Light a match to the brandy. Keep your head back and swish the pan until the flames die out. Then add

>1 *cup warm heavy cream.*

Let it come almost to a boil before returning the chicken to the skillet. Cook 5 to 10 minutes over medium-low heat, stirring occasionally until the sauce has reduced and thickened slightly. Add the avocado cubes and stir until just blended. Add salt and pepper to taste and serve at once.

CHICKEN CORDON BLEU (Serves 4)

Every cook claims to have the best recipe for this classic, including me.

Preheat the oven to 350°.

Prepare

>2 *whole chicken breasts.*

Flatten the boned, skinned, and halved breasts as described for Chicken Kiev (page 163). On each flattened half place

>1 *thin slice prosciutto or, when available at a German butcher, Lachs Schinken*
>1 *thin slice Gruyère or Emmenthaler cheese.*

The ham and cheese slices should be slightly smaller than the chicken halves so you can fold a bit of the chicken over the edges. Roll up the breasts and pinch the flesh together. Follow the breading procedure (page 21) by rolling the pieces first in flour, then in beaten egg, and finally in bread crumbs.

Clarify

>4 *tablespoons butter (page 46).*

Brush the bottom of a shallow baking dish with some of this butter and set aside. Pour the remaining butter into a large skillet and sauté the chicken rolls over medium-high heat on all sides till golden brown. Place them side by side into the buttered dish.

Bake for 15 minutes.

Meanwhile make

>1 cup Cheese Sauce (page 39).

When the chicken is done, pour the hot sauce over it and run the dish under the broiler for a minute or so until the top is lightly brown.

WALNUT CHICKEN BREASTS (Serves 6)

Cut into 1-inch cubes

>2 whole chicken breasts, boned and skinned.

Marinate overnight in

>¼ cup soy sauce
>¼ cup Madeira
>1 teaspoon sugar
>a pinch of salt.

Cover with plastic wrap and refrigerate.

Half an hour before dinner, remove the chicken and dry with toweling.

Reserve the marinade. On a sheet of wax paper spread

>1½ tablespoons cornstarch.

Roll the chicken to coat it lightly with the cornstarch.

In a bowl lightly beat

>1 egg.

Add the chicken to the bowl piece by piece and toss lightly in the egg. Return it to the wax paper.

In a heavy skillet heat

>2 tablespoons peanut oil.

Add

>¾ cup walnut halves.

Stir the nuts in the hot oil until they get crisp. Remove them to toweling.

Into the skillet stir

>2 pressed garlic cloves
>½ teaspoon ground ginger.

Add the chicken cubes and brown them on all sides over medium-high heat. Do it in two batches if necessary. Remove the chicken from the skillet before stirring in

the marinade
¼ cup water.

Bring it to a boil, stirring to deglaze. Return the chicken to the skillet and turn down the heat to simmer for 5 minutes. Add the sautéed walnuts. Cook for another minute and serve at once.

CHICKEN CUTLETS KIEV (Serves 4)

When I was eighteen and on tour with the Lunts, an actor took me to the Russian Tearoom in Philadelphia and I tasted my first Cutlets à la Kiev. I think I've learned to make it so that it almost lives up to that first memory.

For this recipe as well as for the following Chicken Cordon Bleu, the halved chicken breasts must be not only boned and skinned, but flattened out. Before flattening, the suprême looks like a little puffy envelope. The fold of this envelope is joined by a thin membrane. Sever the membrane with a sharp knife, and pull back the flap until the breast lies flat and even. Place the open breast between two sheets of wax paper and use the flat side of a cleaver, a large mallet, or the flat bottom of an iron skillet to pound it very thin and stretch it out. When you remove the wax paper, if the chicken has little holes, simply patch by pulling the flesh together and pressing firmly with your fingers. If you're fearful, let the butcher do it.

You will need

> *2 whole chicken breasts prepared as described above.*

In a bowl put

> *1½ sticks softened butter (12 tablespoons)*
> *2 tablespoons chopped chives*
> *1 tablespoon chopped parsley*
> *1 teaspoon salt*
> *a few gratings of pepper*
> *1 teaspoon salt.*

Mash everything into the butter with a fork.

Divide the seasoned butter into 4 pieces and shape them to the size of a fat man's third finger. Place 1 butter finger in the center of each flattened chicken half. Wrap the breasts snugly around the butter and press the edges and ends together so no butter will escape during cooking.

Follow the breading procedure on page 21 by rolling the cutlets one at a time first in the flour, then in the beaten egg, and finally in the bread crumbs. Put them side by side on a plate, cover with wax paper, and refrigerate a minimum of 3 hours.

Just before dinner, in a large deep skillet heat to 360°

2–3 inches of peanut or vegetable oil.

Use your thermometer. Fry the cutlets 5 to 6 minutes until they puff slightly and turn golden. Turn them once if they're not covered by oil. Drain on toweling and serve at once with lemon wedges and sprigs of parsley. If the butter squirts out as you stick in your fork, remember it's part of the delight.

Duck

ROAST DUCKLING (Serves 4)

I feel very proprietary about Long Island ducklings. Although they're known throughout America, they're not eaten nearly enough, in my opinion. If you don't have access to a duck farm, you'll probably have to order a duckling from your butcher, because they're not always on hand.

Duck is fattier than chicken and there's less meat on it so you'll need a

5–6-pound duckling.

If I'm planning dinner for 6, I usually roast two 4-to-5-pounders. In the wild event that there's any left over, it's delicious cold.

Wipe the duck inside and out with a clean damp sponge and dry it with toweling. Pull the loose fat from the skin inside the cavity and save for rendering (page 17). Now begin by making the stock for the gravy.

The Stock

Chop into small pieces

> *neck, heart and gizzard, and wing tips*
> *1 small onion*
> *1 carrot.*

In a large skillet heat

> *2 tablespoons fat (rendered goose or duck fat is best).*

Sauté the duck pieces and vegetables over medium heat until brown. Pour off the fat.

Add

> *1½ cups beef broth or a can of condensed beef bouillon*
> *3 parsley sprigs*
> *a pinch of thyme.*

Cover and simmer for 1 hour. Skim off any scum and strain through a sieve, pressing down on the contents to extract flavor. Let the stock cool. Just before using, skim off the fat. (If you don't use it all in the gravy, add it to chicken stock you may already have in the refrigerator.)

Preheat the oven to 425°. A 5-to-6-pound duck requires about 1½ hours of roasting.

On a plate mix together

> *½ teaspoon coarse salt*
> *generous gratings of pepper*
> *¼ teaspoon thyme.*

Rub the inside of the duck with this mixture and truss it (page 141). Use a needle or sharp-tined fork to prick the skin of the duck around the thighs, the bottom of the breast, and a little on the back. This procedure allows the fat to run out while roasting. Slice

> *1 onion*
> *1 carrot.*

Sprinkle the vegetables across the bottom of the roasting pan. Set the duck on top of them and put the pan into the hot oven for 15 minutes, turning down the heat to 350°. Every 20 minutes or so, draw out some fat from the pan with a bulb baster and baste the breast with it. If too much fat accumulates in the pan, remove it with the bulb baster.

When the duckling has been in the oven for 1½ hours, test it by jiggling a drumstick to see if it moves in the socket. Or prick the top of the thigh; if the juice runs out yellow, not pink, the duck is done. Roast longer if needed. Remove the duck from the pan and put it on a platter. Turn off the heat and replace the duck in the oven with the door ajar while you make the sauce.

TWO FABULOUS DUCK SAUCES

PINEAPPLE SAUCE

You'll need

> *2 cups pineapple cubes*
> *¼ cup pineapple juice*
> *¼ cup rosé or dry white wine*
> *½ cup of the degreased duck stock.*

Frozen pineapple chunks work almost as well as fresh ones. If you use them, thaw them in a colander over a bowl. If you don't have ¼ cup drained juice, supplement with canned juice. Or cut up a fresh pineapple into 1-inch cubes and scrape the juice from the cutting board into a measuring cup, supplementing with canned juice if needed. After draining, pat the cubes as dry as you can.

When the duck is resting in the oven, pour off the fat from the roasting pan and set the pan on the stove. Add

> *2 tablespoons butter.*

Over medium heat, sauté the pineapple cubes until lightly brown on all sides. Remove them with a spoon and arrange prettily around the duck on the platter.

Add the pineapple juice, wine, and duck stock to the roasting pan. Bring the liquid to a boil over high heat, stirring briskly, boiling it down until it has reduced a *little*. Turn off the heat while you blend till smooth

> *1 tablespoon arrowroot or cornstarch*
> *2 tablespoons cold water.*

Whisk the mixture into the sauce and simmer over low heat until it thickens. Strain through a sieve and pour it over the duckling and the pineapple cubes.

ORANGE SAUCE

If you don't already have the base for this sauce in the refrigerator for Lily's Orange Pancakes (page 30), make some. You'll need

> *1½–2 cups Orange Sauce.*

Stir in

> *1 cup degreased duck stock (page 164).*

Bring it to a boil in a saucepan and let it simmer 5 to 10 minutes until it reduces a little and thickens again. You can mask the duckling with the sauce before carving, or you can serve it separately to let the guests slosh it over their own portions.

BRAISED DUCKLING IN RED CABBAGE (Serves 4 or 5)

On a cold winter's night, this dish is not only tasty but somehow comforting to the soul.

In the morning, cook red cabbage (page 230). It will take several hours. Let it rest at room temperature until time for the duck.

Wipe and dry

> *a 5–6-pound duckling.*

Rub the cavity with

> *1 teaspoon coarse salt*
> *¼ teaspoon grated pepper.*

After pulling the loose fat from the cavity, truss the duck (page 141) and prick the skin all over with a needle or sharp-tined fork. In a large skillet containing

> *4 tablespoons oil or rendered duck fat*

brown the duckling evenly on all sides. This will take about 15 minutes.

Sprinkle the outside of the duck with

> *1 teaspoon coarse salt.*

Tuck the duck into a large casserole embedded in the cooked red cabbage. Cover tightly and simmer slowly for 1½ hours. Jiggle a drumstick to see if it moves slightly in the socket. If so, it's done.

Lift the bird from the cabbage and let most of the juice run off before setting it on a hot platter. Put the cabbage in a colander over a bowl to let the juice drain. Arrange the cabbage around the duckling. Skim floating fat from the juice before pouring it back into the casserole. Boil it down briskly to reduce a little. Serve it in a pitcher. Sprigs of parsley look sprightly tucked around the edge of the red cabbage.

Turkey

ROAST TURKEY

I believe the days of serving a sit-down dinner for dozens of people have disappeared for most of us and I'm always annoyed at recipes calling for a twenty-pound turkey. I think I've worked out a lovely one for just a chosen few and even devised a beautiful hash which includes the stuffing in case there's any left over.

Use

> *a 10–12-pound turkey.*

Remove the excess fat from the cavity plus the bag of giblets and piece of neck. Damp-wipe the bird inside and out.

The Stock

Reserve the liver. Chop the gizzard, heart, and neck into small pieces and sauté them in a skillet in

> 2 tablespoons fat.

Add

> 1 onion, coarsely chopped
> 1 carrot, coarsely chopped.

When meat and vegetables are browned on all sides, remove them to a saucepan and add

> 1 can condensed beef bouillon
> a few parsley sprigs
> a pinch of thyme
> a pinch of salt and pepper.

Cover tightly and simmer for 1 hour over low heat.

Strain the stock through a sieve and set aside. Degrease when cool.

The Stuffing

In a large skillet over low heat gently sauté the turkey liver in

> 1 tablespoon butter.

When it is lightly browned on both sides, but still soft, remove it from the skillet and chop it finely. Put chopped liver in a large bowl. To the skillet, add

> 1 tablespoon butter
> ¾ cup coarsely chopped walnuts.

Stir the walnuts for a few minutes till lightly toasted. With a slotted spoon, remove and place in bowl with liver. To the skillet add

> 2 tablespoons butter
> 1 cup finely chopped onion
> 2 pressed garlic cloves.

Stir and sauté over low heat for a few minutes before adding

> ½ pound finely chopped mushrooms.

Continue stirring and cooking until the mushrooms have given off most of their liquid. Remove the onion and mushroom mixture to the bowl with the nuts and chopped liver.

To the skillet add

> 2 tablespoons butter
> ½ cup finely chopped celery stalks
> ½ cup finely chopped carrots
> ¼ cup finely chopped parsley
> 1 teaspoon salt
> a few gratings of pepper
> 1 teaspoon dried tarragon.

Sauté for several minutes or until the vegetables are soft. Then add

> 2 cups crumbled, coarse, day-old bread.

Blend the mixture well and continue to cook. Meanwhile, beat up

> 1 jumbo egg in
> 1 cup condensed chicken broth.

Pour this mixture over vegetables and bread crumbs and blend well before removing from heat and adding to the contents of the large bowl. Peel, core, and dice

> 2 large green apples.

Fold the diced apples into the stuffing, plus

> ½ cup raisins or currants.

Rub the turkey inside and out with

> 1 stick softened butter (8 tablespoons).

Spoon the stuffing into the cavity and into the hole under the flap at the neck. Truss the bird (page 141).

Roasting the Turkey

I think turkey meat is often too dry so I guard against it in a number of ways.

Preheat the over to 425°.

Simmer

> 8 slices fatty bacon in
> water

for 10 minutes. Drain.

Place the turkey on a rack in the roasting pan and arrange the bacon over breast and drumsticks. Then cut out a double thickness of cheesecloth large enough to drape over the entire bird and drench it in a saucepan containing

> 1 stick melted butter (8 tablespoons).

Cover the bird with the soaked cheesecloth. Place the turkey into the preheated oven; after 15 minutes, reduce heat to 350°.

Use a bulb baster to baste the turkey with the pan drippings every 20 minutes or so. Allow 20 minutes of roasting per pound, or about 3½ to 4 hours total cooking time.

When done, remove the turkey to a platter and sprinkle with coarse salt and grated pepper. Return it to the oven to keep warm but make sure the heat is off and the door ajar.

The Gravy

Pour off all but a few tablespoons of fat from the roasting pan and deglaze it with

>½ cup dry white wine.

Stir with a wooden spoon scraping bottom and sides of pan. Add

>1½ cups turkey stock.

In a small bowl, stir till smooth

>1 tablespoon cornstarch
>2 tablespoons cold water.

Stir the mixture into the contents of the roasting pan. Cook till thickened.

Season to taste.

>or

Heat

>1 cup strained turkey stock with
>1 cup Lily's Orange Sauce (page 30).

I like this last one a lot!

TURKEY HASH (Serves 3 or 4)

In a large, heavy skillet melt

>4 tablespoons butter.

Add

>1 large onion, finely chopped
>2 green peppers, seeded, deveined, and finely chopped.

Cook over medium heat and stir till tender.

Add

> *3–4 cups finely chopped cooked turkey meat*
> *1–2 cups stuffing*
> *a few dashes of Worcestershire sauce.*

Blend well. Add

> *1 cup turkey stock or chicken broth.*

Cover and cook 10 minutes till heated through.

THE FAMOUS CHRISTMAS GOOSE (Serves 6)

Give your butcher a week's notice to order this beauty. Ask for

> *a 9–10-pound goose.*

It will probably arrive frozen, but that won't influence flavor or texture.

Let it thaw at room temperature during the night. Make the stuffing first.

The Stuffing

In a saucepan bring to a boil

> *1 cup dry red wine.*

Remove the wine from heat and add

> *1 pound mixed dried apricots and pitted prunes*
> *a handful of black or white seedless raisins.*

Let the fruit soak and puff up in the wine for ½ hour. Then core and peel

> *2 green cooking apples.*

Chop the apples coarsely and sprinkle with a little lemon juice. Put them in a bowl with

> *¼ cup slivered, blanched almonds*
> *1 chopped onion.*

Strain the soaked fruit, reserving the liquid. Combine the apricots, prunes, and raisins with the apples, nuts, and onion. Sprinkle the mixture with

> *2 tablespoons brandy*
> *2 tablespoons of the wine in which the fruit was soaked.*

Stir until everything is moist and well blended. Set aside. (If any of the stuffing is left over put it in a baking dish, dot with butter, cover with foil, and bake in the oven the last half-hour with the roasting goose.)

The Stock

Chop

> *neck, heart, gizzard, and wing tips.*

Put them in a saucepan with

> *1 sliced onion*
> *1 sliced carrot*
> *1 chopped celery stalk*
> *a pinch of thyme*
> *a pinch of salt and pepper*
> *1½ cups of beef broth or 1 can condensed beef bouillon.*

Simmer covered for 1½ hours. Strain and set aside.

The Liver

Goose liver is a delicacy. Sauté it gently over medium-low heat for 10 minutes in

> *2 tablespoons butter with*
> *1 teaspoon minced shallot.*

Cut it into pieces and put it into the blender with

> *1 tablespoon brandy*
> *salt and pepper to taste.*

Serve it as an hors d'oeuvre on toast rounds.

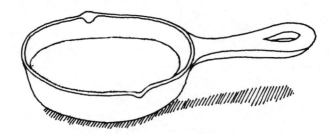

Rendering the Fat

I've sometimes thought of preparing a goose just to have the fat. In Germany it's called *Gänse Schmalz,* and the name brings back lyric memories of black bread thickly spread with smooth, white *Schmalz,* sprinkled with salt and topped with a sliced cucumber or onion. As a base for a goulash or used to brown poultry and meat it's unbeatable. From one goose I often get as much as 2 quarts of rendered fat. If you use only the loose fat from the cavity of the bird, you'll get a small amount of pure white fat. But I also strain the fat from the roasting pan through layers of cheesecloth, simmer it again with chopped apples and onions, strain once more, and then store it in a container in the refrigerator.

To render the solid fat from the cavity, cut it into large hunks and put it into a heavy pot or the top of a double boiler. Add a tablespoon of water, a cored chopped apple, and a sliced onion. Simmer for several hours over very low heat and then strain through layers of cheesecloth. Store it in the refrigerator in an old coffee tin with a tight lid. It will keep for a year.

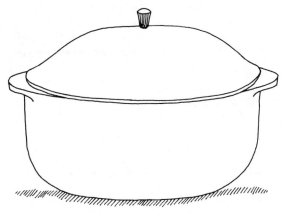

Preparing the Goose

Preheat the oven to 350°.

Wipe and dry the goose. Pull out loose fat for rendering. Rub the goose inside and out with

> *½ lemon*

squeezing lightly as you do so.

Rub the goose inside and out with a mixture of

> *2 teaspoons coarse salt*
> *½ teaspoon grated pepper*
> *¼ teaspoon thyme.*

Spoon the fruit stuffing loosely into the cavity. It will swell during the cooking. If you like, you can also spoon stuffing under the long skin at the neck before skewering the neck skin to the back of the goose. Truss the goose (page 141). Prick the goose's skin all over with a needle or sharp-tined fork to allow the endless amounts of fat to run out while roasting.

Place the stuffed goose on its side on a rack in a roasting pan and set it in the hot oven. The stuffed bird should cook 20 minutes per pound (about 3 hours). It needs no basting. After 40 minutes, turn the goose on its other side. Draw the excess fat from the pan with a bulb baster. Roast for another 40 minutes and set the goose breast side up. Again draw off excess fat. When the 3 hours are up, jiggle a drumstick. If it moves in the socket, the goose is done.

Allow the goose to rest on a serving platter while you make the sauce.

The Sauce

Pour out the remaining fat from the roasting pan. Set the pan on the stove and pour in

> *the strained stock*
> *½ cup red wine.*

Bring it to a boil, stirring briskly to deglaze the pan. Let it reduce to 1 cup.

Add

> *salt and pepper to taste*

and strain through a sieve. Serve separately in a pitcher.

Bring the goose to the table. *Fröhliche Weihnachten!*

X. Meat

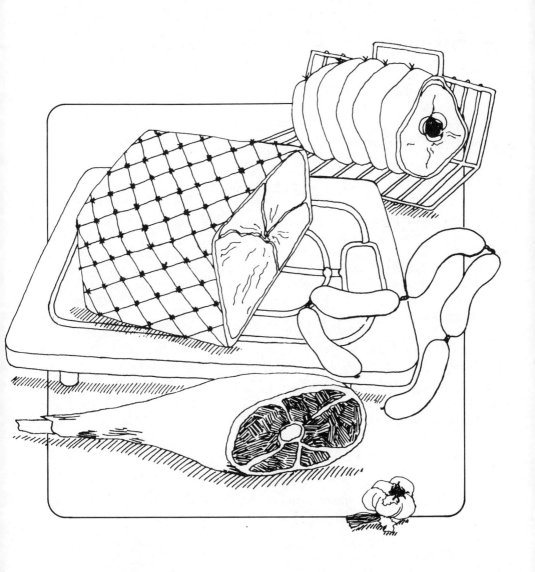

I was born in Germany shortly after the First World War during a period of inflation and near starvation. Meat was almost unheard of. A few lucky people occasionally received food parcels from abroad, and once my aunt, who was living in Norway, sent us a guinea hen. Shortly after having devoured this hen, I was at a neighbor's house for supper and raved, "What? No meat?" The neighbors were flabbergasted, and wondered if we ever had meat at home. "Every night!" I announced proudly. "What kind of meat?" they asked skeptically. I drew myself up to my full three feet and boasted, *"Hasen, Hühner, . . . und Hünde!"* (Hare, hens . . . and hounds.) Till the day they died, my parents held this story up to me whenever I bragged or put on airs.

My appetite for meat has never abated, though it's being curbed by world food shortages. I remind myself that we're probably the only nation in the world where meatless days are considered a sacrifice.

Beef

BEEFSTEAKS

When making room in our budgets for good old American steak, we might as well make sure we're getting the best. I depend on the butcher to provide me with the finest because I panic a little when faced with a variety of steaks. If the meat is packaged, I know I have to look for the stamp that says "prime" or "choice" and that the brighter scarlet steak is usually not as well aged as the darker one, and yet I'd rather leave the decision to the man who cuts them up.

My preference is for a small porterhouse, sirloin, or shell steak. When a whole tenderloin of beef is on sale, I put it to other use (page 180) rather than cutting it up for filet mignon, tournedo, or châteaubriand.

To broil, start with a hot broiler, place the steak about 4 inches from the heat, leaving the broiler door ajar to maintain proper heat and ventilation. Cook 3 to 4 minutes on each side.

PAN-BROILED STEAK

I usually pan-broil steak on top of the stove. The steak seems far more tender, never dries out, and I have better control over it.

Half a pound of steak per person is a generous serving. It should be 1 to 1½ inches thick, no more. Trim off excess fat and wherever you see gristle around the edges, cut little gashes at half-inch intervals so the steak won't curl up as it cooks. Pat the meat with toweling to dry thoroughly on both sides. For every 2 pounds of steak in the skillet, heat

> 1 tablespoon butter
> 1 tablespoon oil.

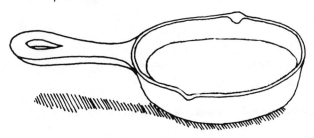

When the butter has foamed and the foam subsided, add the steak. Sauté over medium-high heat for 3 minutes on each side, if you want your steak rare; add a minute for medium rare. Control the heat so the butter stays hot without burning. As melted fat accumulates during the cooking, re-move it from the pan with a bulb baster so you won't have fried steak instead of pan-broiled. When little drops of blood come to the surface of the beef, it's done.

Place the steak on a hot platter and season with sea salt and grated pepper. Pour the fat out of the skillet and add

> ¼ cup beef stock or canned condensed bouillon
> 2 tablespoons dry vermouth or red wine.

Boil down the liquid over high heat as you deglaze the pan. Remove from heat to whisk in

> 2 tablespoons butter or cream.

Pour over the steak and serve.

Variations
1) The steak can be seasoned by rubbing a pressed garlic clove into the skin and then sprinkling with grated pepper before cooking. (Add salt *after* it's done.)
2) When the steak is almost finished, smother it with sautéed onions or with sautéed sliced mushrooms.
3) Add 2 tablespoons sautéed minced shallots or scallions to the sauce. Chopped dill or parsley or watercress leaves make a nice garnish.

STEAK TARTAR (Serves 3 or 4)

Herbert and I eat steak Tartar more often than any other meat. My butcher calls it TaTa. I serve it to guests only if I know they like it as much as we do.

No prepackaged chopped meat will do. All of it is fatty. Get top or bottom round steak with every smidgeon of visible fat removed before grinding. Explain to the butcher what you want it for. If you own a meat grinder, it can be made more reasonably at home and will probably be better, too.

It's delicious just sprinkled with a little sea salt and freshly grated pepper. Traditional ways of jazzing it up include the addition of herbs, sauces, oil, capers, mustard, and egg. Here's an example.

On a platter mound

1 pound ground round (totally fatless).

Make an indentation in the top of the mound and drop in

1 raw egg yolk.

Sprinkle the meat with a little

Worcestershire sauce.

Surround the mound with

1 diced onion
2 chopped anchovy filets.

Sprinkle with

chopped parsley
a few drained capers
salt and pepper to taste.

Bring it to the table and use a fork to blend the ingredients. Serve Tartar on thinly sliced black bread or with hunks of crisp French bread.

HAMBURGER STEAK (Serves 4)

Get ground round steak for hamburgers, especially when buying prepackaged meat, unless you like fatty ones. Use about

2 pounds ground meat.

Shape the hamburger into generous-sized patties about an inch thick and grate a little pepper over them. In a large skillet heat

1½ tablespoons butter
1 teaspoon oil.

When the butter foam has subsided, add the patties. Don't crowd them in the pan. Sauté 2 to 3 minutes on each side. Make sure the fat doesn't burn.

Sprinkle with salt and serve at once.

Additional seasonings can be chili sauce, Worcestershire sauce, horse-radish, mustard, or snail butter (page 47).

Variations
1) Hamburgers can be topped with sliced sautéed onions or mushrooms.
2) Mince a little onion and mix into the patty before cooking.
3) Coarsely chop a handful of walnuts and put some in the center of each patty before cooking.
4) Use chopped pimento olives in the same manner as the walnuts.
5) Make cheeseburgers by topping the cooked patties with slices of American, cheddar, or Swiss cheese. Run under the broiler until the cheese melts.
6) Top cooked hamburgers with slices of sautéed bacon.

PENNIE'S MEAT LOAF (Serves 4)

My gorgeous actress girl friend, Pennie du Pont, gave me this recipe. Everyone has his favorite meat loaf. This one's mine.

Preheat the oven to 350°.

In a bowl combine

> 2 pounds ground chuck (or 1 pound ground chuck plus 1 pound ground pork)
> 1 small onion, grated
> 2 tablespoons Dijon mustard
> 2 tablespoons chili sauce
> 1 whole egg
> ¼ cup dry bread crumbs
> ½ teaspoon lemon juice
> salt and pepper to taste.

When everything is well blended, press half of the mixture into the bottom of an oiled standard loaf pan. Cover the meat with

> 2–3 thin slices of boiled ham.

Over the ham sprinkle

> ½ cup coarsely grated mozzarella.

Cover the mozzarella with

> 2–3 thin slices of ham.

Fold over the edge of the ham a little to encase the cheese. The ham "roll" should be at least ½ inch smaller in length and width than the loaf pan. Now place the other half of ground meat on top of the ham. Press down on it and smooth it off. Dot with butter and cover the pan snugly with foil. Bake for 1 hour.

Before serving, remove the foil and let the pan rest for 5 minutes. Tilt the pan to pour off the juices before inverting the loaf onto a platter. Use a serrated knife to slice it gently so it won't crumble.

Refrigerate the juice from the pan. Use the congealed fat as a base for browning meat and add the juice to a beef stock or bouillon.

While I'm at it I usually make two meat loaves and refrigerate or freeze the second one. It will keep for a week in the refrigerator after it's been cooked. It's delicious cold. Freeze it *before* cooking, then thaw and cook when the time comes.

ROAST FILET OF BEEF (Serves 4 to 6)

Jumping from a meat loaf to a filet of beef may seem like going from the ridiculous to the sublime. The meat loaf is *not* ridiculous, but the filet *is* sublime!

On occasion when a whole beef tenderloin or filet of beef is on a special sale, I grab one. They come untrimmed, packed in large plastic bags, and seem to be available in this form all over the country. If you haven't seen them, ask your butcher if he can order one—after he's told you the price.

Trimming the Filet

Initially I prepare the filet in the same way, whether it's to be roasted or used for Tafelspitz (page 182) or Filetto Tonnato (page 191). It must also be trimmed if you feel rash enough to cut it up for steaks.

When first unwrapped, the filet will be about 2 feet long and 6 or more inches in diameter. Almost a third of its weight may consist of fat. With a sharp knife, cut, loosen, pull, and shave off as much as possible. (Save for rendering.) Without the fat, you'll see that the shiny underpart of the filet is covered by a thin, very tough membrane. Use your sharpest knife to shave it off, being careful not to pull off the meat. This takes a little time but is essential.

The defatted filet will be rounder at the butt end and taper down to the tail or skinny flap at the other end. The butt is called the rump, the center comprises the châteaubriand, and the other end is sometimes used for tournedos and filet mignon. A skinny strip of beef running along the side of the filet may have been almost severed after the fat has been removed. I tuck this strip against the meat and cook it with the filet. Before carving, I remove it. It's delicious for a cold snack.

Before cooking, I usually cut the filet into two pieces for two separate meals, using a little less than half for the rump end and a longer one for the thinner part with the tail. Each half should serve 4 to 6 people. The part not to be cooked at once is snugly wrapped in foil and placed in the freezer. Each piece will now be approximately 8 to 10 inches long and 3 to 4 inches in diameter.

Roasting the Filet

Preheat the oven to 450°.

If using the tail end, tuck under the flap so the shape of the filet will be uniform in diameter. Rub all around with freshly ground pepper. To coat thinly, all over the filet spread the contents of

> 1 4–6 ounce can of Strasbourg type liver pâté.

Cover with

> 6 slices of lean raw bacon.

If you're afraid of too strong a bacon flavor, simmer the bacon in water for 10 minutes and drain it before placing it on the filet.

Place the beef on a rack over the roasting pan and put it into the hot oven for about 35 minutes. It should be beautifully pink inside, not gray and overcooked! Serve on a hot platter carved into one-inch slices. I think it beats all the Beef Wellington and en crôutes recipes by a mile.

Pan juices are a perfect moistener. If you want an added pleasure, serve with Béarnaise Sauce (page 42).

ROAST BEEF (Serves 4 or 5)

A rib roast of beef is always simple to cook, always delicious, and always unbelievably expensive (when you consider the waste weight of fat and bones). If you feel plush, this is the best way to cook it. Ask the butcher to prepare a

> 2-rib standing roast.

Preheat the oven to 500°.

The beef should be at room temperature and unseasoned when you place it fat side up on a rack over the roasting pan into the center of the oven. Immediately turn down the heat to 350°. Roast it 18 minutes per pound. When cooked, remove from the oven and sprinkle with seat salt and freshly ground pepper.

BOILED BEEF

Boiled beef is unbelievably good when properly cooked, not at all the ordinary fare most Americans think. European countries have their traditional recipes and every European seems convinced that his version is the best. In Austria it's *the* national dish, and there are countless variations. Herbert introduced me to his favorites, Tafelspitz (page 182) and Beinfleisch (page 186). France has its famous Pot au Feu (page 184), Italy has Bollito Manzo, Holland has Hotspot met Klapstuck (page 185), and of course, Germany has Gekochtes Rindfleisch (page 186).

The basic cooking principle remains the same; raw, unbrowned meat is covered with water. Soup bones and vegetables are added. While boiling, scum floating to the top of the broth is skimmed off at intervals. The difference consists in the cuts of meat and the vegetables and seasoning. Occasionally other meat such as lamb, chicken, and sausage is added. When you've made a few kinds of boiled beef, you can start experimenting to develop your own creation.

TAFELSPITZ (Serves 4 to 6)

Herbert ordered this for me at a restaurant in Vienna. It was unforgettably tender and flavorful. I'm convinced a filet of beef was used, although tenderloin is not suggested in any of my Austrian cookbooks. In any event, this invention comes up to my memory of that first taste.

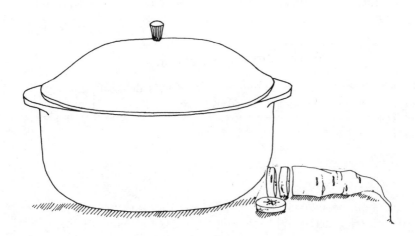

Prepare

> *half a filet of beef*

as described on page 180.

Put the meat into a heavy pot large enough for the meat and

> *1–2 pounds sawed-up soup bones (neck, knuckle, marrow bones).*

Cover the meat and bones with cold water. Cover the pot and bring the water to a boil. Use a skimmer to remove the floating scum. Then add

> *1 teaspoon salt*
> *1 pound chicken backbones, necks, wing tips, and gizzards.*

Bring the water back to a boil and skim again.

Meanwhile sauté

> *1 chopped onion*
> *1 large chopped parsnip*
> *4 chopped carrots*
> *2 sliced celery stalks*
> *1 sliced leek (white part only) in*
> *4 tablespoons butter.*

Stir occasionally over low heat for 10 minutes, then add the vegetables to the pot. Return the water to a boil and skim again. Add boiling water to cover everything, if needed. Add

> *6 peppercorns*
> *a few parsley sprigs*
> *1 bay leaf*
> *a pinch of thyme.*

Lower the heat to allow the beef to simmer. The preparation to this point will have taken about ½ hour. Simmer for another hour, then pierce the meat. It should be very tender. If needed, simmer a little longer.

Remove the meat from the pot with a slotted skimmer and serve on a hot platter with White Sauce (page 38) or with Horseradish Dressing (page 49).

If you're planning to use the broth as a first course, put the meat into a covered pot with a little of the broth and keep it hot in a 200° oven. Degrease the broth and strain it through several layers of cheesecloth. Serve with Croutons (page 90) or cold diced avocado. Otherwise, do the degreasing and straining later and keep the broth in a covered bowl in the refrigerator for another meal.

This Tafelspitz may make you famous!

POT AU FEU (Serves 8)

Or the *pot's* on the *fire*. I feel cozy just thinking about it. The dish constitutes an entire meal from soup to everything except nuts. The total cooking time takes 3½ to 4 hours.

Start with

> *4 pounds boneless beef in one piece (rump, round, chuck, or brisket)*
> *2 pounds sawed-up soup bones (marrow bones and a veal knuckle are best).*
> *1–3 pound whole chicken.*

Since the broth won't be strained, you'll need a *spice bag* that can be lifted out when necessary. I use a little muslin bag from the hardware store. Otherwise, cut an 8-inch square from several layers of cheesecloth, put the spices in the center, and tie with a string long enough to fish out easily.

Fill this spice bag with

> *6 peppercorns*
> *a bay leaf*
> *3 halved garlic cloves*
> *a few parsley sprigs*
> *a few celery leaves*
> *½ teaspoon thyme.*

Choose a heavy pot large enough to hold the beef, the bones, the chicken, and the vegetables that are to follow. If you're lucky, the pot will also be attractive enough to bring straight to the table.

Cut all extra fat from the meat before putting it into the pot with the bones. Pour cold water over everything to cover it by a few inches. Cover the pot and bring the water to a boil. Skim off floating scum. Lower the heat to allow the broth to simmer. Drop the filled spice bag into the pot and add

> *2 teaspoons salt.*

Use a small nylon laundry bag or make another larger cheesecloth bag to hold

> *2 large chopped carrots*
> *2 large chopped onions*
> *2 scraped and sliced parsnips*
> *2 sliced leeks.*

Tie the bag securely and drop it into the pot. Skim the broth every half-hour or so.

When the beef has simmered a total of 2 hours, add the chicken and more water to cover. Simmer and skim for another half-hour. Then add

4 washed and trimmed leeks (white parts only)
8 medium-sized carrots, scraped (or 24 baby carrots)
8 medium-sized peeled potatoes (or 24 scrubbed tiny new potatoes)
2 dozen small white onions, peeled (optional).

After another 30 minutes of simmering, pierce the meat, chicken, and vegetables to make sure they're all tender. Lift out the two bags of herbs and vegetables and discard them. Fish out the soup bones and bring the pot to the table.

Start the feast by ladling broth into soup bowls. Have a platter ready when you fish out the meat and chicken and use a slotted spoon to remove the vegetables.

Mustard Sauce (page 39) is lovely poured over the meat and chicken, but it's not essential. Eat hearty!

HOTSPOT MET KLAPSTUCK (Serves 6)

I'm not sure what the Dutch name means, but this is a marvelous meal-in-one for a winter evening.

Trim excess fat from

3–4 pounds boneless chuck or rump in one piece.

Place in a kettle and cover with cold salted water. Bring it to a boil and skim the floating scum. Reduce the heat and simmer 2 to 2½ hours, depending on the size of the meat. Skim occasionally. Then add

8 carrots, scraped and sliced
8 potatoes, peeled and cut in half
6 medium-sized onions, peeled and quartered.

Simmer 40 minutes longer. Pierce the meat and vegetables with a sharp knife to see that they're tender. Remove the vegetables with a slotted spoon and push them through a food mill or ricer onto a platter to form a lovely pale orange mound. Top the mound with

2 tablespoons dotted butter
generous gratings of pepper.

Slice the meat and arrange it overlapping on a hot platter. Grind lots of pepper over it.

If you want to serve the broth at the same meal, skim off as much fat as possible before doing so.

RINDFLEISCH MIT SCHNITTLAUCH OR
BEINFLEISCH MIT KREN

A rose by any other name would smell as sweet. So, I'm giving this dish two names, both applicable, to get myself off the hook. Literally translated, *Beinfleisch* means leg meat *Rindfleisch* means beef meat. (Kren is horseradish and *Schnittlauch* are chives.) In any event it's beef for boiling. I prefer the shin or lower shank sliced into 2-inch pieces. It has the marrow bone in the center. Otherwise use the same cuts of beef as for Pot au Feu (page 184) and add a pound of sawed-up soup bones.

Put

> *3–4 pounds of one of the above cuts of beef*

into a heavy pot and cover by an inch with cold, lightly salted water. Bring it to a boil and skim off floating scum. Add

> *2 carrots, scrubbed and sliced*
> *1 celery stalk with leaves, chopped*
> *1 large onion, chopped or quartered*
> *1 leek, chopped*
> *1 parsnip, scraped and sliced*
> *3 parsley sprigs*
> *a few peppercorns.*

After the water has returned to a boil, turn down the heat and skim it again. Simmer the meat 2½ to 3 hours or until tender when pierced. Serve with Horseradish Dressing (page 49).

Or keep the meat hot with a cup of broth in the pot in a 200° oven while you make:

Chive Sauce (Schnittlauch)

Strain the broth through several layers of cheesecloth and degrease it. In a heavy skillet melt

> *4 tablespoons butter*

and blend in

> *3 tablespoons quick-mix flour.*

Cook and stir for a minute. Add

> *2 cups strained and degreased broth.*

Whisk over medium heat until the sauce begins to thicken. Add

> *½ cup heavy cream.*

Whisk a little longer before turning down the heat. Simmer for 5 minutes.
Add

> 4 tablespoons chopped chives
> a few gratings of nutmeg.

Taste to see if it needs more

> salt and pepper.

Pour some of the sauce over the meat and serve the remainder in a pitcher.

Note: Keep leftover strained broth in the refrigerator. It's pure beef stock.

SAUERBRATEN (Serves 8)

If you've never tasted Sauerbraten, I'll make a flat claim that you haven't lived until you've tasted mine. The work time is short, the marinating time long. While the meat is resting in the marinade it must remain cool in order not to spoil. If there's not enough room for it in your refrigerator, wait until the outside temperature is between 40° and 60° to store the marinating meat on a fire escape in the city or a tool room or cool basement in the country.

Ask the butcher to roll and tie

> 5 pounds of eye-round of beef.

(If you've heard that it must be larded, rest assured, I don't have it done.) Place the meat in a glass, enamel, or porcelain bowl that will hold it snugly and surround with

> 2 sliced onions
> 2 sliced leeks (white parts only)
> 2 sliced carrots
> 1 sliced parsnip
> 6 whole cloves
> 12 peppercorns
> 12 crushed juniper berries.

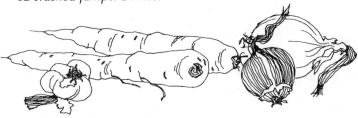

(Don't eliminate the juniper berries, because they *make* the Sauerbraten. They're available in the spice department of any good grocery store.)

Sprinkle everything with

> 2 *teaspoons coarse salt*

and pour on

> 1 *quart boiling red wine vinegar.*

Cover the dish with plastic wrap, then with a lid, and keep cool for one week as described. Turn the meat in the marinade once or twice a day.

On the day of your party, take the meat from the marinade and drain it in a colander for ½ hour before drying it thoroughly with toweling so it will brown well. Put the marinade into a heavy pot large enough to hold the meat and set it over a very low flame.

Meanwhile, brown the meat evenly on all sides in a large skillet in

> 2 *tablespoons fat (goose fat is ideal; bacon fat will do).*

The browning should take about 15 minutes. Regulate the heat so the fat won't burn. Remove the meat and arrange it among the vegetables in the hot marinade. Cover tightly and simmer for 2½ hours, turning the meat over once after an hour or so. Pierce to see if it's tender. It may need as much as another 30 minutes of simmering.

When done, remove it carefully from the pot and cut off the strings. Keep it hot on a platter in a 200° oven while you make the sauce.

The Sauce

To the marinade in the pot add

> 1 *cup dry red wine.*

Boil it down a little and strain through a fine sieve, pressing down hard on the vegetables to extract flavor. Let rest for a few minutes before skimming off all possible fat. In a skillet melt

> 1 *stick butter (8 tablespoons)*

and add

> 4 *tablespoons quick-mix flour.*

Over low heat, blend and cook for a few minutes. Add

> 2 *tablespoons sugar*
> *the strained marinade.*

Cook and stir until the sauce thickens. Serve it at the table in a pitcher.

Don't forget, it's not a Sauerbraten party without red cabbage (page 230) and Potato Pancakes (page 252). *Guten Appetit!*

HASKEL'S POT ROAST (Serves 4 to 6)

Haskel Frankel, the fine writer who assisted me with my book *Respect for Acting*, once made me this unusually good pot roast. It contains *canned* beef gravy, which made me shudder, but the results are so special that I haven't tampered with his recipe.

Start the preparation the day before serving the pot roast.

Preheat the oven to 350°.

Use toweling to dry

> 3 to 4 pounds beef rump or bottom round.

In a heavy skillet sauté

> 1 chopped onion in
> 1½ tablespoons bacon grease or goose fat.

When the onions are translucent, add the beef and brown it on all sides over medium-high heat. Be sure the fat stays hot without burning. Transfer the beef to a large, heavy casserole, discarding the onion. You need only a little liquid. To the casserole add

> ¼ cup dry vermouth or red wine
> 1 tablespoon wine vinegar
> a pinch of curry powder.

Cover the pot and cook it in the oven for 2 hours, turning the meat once. If more liquid accumulates during cooking, remove it with a bulb baster and reserve it for gravy.

Let the pot with the meat cool before refrigerating overnight.

The next day, remove the congealed fat from the liquid. Replace the covered casserole in a 350° preheated oven for 1½ hours or until tender when pierced.

Slice and serve with gravy.

The Gravy

Combine the liquid from the pot with

> 1 can of beef gravy (Eeeeek!).

Heat and serve. (Heavenly!)

BRAISED BEEF (Serves 6 to 8)

Don't get confused by the name. Unlike boiled beef, the meat is browned
before it's cooked in lots of wine. Although its potted, it requires much
more liquid than the average pot roast. Texture and flavor are quite
different.

Marinate

> 4 pounds boneless beef in one piece, rump, bottom round, or
> eye-round

in an enamel or Pyrex dish overnight with

> 2 sliced onions
> 4 sliced carrots
> 2 stalks chopped celery
> 3 cloves garlic, halved
> 1 teaspoon thyme
> 3 tablespoons chopped parsley
> 2 whole cloves
> 1 bottle dry red wine
> ¼ cup brandy
> ¼ cup olive oil
> 2 teaspoons salt.

Turn the meat until saturated before covering with plastic wrap and refrigerating.

The next day, bring it to room temperature. Turn it several times. Plan
on 2½ to 3 hours of cooking time. Remove the meat from the marinade
and set it in a colander to drain for an hour before drying with toweling.
Preheat the oven to 350°.

In a large, heavy casserole, brown the meat on all sides in

> 4 tablespoons goose fat or bacon grease.

Pour out the browned fat and add the marinade plus the vegetables, and
boil down the liquid until it has reduced to half. Then add

> 1 can condensed beef bouillon or 1½ cups strong beef stock.

The liquid should come halfway up the sides of the meat in the casserole.
Skim off scum if there is any. Put the lid tightly on the pot and place the
whole thing into the hot oven. Turn the meat after 1 hour, and cook for
another 15 minutes before adding

> 8 large, scraped carrots
> 24 tiny white peeled onions (dip in boiling water for 30 seconds to
> slip off the skins).

Simmer in the oven for another ½ hour and pierce both meat and vegetables to make sure they're tender.

Carefully remove the meat from the casserole with a slotted spoon and arrange on a platter surrounded by the carrots and onions. Return the platter to the oven with the heat turned off and the door ajar.

Make the sauce by skimming all possible fat from the liquid in the pot. Strain it through a fine sieve. Boil it down in a saucepan to reduce to 2½ to 3 cups. Meanwhile blend till smooth

> 1 tablespoon cornstarch
> 2 tablespoons Madeira.

Whisk the mixture into the reduced liquid over medium heat till thickened. Serve the sauce in a pitcher and let the guests pour over meat and vegetables.

FILETTO TONNATO (Serves 6)

A summer event of such perfection must be tasted to be believed. The classic recipe, Vitello Tonnato, calls for veal, but price has made this an almost impossible dream. However, you can use 4 pounds boned leg of veal instead of my "substitute," beef tenderloin.

Two or three days before needed, trim a filet as described on page 180. Use the longer half, instead of the rump end. Place the filet in a heavy, lidded casserole into which it fits snugly and surround it with

> 2 sliced carrots
> 1 large sliced onion
> 1 stalk chopped celery, leaves included
> 1 7-ounce can of tuna in oil (preferably Italian)
> 1 can anchovy filets in oil
> 1 large sliced sour pickle
> 2 halved garlic cloves
> a few parsley sprigs
> a few gratings of pepper
> a pinch of thyme.

Over meat and vegetables pour

> 1¼ *cups strong chicken stock or 1 can condensed broth*
> 1–2 *cups dry white wine.*

The amount of wine depends on the size of the pot. The liquid should cover the meat.

Cover the pot and bring the liquid to a boil. Skim off floating scum if necessary. Reduce heat and let simmer covered tightly for 1½ hours. Pierce with knife to make sure it's tender. (Veal may have to simmer longer.)

Let the pot cool before placing in the refrigerator for a minimum of 24 hours. Three days are preferred, to let the meat steep in the wine, tuna, and vegetables.

On the day of the feast, remove congealed fat from the pot, take out the meat, and wipe off clinging tuna or vegetables. Wrap in foil and replace in the refrigerator. Boil down the liquid until you have about 1½ cups. Strain through a fine sieve, pushing down hard on the fish and vegetables to extract flavor. Discard the pulp (or put it in the blender with one 3-ounce package of cream cheese and use as a cocktail spread or for stuffing cucumbers). If you used veal the broth will have jelled when cool, but if you're using beef, you'll need gelatin to make a proper sauce. Soften

> 1½ *teaspoons gelatin (half the package) in*
> 2 *tablespoons cold water.*

After 5 minutes dissolve it until all visible granules have disappeared in

> ¼ *cup scalding water.*

Stir the gelatin mixture into the strained broth and chill until it starts to set around the edges. Into the blender put

> 1 *cup Fanny's Mayonnaise (page 42) with*
> *the jellied broth.*

Blend for a few seconds at low speed. Refrigerate for an hour to let it thicken again.

To assemble, carve the cold filet into ½-inch slices and arrange on a platter over a bed of cold rice (page 255). Spoon some of the sauce over the slices to mask them completely. Place the remaining sauce in a pitcher to serve separately. Slice a lemon into transparently thin pieces and arrange around the edge of the platter on the rice. Garnish with black Italian olives, making a design on the meat or rice. A few sprigs of parsley will add color.

    The sauce and the arrangement of the platter can all be done earlier in the day. Just cover the platter with plastic wrap, refrigerate, and serve when your guests are ready for their festival.

SLICED BEEF EN GELÉE

Cold, sliced leftover beef is always delicious, whether it has been boiled, potted, braised, or roasted. Here's a way of dressing it up so that newly arrived guests will never dream it was left over.

Cut the beef into thin slices and arrange them neatly, overlapping slightly on a platter. Sprinkle the slices with freshly chopped (or pinches of dry)

> *basil leaves*
> *tarragon leaves*
> *thyme snippets.*

Sprinkle with

> *grated pepper*
> *sea salt.*

Around the meat arrange thin strips of

> *carrots*
> *green peppers.*

Soften

> *1 envelope gelatin in*
> *2 tablespoons lemon juice.*

In a saucepan bring to a boil

> *1¼ cup beef stock or 1 can condensed beef bouillon.*

Turn off the heat and stir in the gelatin mixture until completely dissolved. Add

> *½ cup cold water*
> *a dash of Worcestershire sauce*
> *a pinch of cayenne or black pepper.*

Cool the mixture until it gets gooey, about ½ hour. Whisk it well to incorporate the jelled part around the edges and pour the mixture evenly over the slices of beef. Chill 3 to 4 hours before serving.

THREE HEAVENLY STEWS

Don't be misled into thinking of stew as something drab to serve haphazardly around the kitchen table. It can be phenomenal, even exotic.

IRANIAN STEW (Serves 6)

Like most stews, this tastes even better a day or two after cooking. On a chilly night, serve it together with a loaf of crunchy bread, a bottle of red wine, followed by a green salad, and it's already an event.

You'll need

> 3½ pounds cubed chuck steak (trimmed of excess fat)
> 2 cups chopped parsley (stems removed)
> ½ cup sliced scallions, white part only (about 2 bunches)
> ½ lemon.

In a heavy pot melt

> 4 tablespoons butter.

Add the chopped parsley and scallions. Keep the pot over very low heat and stir the vegetables occasionally while you brown the meat.

Dry the cubed meat with toweling and grate pepper over it. In a large skillet melt

> 1 tablespoon butter
> 1 tablespoon oil.

When the fat is hot, brown 8 to 10 pieces of meat evenly on all sides over medium-high heat and add them to the vegetables in the pot. Proceed with the next batch. Don't crowd the skillet. Add more butter between batches as needed. When the meat is all in the pot with the scallions and parsley, sprinkle it with

> 1 teaspoon salt
> ¼ cup lemon juice

and add

> the half lemon, rind included.

Deglaze the skillet with

> 1 cup beef stock or canned bouillon.

Boil briskly to incorporate bits of meat from the pan. Add the broth to the pot. Cover and simmer 1½ hours. Then drain

> 2 cans of red kidney beans

and add them to the meat in the pot.

Simmer 10 minutes until the beans are heated through. Pierce the meat to make sure it's tender. Serve in a large tureen.

BEEF CARBONNADE (Serves 6)

Belgian stew simmered in Guinness Stout or dark beer is zesty and, like the Iranian stew, improves with age. You can make it a day or two ahead of time.

Cut

> *3–3½ pounds boneless chuck into 1½-inch cubes.*

Remove all excess fat. Dry with toweling and sprinkle with grated pepper.

In a large casserole melt

> *4 tablespoons butter.*

Over low heat add and cook

> *1 cup thinly sliced onions.*

Meanwhile, in a large, heavy skillet heat

> *1 tablespoon butter*
> *1 tablespoon oil.*

Brown the meat evenly on all sides in the hot fat, about 10 pieces at a time. Don't crowd the pan, and add butter between batches as needed. Place the browned meat into the casserole with the onions.

Preheat the oven to 350°.

When all the meat is in the casserole, to the skillet in which it was browned add

> *2 tablespoons butter*

and when it foams blend in

> *2 tablespoons quick-mix flour.*

Cook the mixture until golden. Then whisk in

> *1½ cups Guinness Stout (dark beer is a good substitute)*
> *1 can condensed beef bouillon.*

Lower the heat and whisk the sauce until it begins to bubble. Simmer about 15 minutes, until it has reduced and thickened a little. Then add

> *2 tablespoons sugar*
> *2 tablespoons vinegar*
> *2 cloves pressed garlic*
> *a pinch of thyme*
> *a few parsley sprigs*
> *salt and pepper to taste.*

Stir and simmer the sauce another minute or so before pouring into the casserole. If the sauce doesn't come halfway up the meat, add more beer. Cover tightly and place in the hot oven for 1½ hours or until the meat is tender when pierced. Let it cool before refrigerating for a day or two. (Or it can, of course, be served at once.)

When ready to serve, fish out the parsley and reheat. It will make you happy!

UTA'S HUNGARIAN GOULASH (Serves 4 to 6)

This recipe should be the climax to the entire chapter about meat since it was the dish which started me on the road to confidence in the kitchen.

In a heavy casserole with a lid melt

> 4 tablespoons butter.

Set it over a very low flame and add

> 2 cups chopped onions.

Stir the onions in the butter occasionally while you brown the meat.

Use

> 3–3½ pounds boneless chuck cut in 1½-inch cubes.

Trim excess fat and dry the cubes thoroughly. Sprinkle with freshly ground black pepper.

In a large skillet melt

> 2 tablespoons goose fat
> or
> 1 tablespoon butter and
> 1 tablespoon oil.

Brown the meat in the hot fat in small batches adding more fat as needed.

Then add the meat to the casserole. Into the empty skillet put

> 1 tablespoon butter
> ¼ cup ketchup
> 3 tablespoons imported paprika
> 1 teaspoon salt.

Heat and stir the mixture for several minutes before adding

> 1¼ cup strong beef stock or 1 can condensed beef bouillon (as a
> variation try ¾ cup beef stock and ⅓ cup dry red wine).

Stir the sauce and pour it over the meat and onions. Cover tightly and simmer 1½ to 2 hours, until the meat is tender when pierced.

Sometimes for the last half-hour of cooking, I add

>*6 small peeled potatoes*

burying them in the goulash.

For the last few minutes of cooking add

>*1 cup sour cream.*

Blend into the sauce and cook until heated through. Garnish with a colorful sprinkling of paprika and parsley leaves. Eat at once . . . or the next day . . . or the next. . . .

Veal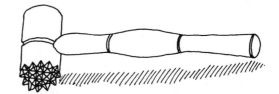

Years ago this section would have been lengthy. Soon veal may no longer be available, or at least not within our budget. I worry about the Austrians and the Italians. What *will* they do without their Schnitzel or their Scallopini? Veal scallops are still possible, because one pound of boneless leg, cut thin and flattened into scallops, will serve 4 to 6 people.

PREPARING VEAL SCALLOPS

American veal is not milk fed as it is in Europe, so I "feed" it by soaking the scallops in milk overnight or for a minimum of four hours. They turn as tender and white as they ought to be. They may also be marinated in lemon juice, but I prefer the milk treatment.

Most scallops need to be flattened until they're ⅛ inch thin. The butcher presents them to me already flattened and placed neatly between separate layers of wax paper. In case you have to flatten them yourself, place between sheets of wax paper and pound them with the side of a cleaver, a heavy mallet, or the flat bottom of an iron skillet. Do this *before* marinating in milk or lemon juice.

You'll need 2 scallops per person for most recipes. Depending on circumference, 1 pound of veal usually supplies 8 to 10 scallops. When serving more than 4 people, your largest skillet will be too small to do the cooking all at once. Use two skillets or do it in batches. Keep the cooked veal hot on a platter in a 200° oven until the rest is completed.

WIENER SCHNITZEL (Serves 4)

Herbert would eat these every night if I let him.

Overnight in milk, marinate

> *8 flattened veal scallops.*

Next day drain and dry them and sprinkle with salt and pepper. Follow the breading procedure on page 21 by dusting with flour, coating with beaten egg, and dredging with bread crumbs. At this point, the scallops can be covered with wax paper and refrigerated until cooking time.

In a large, heavy skillet melt

> *1 stick butter (8 tablespoons).*

Over medium-high heat fry a few Schnitzel at a time about 2 minutes on each side. Serve with thin lemon slices and sprinkle with chopped parsley.

(A Viennese variation is to top each Schnitzel with a fried egg.)

SACHER SCHNITZEL (Serves 4)

I had a similar experience in Vienna at the Café Sacher to the one I had with their Backhendl. Since they don't hand out recipes, I ended up using the same batter, Uta's Fluffy Batter (page 118). Don't forget to make the batter in the morning and fold in the beaten egg white just before you start cooking. Double the batter recipe for

> *8 flattened, milk-marinated scallops.*

Drain and dry the scallops and dust them lightly with flour.

In a deep skillet heat to 350°

> *1 inch peanut or vegetable oil.*

Dip each scallop into the batter till coated and then slide into the hot fat. Fry for a few minutes until fluffy and golden. Fry in at least two batches; don't crowd the pan. Drain on toweling and serve sprinkled with lemon juice. Sprinkle with parsley.

NATUR SCHNITZEL

This speedy Austrian way of cooking veal scallops is pure and beautiful. Use

> *2 scallops per person.*

After removing them from the milk marinade, dry them with toweling, sprinkle with salt and pepper, and dust on both sides with a little flour.

For every 2 scallops, use

> *1½ tablespoons butter.*

Sauté them quickly over medium-high heat for a minute or so on each side until golden.

Remove them to a platter and make a sauce by adding to the skillet

> *¼ cup dry Madeira wine.*

Stir briskly and pour over the meat. Garnish with parsley sprigs and lemon wedges.

VEAL SCALLOPS IN LEMON BUTTER (Serves 4)

Marinate in milk overnight

> *8 flattened veal scallops.*

Drain and dry.

Clarify

> *6 tablespoons butter (page 46).*

In a heavy skillet heat

> *2 tablespoons of the butter.*

Over medium-high heat, sauté four scallops at a time for 2 to 3 minutes on each side.

Transfer them to a warm plate and sprinkle with salt and pepper. Keep them hot in a low oven.

Add the remaining butter to the skillet and sauté

> *1 tablespoon minced shallots.*

After a minute add

> *1 tablespoon quick-mix flour.*

Cook and stir the mixture for another minute over low heat. Add

>½ cup chicken stock or canned condensed broth.

Cook and whisk until the sauce thickens. Add

>2 tablespoons lemon juice
>a pinch of salt and pepper.

Pour the sauce over the scallops and garnish with lemon wedges and parsley sprigs.

VEAL CORDON BLEU (Serves 4)

Sprinkle

>8 prepared veal scallops (page 197)

with salt and pepper.

Cut

>4 thin slices of prosciutto or boiled ham
>4 thin slices of Gruyère or Emmenthaler cheese.

Make sure the slices of ham and cheese are slightly smaller in circumference than the veal. On each of four scallops place a slice of cheese and one of ham, then cover with another scallop. Squeeze the edges of these "sandwiches" together as tightly as possible. Dust lightly on each side with a little quick-mix flour, then dip in beaten egg and finally dredge with dry white bread crumbs.

In a large skillet heat

>4 tablespoons butter.

When the butter foam has subsided, sauté the veal "sandwich" on each side about 4 minutes. Add more butter if needed. Serve at once.

Note: Mushrooms and veal are a wonderful combination. Sometime, for a luncheon, serve the Natur Schnitzel or Wiener Schnitzel (page 198), Scallops in Lemon Butter (page 47), or even the Veal Cordon Bleu (above) on sautéed toast and smother with sautéed sliced mushrooms!

VEAL SYLVIA (Serves 8)

Once, before it's too late, try this wildly expensive veal roast. It's worth a week of fasting. Traditionally it's called Veau Sylvie. I don't know who *that* Sylvie is, but I pretend this roast is named for Sylvia Weaver, the dynamic wife of the great actor Fritz Weaver. She *should* have such a dish named for her.

Begin with

> *4 pounds boneless top round of veal*

rolled into a cylindrical shape. This cut has the least amount of sinews and muscles and will hold together well. Boned rib works equally well but is even more expensive.

Place the veal on a board and use a long sharp knife to slice downward into the veal every 1½ inches. Slice to within ½ inch of the bottom so the meat will still be in one piece and open up like the pages of a book. Marinate overnight in

> *3 tablespoons olive oil*
> *¼ cup brandy*
> *¼ cup dry Madeira*
> *2 thinly sliced onions*
> *2 thinly sliced carrots*
> *1 teaspoon salt*
> *freshly grated pepper*
> *a pinch of thyme*
> *parsley sprigs*
> *a bay leaf.*

Turn the meat in the marinade to make sure it's saturated. Cover with plastic wrap and refrigerate. The next day turn it several times while it returns to room temperature. Drain the meat in a colander and pat dry with toweling. Reserve the marinade.

Preheat the oven to 425°.

Between each leaf of sliced veal place a sandwich of

> *1 thin slice boiled ham*
> *1 thin slice Gruyère cheese*
> *1 more thin slice of ham.*

When all the slices of veal have been stuffed, push the roast together and tie it securely lengthwise with kitchen string.

Strain the marinade, reserving the liquid. Cook the remaining vegetables in a heavy casserole over low heat for 5 minutes in

> *3 tablespoons butter*
> *1 tablespoon oil.*

Push the vegetables to the edge of the pot and set the veal in the center, sliced side upward. Turn up the heat to let the bottom of the veal brown for 5 minutes. Then place the uncovered casserole into the hot oven to let the top brown for 15 minutes. Remove the casserole from the oven, baste the veal with pan juices, and pour in the reserve marinade. Sprinkle the meat with salt and pepper and cover with

>*3 strips of blanched bacon (simmered in water 10 minutes).*

Cover the casserole and replace in the oven turning the heat to 325°. Cook 1½ to 2 hours, basting with the pot juices every now and then. Pierce the roast to make sure it's tender before removing from the casserole. Degrease the juices in the casserole and boil down to about 1 cup. Strain through a fine sieve and serve in a pitcher. Don't let this veal spoil you for everything else!

VEAL STEAK PAPRIKA (Serves 4)

Wipe and dry

>*1½ pounds of veal steak (sirloin or round, cut 1½ inches thick).*

Peel

>*2 onions and slice them paper thin.*

In a large, shallow casserole with lid, heat

>*4 tablespoons butter.*

Blend in

>*1½ tablespoons imported sweet paprika.*

Add

>*the sliced onions.*

Gently cook the onions over low heat in the red butter for 10 minutes, turning and stirring until they're soft. Use a slotted spoon to move them to a side dish. Lightly dust the veal steak on both sides with a little flour. Then brown it on both sides in the remaining butter in the pan over medium-high heat, about 3 minutes on each side. Sprinkle with salt and pepper and pile the cooked onions over the steak. Over everything pour

>*½ cup chicken broth.*

Cover the casserole and turn down the heat. Simmer for 15 minutes.

Add

1 cup sour cream.

Blend it into the sauce and heat through.

Garnish with a sprinkling of paprika and a few parsley sprigs.

Lamb

When a sheep is less than a year old it's a lamb. After that it's a mutton. I'm on guard about this difference because after six months in a London boarding house when I was in my teens, where they served mutton every other night prepared in any number of revolting ways, I developed a prejudice. Now I keep in mind that a leg of lamb weighing over eight pounds is approaching "muttonhood."

PREPARING A LEG OF LAMB

The butcher usually cracks the bones and slices partway into the top of the leg of lamb. That top part is the sirloin. I cut it off to use for a separate roast, or I complete the slicing to make 4 or 5 lamb steaks, which I prepare in exactly the same way as the pan-broiled beef steaks on page 176. Since I'm usually planning to roast the leg first, I wrap the sirloin in foil and freeze it for another time.

The butcher rarely removes enough fat to suit me. I trim off almost all of it. The filament or transparent membrane on top of the lamb should *not* be removed or the lamb will dry out. If the purple government stamp is visible on the membrane, scrape it off, trying not to cut into the membrane. Now it's ready for seasoning. A leg of lamb is one of the easiest things to cook, and yet it always seems to have an air of grandeur.

ROAST LEG OF LAMB (Serves 6)

As described above, prepare a

     6–7 pound leg of lamb.

Preheat the oven to 425°.

Mix

> 4 tablespoons softened butter
> 1 tablespoon olive oil
> 2 or 3 pressed garlic cloves.

Rub the mixture into the skin of the lamb.

Chop

> 1 large carrot
> 1 large onion.

Sprinkle the vegetables loosely over the bottom of the roasting pan. Set the lamb on a rack over the pan and put it into the hot oven. A 6-pound roast will be done in one hour. A 7-pound leg will take 1 hour and 10 minutes. The lamb should be crisp and brown on the outside and slightly pink in the center. It will also be tender and juicy. Longer roasting produces grayness and dryness.

Place the lamb on a platter and sprinkle with salt and pepper. Let it rest for 10 minutes before carving. Meanwhile make the sauce.

The Sauce

Pour and then skim off as much fat from the roasting pan as possible, leaving behind the brown juices. If the vegetables have turned black, discard them. Otherwise leave them in the pan. To the pan add

> 1½ cups beef stock or 1 can condensed beef bouillon.

Boil it down to reduce by about one-third. Strain it through a fine sieve. Season the sauce with salt and pepper and serve in a pitcher.

Sauce Variations
Mint Sauce

After the juices in the roasting pan have been degreased, remove the vegetables with a slotted spoon and add

> 1 cup beef stock
> 1 tablespoon sugar
> ¼–½ cup chopped mint leaves
> salt and pepper to taste.

Bring to a boil, lower the heat, and simmer 5 minutes. Serve in a pitcher.

Dill Sauce

Degrease the roasting pan except for 1 or 2 tablespoons fat. Remove the vegetables with a slotted spoon. Blend in

2 tablespoons quick-mix flour.

Cook for several minutes stirring and scraping the pan to loosen food particles. Add

2 cups beef stock or 1½ cans condensed beef bouillon.

Whisk the sauce over medium-high heat until it starts to thicken. Add

3–4 tablespoons chopped dill
1 tablespoon white vinegar
1 tablespoon sugar
1 teaspoon lemon juice
a pinch of salt.

In a bowl lightly beat

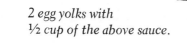

2 egg yolks with
½ cup of the above sauce.

Whisk the egg mixture back into the sauce in the pan. Add salt and pepper to taste. Strain through a fine sieve and serve it in a pitcher.

Roast Leg of Lamb Variations   Prepare the lamb as described on page 203. After rubbing with the butter and garlic mixture, smear 4 tablespoons Mary La's Mustard (page 49) over the top. The sugar in the mustard may burn as it runs off into the bottom of the pan, but it won't affect the lamb. You may not be able to use the pan juices for sauce, but the sweet mustard coating gives it such flavor, you won't need any.

> Or

Instead of the initial mixture of butter, oil and garlic, make a paste of

⅓ cup Dijon or Düsseldorf mustard
2 or 3 pressed garlic cloves
a pinch of thyme or tarragon
a pinch of ground ginger
2 tablespoons soy sauce.

Smear the paste over the lamb and proceed with the roasting as described.

MARINATED ROAST LEG OF LAMB

This lamb is tangy with an almost venisonlike flavor. Prepare the leg as described on page 203 but have the butcher crack the ankle bone so it can be folded back when the lamb is placed in an enamel, glass, or porcelain bowl to fit snugly. Then you won't need excessive amounts of marinade.

Into a large pot put

> ½ cup olive oil
> 2 sliced onions
> 3 sliced carrots
> 2 chopped celery stalks
> 2 halved garlic cloves.

Cover the pot and simmer the mixture for 10 minutes. Then add

> 1 cup vinegar
> 1 bottle of dry red wine
> 1 tablespoon salt
> 8 peppercorns
> parsley sprigs
> 1 teaspoon dry tarragon
> 12 juniper berries
> 1 bay leaf.

Simmer 20 minutes longer. Allow the marinade to cool before pouring it over the lamb in the bowl. Cover with plastic wrap and let rest at room temperature for 3 days, turning the lamb twice a day. The temperature can be between 60° and 70°, but don't try this during a heat wave or the marinade will sour and the lamb will spoil.

The day of your party, place the lamb in a colander to drain for an hour, then dry with toweling. Reserve the marinade. Rub the lamb with

> 3 tablespoons softened butter.

Roast the lamb as described on page 203. Add 20 minutes to the roasting time.

The Sauce

Degrease the roasting pan as much as possible.

Boil the marinade to reduce to 1 cup and add it to the pan. Also add

> 1 cup beef stock or canned condensed bouillon.

Simmer the sauce for a few minutes while you make a paste of

> 2 tablespoons cornstarch
> 3 tablespoons cold water
> 2 tablespoons sugar.

Whisk the paste into the sauce and simmer until it thickens. Strain through a sieve. Taste for additional seasoning and serve in a pitcher with the lamb.

Variation Try the Marinade on page 50 and marinate the lamb overnight before roasting.

BRAISED LEG OF LAMB (Serves 6)

A juicy and tender way to prepare lamb, braising is also ideal if you don't have a self-cleaning oven. In order to absorb the flavors of the braising liquid it must cook much longer than a roast. You have three options:

> A 6-pound leg of lamb (in which case ask the butcher to saw through the ankle bone so it can be folded back and allow the lamb to fit snugly into a casserole).
>
> *or*
>
> A 6-pound boned leg of lamb, rolled and tied, with the lamb bone sawed up to use for cooking.
>
> *or*
>
> A 5-pound shoulder of lamb, tied up to form a compact piece, plus a sawed-up lamb bone.

The boned lamb or the shoulder require a smaller casserole and less braising liquid.

Preheat the oven to 350°.

Dry the meat and brown it on all sides in a heavy skillet in

> *4 tablespoons oil, bacon grease or, best of all, goose fat.*

Sprinkle the lamb with salt and pepper and place it snugly into a casserole.

Use the same skillet and remaining fat to brown the lamb bones. Sprinkle with salt and pepper and tuck them around the lamb in the casserole.

At this point, if the skillet seems dry, add

> *2 tablespoons goose fat or butter.*

Over medium-high heat brown

> *2 large sliced carrots*
> *2 sliced onions.*

Remove the vegetables with a slotted spoon and sprinkle them around the lamb and bones. Pour the fat out of the skillet and add

> *1 cup dry red wine.*

Boil it down briskly, using a wooden spoon to deglaze the pan and incorporate clinging meat particles. Then add

> *1–3 cans condensed beef bouillon.*

(The liquid should come well up the sides of the lamb in the casserole.)

Simmer the liquid in the skillet a minute and then add

2 whole garlic cloves
a pinch of thyme
a pinch of tarragon or rosemary
a bay leaf
a few parsley sprigs.

Simmer a few minutes longer and pour the mixture over meat and bones and vegetables in the casserole. Place a piece of foil over the pot before putting on the lid.

Braise in the hot oven for 2 hours. Pierce for tenderness. Braise another ½ hour if needed. Remove the lamb from the casserole and drain in a colander. Cut off the strings and set on a hot platter.

Skim as much fat as possible from the braising liquid in the pot. Boil it down rapidly for a few minutes, strain through a sieve, and serve.

BRAISED LAMB WITH BEANS (Serves 6 to 8)

Before you begin to prepare the preceding lamb, in a large pot boil

1½ quarts water.

Add

2 cups small white dry beans.

Let the water return to a boil and immediately turn off the heat. Let the beans soak for 1 hour. Then add

1 tablespoon salt.

Bring the water back to a boil, turn down the heat, and let simmer 1 hour. turn off the heat. Preheat the oven to 350°. Prepare the lamb as above.

When the lamb has been braising in the oven for 1½ hours, drain the beans and add them to the liquid in the casserole. Cover with the foil and lid and continue braising for another ½ hour or so.

When everything is tender, remove the lamb as described. Remove the beans with a slotted spoon and arrange around the lamb. Proceed with the braising liquid to make the sauce as before.

Pork

Although pork is a fatty meat, I love it. It should always be cooked slowly and thoroughly. The meat should be grayish-white when finished, never pink, and the juices should run clear.

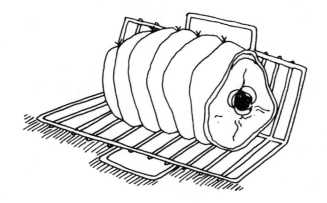

ROAST LOIN OF PORK

A plain roast pork is beautiful to taste, to look at, and to cook!

Get

1 rib end loin of pork.

My loin usually includes 2 ribs per person. Ask the butcher to crack the ribs and saw partway through into the bone so that when you carve, you can simply slice off as many ribs as you like per serving.

Preheat the oven to 350°.

Rub the roast with a mixture of

2 pressed garlic cloves
1 teaspoon dried tarragon
salt, pepper, and nutmeg.

Dust the fatty top with 2 tablespoons flour.

Place the pork on the rack over your roasting pan, fat side up, and set it in the hot oven to roast 30 to 35 minutes per pound. The fat makes it self-basting.

CASSEROLE ROAST PORK WITH PRUNES AND APPLES (Serves 6)

This recipe comes from Scandinavia; Denmark, I hope, in honor of my Danish mother. It elicits admiration from all who sample it.

Use the center cut of

a loin of pork (4–5 pounds).

Ask the butcher to bone it and slice a pocket for the stuffing to within ½ inch of each end.

In a saucepan bring to a boil in water to cover

> 12 pitted prunes.

Turn off the heat and let the prunes soak for 30 minutes.

Peel, core, and cube

> 1 large green cooking apple.

Sprinkle the apple cubes with

> 1 tablespoon lemon juice.

Rub the pork, including the inside of the pocket, with salt and pepper. Stuff the pocket with the apple cubes and pitted prunes, alternating. Sew up the pocket with a large needle and kitchen twine. Tie the loin with twine to give it a cylindrical shape.

Preheat the oven to 350°.

Choose a heavy casserole into which the meat will fit snugly and in it heat

> 4 tablespoons butter
> 1 tablespoon oil.

When the butter foam has subsided, brown the pork carefully on all sides, turning it with wooden spoons. Then tip the casserole to pour off all fat, or remove the fat with a bulb baster. Pour in

> ½ cup dry white wine
> 1 cup heavy cream.

Bring the liquid to a simmer on the stove. Cover the casserole with foil and then a lid. Cook in the hot oven for 1½ hours.

Pierce the meat to make sure it's tender before removing it from the casserole with wooden spoons. Place it on a platter and remove the twine. Keep it warm in the oven with the heat turned off and the door ajar.

To make the sauce, skim as much fat as you can from the liquid in the pot. Bring to a boil, uncovered, to let the liquid reduce to a little more than 1 cup. Add

> 4 tablespoons currant, apple, or beachplum jelly.

Whisk the jelly into the sauce until dissolved. Serve it in a pitcher. Carve the meat at the table so the guests can see the apples and prunes emerging from the center of each slice. It's truly beautiful.

BAKED HAM WITH TWO GLAZES (Serves 6 to 8)

Until I learned about Hungarian Goulash, I made ham so often that at the merest hint of a dinner invitation my friends would say, "Baked ham and beans, eh?" Finally I learned to serve it only once in a while, and not always to the same people. It gives the impression of elaborate preparation and is a sure-fire success for a beginning cook.

Start out with a processed, precooked ham in a can. I prefer the Danish and Polish brands even though I'm not the least bit un-American. The initial baking only consists of further tenderizing and heating through. Cans are available in sizes to serve from 2 to 10 people. Cooking time and glazing ingredients can be cut down proportionately. It's hard to goof.

Buy a

> *5-pound ham.*

Remove it from the can and wipe off the surrounding jelly. If it has any fat, place it fat-side up in a small roasting pan into which it fits comfortably. Bake for 1 hour in a 325° preheated oven basting every 15 minutes with appropriate glaze liquid.

Remove from the oven to let it cool just until it can be handled.

Meanwhile, turn up the oven to 425° for the glazing.

If the top of the ham is fatty, criss-cross the fat with a knife to make diamond shapes about ½ inch in diameter. If there's no fat, skip it.

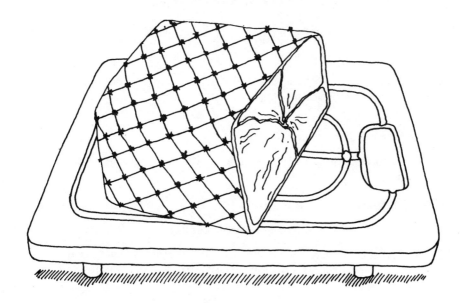

Bourbon Glaze with Oranges

Bake the ham for 1 hour basting every 15 minutes with spoonfuls of

½ cup bourbon or blended whiskey.

In a small bowl mix

*¾ cup brown sugar
2 teaspoons dry mustard
3 tablespoons bourbon or blended whiskey.*

Stir the mixture till gooey and brush it over the top and sides of the ham. Make a design by studding the ham with whole cloves. (If you've scored it, put a clove in each diamond tip.)

Pull apart the sections of a peeled

navel orange.

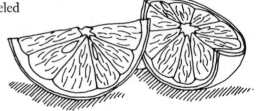

Place the wedges on top of the ham in a pretty pattern. Secure the wedges with toothpicks. Replace the ham in the oven and bake 15 minutes longer or until glazed. Place on a platter and serve.

Apricot Glaze with Pineapple

Bake the ham for 1 hour basting every 15 minutes with

½ cup dry white wine.

Let cool sufficiently to handle and decorate with cloves as described for the Bourbon Glaze. Then mix together

*1 cup apricot jam
1 tablespoon lemon juice.*

Brush the mixture over the top and sides of the studded ham, reserving the spoonfuls.

Surround the base of the ham with

fresh or frozen drained pineapple chunks.

Brush the pineapple with a little of the jam mixture and return the ham to the oven for 15 minutes or until glazed. Arrange on a platter and serve at once.

KASSELER RIPPENSPEER (Serves 6 to 8)

This is a spécialité d'Uta. It dates back to my days in Wisconsin where we were able to get the meat from the German butchers. Easy to fix, fabulous to taste, and unusual. It's always available at Schaller and Weber, that great butcher shop on Second Avenue at 86th Street in Manhattan, but I'm sure any butcher will order you a

4-pound smoked loin of pork.

Ask him to leave the bone attached and, as with the fresh loin, saw the bone partially between the ribs for easy carving. At the start the meat needs no seasoning or browning.

Preheat the oven to 350°.

Choose a casserole into which the pork fits snugly. In the casserole heat

2 tablespoons bacon grease (goose fat is best).

To the fat add

2 large chopped onions
3 sliced carrots.

Cook the vegetables over low heat for 15 minutes, stirring occasionally until soft.

Place the pork, fat side up on top of the vegetables and surround with

6 crushed juniper berries.

Add

2 cans condensed beef bouillon
1½ cups water.

Place the uncovered casserole into the hot oven and cook for 1½ hours. The pork should brown nicely and needs no basting. Remove it to a hot platter.

Skim the fat from the liquid in the pot and strain the juices through a fine sieve. Boil down to reduce to 1½ cups.

Make a smooth paste of

1 tablespoon cornstarch
2 tablespoons dry vermouth.

Whisk the mixture into the sauce and simmer until it thickens. Serve it in a pitcher. Carve the meat at the table. You'll be proud!

POTPOURRI PARTY

This adventure in eating is just as much fun for two people as for a gang; a combination of beef, lamb, liver, sausages, and bacon which everyone can pick out from the platter themselves. For each person you need

> *1 thin slice of calves liver or beef liver*
> *a small slice of porterhouse steak (1 inch thick)*
> *1 loin lamb chop (1 inch thick)*
> *2 Deerfoot or link sausages*
> *1 small Bockwurst*
> *½ a sliced Knockwurst or 1 sliced skinless frankfurter*
> *½ a thinly sliced onion*
> *2 slices lean bacon.*

For the cook the potpourri is also an adventure in timing and organization. Here's my battle plan:

In the morning, make a pot of beans, Kasha, or rice, to be reheated just before serving.

Wash, pat dry, and crisp the lettuce for the salad in the refrigerator. (Add the dressing just before serving.)

Be sure to have a good bottle of red wine on hand, or maybe some imported beer.

About an hour before dinner, start the bacon.

Bacon

Preheat oven to 225°.

Place the bacon strips side by side without touching each other across the rack on your roasting pan. Set the pan in the oven. After 1 hour the bacon will be brown and crisp while the fat has dripped into the pan underneath. No draining necessary.

Set 3 large skillets on the stove and place the meats on a board.

Remove excess fat from the porterhouse steak and cut a thin slice for each person.

Remove excess fat from each lamb chop.

Slice the Knockwurst or frankfurters into 1-inch pieces.

Leave link sausages and small Bockwurst whole.

Place the slices of liver on wax paper.

Thinly slice the onions.

When your guests are halfway through their cocktails, leave them to perform your juggling act in the kitchen.

In one of the skillets melt

2–3 tablespoons butter.

Cook the sliced onions for 10 minutes over low heat until soft. Remove them to a plate with a slotted spoon and reserve the skillet for the liver a little later.

The Lamb Chops

While the onions are cooking, start the lamb chops by searing them in a hot, dry skillet for one minute on each side. Sprinkle with salt and pepper and lower the heat a little to sauté another 5 minutes on each side. Remove them to an ovenproof platter and place them in the oven to keep hot with the bacon.

The Sausages

While the lamb chops were on their second 5 minutes, you will have removed

2 tablespoons bacon drippings

from the pan in the oven, using a bulb baster, and put it into the third skillet. Prick the skins of Deerfoot, link sausage, and Bockwurst so they won't burst while cooking. Sauté all the sausages over medium heat in the bacon drippings to brown them lightly, about 5 minutes or a little longer.

Drain the sausages on toweling and add them to the platter in the oven.

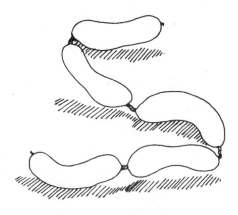

Porterhouse Steak

In the same skillet used for the lamb chops, sauté the strips of steak. There should be enough lamb fat in the pan; otherwise add a tablespoon of butter. Sauté the steak over medium-high heat for 2 minutes on each side. Sprinkle with salt and pepper and add to the platter with the lamb chops in the oven.

The Liver

Sprinkle the liver slices with a little salt and pepper and dust them on both sides with some

quick-mix flour.

Relight the flame under the skillet in which you cooked the onions. There should still be butter in the pan; otherwise add 2 tablespoons. Over medium-high heat, sauté the liver quickly, from 1 to 2 minutes on each side. Pile the onions over them and turn down the heat while they warm through for a minute. Turn off the heat.

Now! Remove the platter from the oven and rearrange it so the lamb chops are in the center, the steak slices fanning out from it with liver slices in between. Alternate the sausages and bacon strips and sprinkle the onions sparsely over everything. Serve and whoop it up!

XI. Fresh, Fresh Vegetables and Grain

(FROM ASPARAGUS TO ZUCCHINI)

Good-by to gray, limp beans or Brussels sprouts, to hurriedly tossed-in-the-pot frozen asparagus or broccoli. Good-by to the boring cans that seemed to save time. No more vegetables only because they're expected or just because "they're good for you." Instead the expectation should be for a vegetable so delicious it can stand alone.

Buy fresh vegetables in season. There are always plenty to choose from so don't be impatient about the others. If possible, grow your own and burst with pride as you reap and serve these fruits of the earth.

Trimming, paring, and cleaning vegetables can become so routine that you won't remember what the fuss was all about. I sometimes do the initial preparation of as many as four vegetables at a time on a free afternoon or evening to have them on hand for their final recipes when the serious cooking begins on the weekend.

To achieve firm, richly colored, cooked vegetables you need no soda or poisonous monosodium glutamate, just lots of boiling water in an open kettle. All my friends who used to be in the front lines defending steamed or pressure cooked vegetables have been converted. If you're not convinced, try it just once.

PARBOILING VEGETABLES

The principle is the same for many green vegetables. After washing and paring as specified, for every

> 1 pound of vegetables

bring to a brisk boil

> 4 quarts water with
> 1 teaspoon salt.

Give the vegetables in the colander a final rinse under the hottest tap water before dropping them into the boiling water in the pot a few at a time in order not to interrupt the boiling. Do *not* cover the pot. At the shortest specified time, taste one of the vegetables for tenderness. When done and dazzling green, drain in a colander under cold running water to stop the cooking process and to refresh them. Spread on toweling and pat dry. If not to be eaten at once, wait until they've cooled and are completely dry before refrigerating in a covered bowl. They'll keep for several days if necessary.

Note: Since I'm starting with A and ending with Z, I'd like to explain a few alphabetical omissions. Artichokes are covered in Chapter V because I serve them as a first course or stuffed as a luncheon course. Beets are not for me except for the tiny ones I stuff for hors d'oeuvres (page 58) and the cold Borscht on page 97. I have an inexplicable aversion for that popular vegetable, the eggplant. The mushroom field has been thoroughly covered in Chapter V and I feel the same about okra as I do about egg-plant. As for turnips, they remind me of my childhood starvation diet in war-torn Germany and I don't even like to smell them cooking. Have pity on my antipathies and join me in my enthusiasm for all the other vegetables!

Asparagus

In an article, James Beard described many complicated ways of cooking asparagus; steamed, tied in bunches, standing upright, wrapped in cheese cloth, etc. If I hadn't finished the article, I'd have missed the last paragraph in which, almost as an afterthought, he claimed that his favorite method is to place the asparagus flat, lying loose, in an open skillet filled with boiling salted water for just a few minutes. He's right. It can't be beat.

Use at least 6 asparagus per person. Don't buy the ones wrapped in bunches, but pick the ones you want from a loose pile for uniformity in thickness. So that the entire spear will cook evenly and come out with a crisp head and tender bottom, the paring method is essential. (I hate it when someone who doesn't know any better leaves the succulent ends on the plate.) To pare, use a small *sharp* knife. Cut off the tough white bottom of each spear. Then hold the asparagus in your left hand with the spear pointing toward you. Start at the bottom and peel upwards, shaving off some of the flesh as well as the skin about halfway up the stalk. When completed, the asparagus should be almost as thin at the bottom as the stalk near the spear. If in doubt, slit the bottom to cook more rapidly. Wash well and drain in a colander. Once you get the hang of it, it's easy and takes little time. If you're not cooking them at once, wrap loosely in toweling, pop them in a plastic bag, and refrigerate, as long as two days.

Just before dinner, fill a large, deep skillet almost to the top with lightly salted water and bring it to a boil. Slide the asparagus in one by one and let boil 8 to 10 minutes, depending on thickness. Taste for tenderness or do what I do: Place a two-tined fork between the stem and the spear, lift it, and if the spear bends *slightly*, it's done. I like asparagus on the crunchy side, not limp. Use a slotted skimmer to move the stalks from the skillet to toweling. Drain for a few seconds and serve at once. If you want cold asparagus, allow them to cool on toweling before arranging side by side on a plate, then cover and refrigerate no more than a day before eating them. When hot, vividly green, and crunchy-tender, they really don't need any embellishment other than a pat of butter and a lemon wedge per serving. Lemon Butter (page 47) for dipping or drizzling is always nice and Hollandaise Sauce (page 41) should never be sneezed at.

STIR-FRIED ASPARAGUS

Sometimes I get a yen for asparagus when the ones in the garden or at the market are still very skinny. They can't be peeled in that condition so I stir-fry them.

Cut off the asparagus bottoms to the green part and wash and dry the stalks. Slice them on the diagonal into 1-inch pieces. I don't own a Wok, so I use my large iron skillet. Heat

> 1 tablespoon peanut or light sesame oil

per pound of vegetable. When the oil is very hot, toss in the asparagus pieces and stir briskly with a wooden spoon for 3 or 4 minutes. Taste a piece gingerly (it's hot!) to see if it's tender yet crisp. Serve with a squirt of lemon juice, salt and pepper, that's all. Can you *wait* for spring?

Beans

"Beans, beans, the musical fruit . . ." I promise not to finish the rhyme. I wax lyrical when I dream of waltzing around the vegetable patch to pick a pot of fresh green beans from the bush. When young and newly harvested they're tender after only a few minutes in boiling water. I once grew lima beans as well but was too impatient for the chore of shelling them. Recently I've learned how to sprout beans for salads or stir-frying. Baked beans, red or white, can be an entire meal, but let me begin with:

GREEN BEANS

They used to be called string beans but they've just about had the strings bred out of them. Pick or buy them when the pods are smooth and green with no fading or brown spots. Once they've started to get lumpy, they're old and tough. (Use those for soup.)

The whole bean is so beautiful that mutilation by "French" cutting or slicing seems unnecessary to me. To serve 4 people you'll need

> 1 pound of string beans.

Simply nip off the tips at each end of the bean and wash them in cold water. Place them in a colander and follow the instructions for parboiling (page 218). When they're young and newly harvested they'll be tender in about

6 minutes. The average bean from the market should boil 10 to 15 minutes. Keep testing to catch them at the right minute.

BEANS WITH BUTTER AND LEMON

Whether the beans have just been parboiled or several days before makes no difference. A few minutes before serving, in a large skillet heat

>*2 tablespoons butter.*

Toss in the beans and stir lightly for a minute over medium heat until heated through and coated with butter. Sprinkle with

>*1 teaspoon lemon juice*
>*a pinch of sea salt.*

Toss them in the pan another few seconds and serve garnished with chopped parsley.

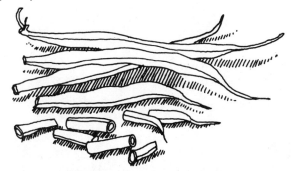

BEANS IN CHEESE SAUCE

Once in a while with a roast pork or lamb served only with the juices, a plain steak, or roast chicken, it's fun to add sauce to the vegetables.

After the vegetables have been parboiled (page 218), make the Cheese Sauce (page 39). Butter a shallow 5-by-9-inch baking dish and spread half the sauce over the bottom. Arrange the vegetables evenly on top of the sauce in layers and cover with the remaining sauce.

Sprinkle with

>*¼ cup coarsely grated Swiss cheese*

and dot with

>*1–2 tablespoons butter.*

Put the dish into a preheated 375° oven for 10 to 15 minutes until the beans are heated through and the sauce is bubbling.

GREEN BEAN SALAD (Serves 6)

In Germany or in Austria bean salad is almost a habit. It's so good I now understand why.

Parboil (page 218)

> 1½ pounds nipped and washed string beans in
> 6 quarts boiling water.

Arrange them neatly in a serving bowl and cover with one of the following dressings.

1) In a bowl beat together

> ½ cup cold chicken broth
> 3 tablespoons olive oil
> 3 tablespoons wine vinegar
> 1 teaspoon sugar
> 1 teaspoon salt
> a few gratings of pepper.

Stir in

> 1 teaspoon chopped dill
> 1 teaspoon chopped parsley.

Pour the dressing evenly over the beans. Cover the bowl and refrigerate at least 3 hours.

2) Dilute

> ½ cup Uta's French Dressing (page 48) with
> 1 tablespoon white wine vinegar
> 1 tablespoon lemon juice.

Stir in

> 1 teaspoon sugar.

Pour the dressing evenly over the beans and sprinkle with

> chopped dill and parsley.

Refrigerate a minimum of 3 hours.

JAZZY CANNED BAKED BEANS (Serves 6 to 8)

The baked ham I used to serve at every party until my friends rebelled was always accompanied by baked beans from a can. To be honest, I still sneak this treat to the table from time to time. I add to it in such a way that everyone assumes I started from scratch. I also bake beans properly, and they are definitely superior to the canned ones.

Preheat the over to 350°.

Into a large mixing bowl empty the contents of

> 3 16-ounce cans of Boston Baked Beans (without tomato sauce).

Stir in

> 2 tablespoons Dijon mustard
> 3 tablespoons dark molasses
> 3 tablespoons brown sugar
> 2 tablespoons chili sauce
> 6 slices sautéed crumbled bacon
> 1 seeded, deveined, and chopped green pepper
> 1 tablespoon chopped onion
> 1 teaspoon salt
> a few gratings of pepper.

Pour the mixture into a buttered crock or casserole and cover with

> 2–3 slices raw bacon.

Bake uncovered in the hot oven for 1 hour.

If you want to serve it as the main dish of a supper accompanied by a loaf of bread, a bottle of wine, and then a salad, add

> 8 skinless frankfurters cut into 1-inch pieces
>> or
> 4 sliced, skinned knockwurst.

Sprinkle the sausage pieces on top of the beans for the last 20 minutes of baking.

PROPERLY BAKED BEANS (Serves 6)

Put

> 1 pound dry beans—red, white, or lima—

into a pot of

> 6 quarts boiling water.

Let the water return to a boil. Turn off the heat and allow the beans to soak 1 hour.

Preheat the oven to 250°.

Drain the beans in a colander and put them into a large mixing bowl with

> 1 large chopped onion
> 4 tablespoons molasses
> 2 tablespoons brown sugar
> 4 tablespoons chili sauce
> 1 tablespoon dry mustard
> 2 teaspoons Worcestershire sauce
> 1 teaspoon curry powder
> 1 teaspoon salt
> ¾ cup dark beer.

Blend the ingredients thoroughly before pouring into a buttered crock or casserole.

Cover the top with

> 6 strips salt pork or bacon.

Use a tight-fitting lid to cover the pot and bake in the warm oven 6 to 7 hours. Check every few hours to make sure the beans aren't drying out. If so, add ¼ cup beer. Remove the lid for the last ½ hour of baking.

Bean Sprouts

Sprouting beans has become a new adventure for me. It seems that not just lentils and beans of all kinds, but most seeds will sprout: wheat, rye, alfalfa, sesame, fennel, etc. It's like having a growing garden right in the kitchen. If this "sport" interests you, go to a health-food store for supplies and information including booklets on the subject. I've had the best result with mung beans, but I'm still a novice.

Cover a handful of beans with water and let them soak in a bowl overnight. Drain them in a colander in which they will remain and refresh them under cold running water. Cover them with a plate, since they seem to enjoy sprouting in dim light or darkness. Repeat the cold water refreshment twice a day, then cover again. In just a few days they're ready to eat—raw with cottage cheese or on a sandwich or mixed in a salad.

Or you can stir-fry them in a heavy skillet in

> 2 teaspoons peanut or light sesame oil.

Stir quickly over high heat for just a minute. They're delightful.

Broccoli

I didn't enjoy broccoli until I learned to prepare it beautifully. Now it's a favorite. Correct paring can be a little troublesome, but it's worth it.

BROCCOLI (Serves 4 to 6)

Quite a lot of vegetable is lost in trimming so get

    2 pounds broccoli.

To retain texture and intensify the color you want a short cooking time, so cut the flower heads from the stem, leaving about an inch of stem on each one. Shave off some of the bitter leaves between the florets. Cut the florets apart so each one is no more than 2 inches in diameter. If the remaining stem is thicker than ½ inch, slit the bottom with a sharp knife to speed the cooking time. To prepare the thick main stalks, cut ½ inch from the tough bottoms. Shave off the outer leaves and all of the skin, leaving the moist flesh exposed. Cube the stems into ½-inch pieces and wash in a colander. Put the florets in a wire basket and wash under cold running water. (Retain parings for soup.)

Parboil (page 218) in

    6 quarts water.

Put the cubed ends in first and simply lower the basket with the florets into the boiling water on top of them. Cook 5 to 6 minutes and taste a piece to make sure it's tender. Lift out the florets and refresh them with cold water first. Finish the draining and drying and refrigerate, for days if you like, unless you're planning the final recipe at once.

BROCCOLI IN BUTTER AND LEMON

In a heavy skillet heat until foaming

>   *2 tablespoons butter.*

Add the parboiled broccoli stems, tossing and stirring for a few minutes until coated with butter and heated through. Sprinkle with

>   *lemon juice*
>   *a pinch of salt.*

Arrange in a bowl. To the skillet add

>   *2 tablespoons butter.*

Add the florets and stir them gently over medium heat until buttered and heated through. Sprinkle with lemon juice and salt and arrange prettily on top of the cubed stems. Grind pepper over everything and serve at once.

BROCCOLI BRAISED IN BUTTER

Preheat the oven to 375°.

Rub a small casserole with butter. Arrange the parboiled cubed stems on the bottom of the dish and the florets around the edge on top of them.

Dot with

>   *3 tablespoons butter.*

Sprinkle with

>   *salt and pepper.*

Draw an outline of the lid on wax paper, cut it out, and smear one side with butter. Place the paper over the broccoli and cover with the lid. Bring the vegetable to a simmer on top of the stove before putting in the hot oven for 10 minutes. Serve at once.

PURÉED BROCCOLI

Preheat the oven to 375°.

Place the parboiled cubed stems into the blender with

>*1 tablespoon cream*
>*1 tablespoon softened butter*
>*pinches of salt, pepper, and nutmeg.*

Blend for 15 seconds till almost smooth and pour into a small buttered casserole. Continue and complete the preceding recipe. *Fabuloso!*

Try the Cheese Sauce method as for beans (page 221).

Brussels Sprouts

At home in Wisconsin these crisp green morsels were served on holidays or for special Sunday dinners. Now I grow them in Montauk, starting the seeds at the end of May so the little heads that grow like pearls along the stems will still be young and tender after the first frost, when they're most delicious. I begin to harvest them at the end of October, when they're as small as marbles. If you have the opportunity to try them at this stage, you'll never forget them. I have them in the garden until Christmas, when they're quite large but still delicious.

When buying them at the market, make sure they're firm and green. Once they've begun to yellow or open up, don't bother with them. Clean and parboil as soon as possible because they'll keep much longer than standing around in cellophane-covered boxes.

To serve 4 people get

>*1 quart Brussels sprouts.*

Cut the remaining knob from the bottom and remove any wilted outer leaves. Make a ¼-inch-deep criss-cross incision in the bottom of each sprout to speed the cooking time. Wash and parboil (page 218) 4 to 6 minutes, depending on the size of the sprouts. Taste one for tenderness. Don't let them get mushy. After draining and drying, they too can go into the refrigerator in a covered bowl for several days or until dinnertime.

BRUSSELS SPROUTS IN BUTTER (Serves 4)

Parboil (page 218)

> *1 quart Brussels sprouts.*

Toss the sprouts in a large skillet in

> *2 tablespoons foaming butter.*

When well coated and heated through, season with salt and pepper and serve at once.

or

Preheat the oven to 350°.

Butter a small casserole and arrange the sprouts in circles, stem side down, in one or two layers. Dot with

> *2 tablespoons butter*

and sprinkle with

> *salt and pepper.*

Trace the lid on wax paper. Cut it out and butter one side. Place the paper over the sprouts and cover with the lid. Put the casserole in the hot oven for 15 minutes until the sprouts are heated through. Serve at once.

BRUSSELS SPROUTS IN CREAM (Serves 4)

Prepare the above recipe, and when the sprouts have been in the oven for 8 minutes add

> *⅓ cup heavy cream.*

Cook another 7 or 8 minutes. Serve and eat luxuriously.

Try the Cheese Sauce method (page 221).

BRUSSELS SPROUTS WITH CHESTNUTS (Serves 6)

This is one of my favorite combinations in late autumn or during the winter when chestnuts are available.

Preheat the oven to 350°.

Parboil (page 218)

> 1½ quarts Brussels sprouts.

Bake

> 24 chestnuts (page 236).

Butter a shallow 8-by-12-inch baking dish. Place the sprouts upright around the edge of the dish in several rows. Sprinkle with

> salt and pepper

and dot with

> butter.

Mound the chestnuts neatly in the center. (They can also be alternated with the sprouts, if you prefer.) Cover everything with the sauce in which the chestnuts were baked. Put a piece of buttered foil or a lid securely over the dish and place it in the oven for 15 minutes until the vegetables are heated through. Serve and sigh with pride and joy.

Cabbage

I have an aversion to regular cooked green cabbage, probably because it was a staple of my diet as a child in war-torn Germany. I've finally discovered a way of disguising it to become a delicacy.

GRATED CABBAGE WITH CREAM CHEESE (Serves 4)

Use

> 1 small, firm head of cabbage.

Remove the wilted outer leaves and slice it downward into quarters. Remove and discard the hard white core at the bottom of each quarter. Use the coarse side of a grater to shred each section and place the shreddings in a large bowl. Cover with boiling water.

Stir in

> 1 tablespoon coarse salt.

After 5 minutes, drain the cabbage in a colander and refresh under cold running water. Let drain and rest. Chop

> 1 large onion.

In a large, heavy pot melt

> 3 tablespoons butter.

Cook the chopped onion in the butter over medium-low heat for 5 minutes and then add

> the drained cabbage.

Cut into pieces

> a 3-ounce package of cream cheese.

Stir the cheese into the cabbage until blended. Simmer until the cheese melts. Add

> 2 tablespoons chopped fresh dill (or 1 teaspoon dill seeds)
> salt and white pepper to taste.

Simmer another minute or so and serve.

RED CABBAGE (Serves 6 to 8)

I can't imagine Sauerbraten or roast goose without red cabbage. It's also excellent with roast pork or lamb. Before I present you with the best recipe handed down by my Danish mother, I must confess that if you can get your hands on an imported German red cabbage called Gundelsheim Rotkohl, you may feel you needn't make it yourself. Simply add 2 tablespoons red wine to each jar before heating it up and passing it off as your own.

The real McCoy is, of course, superb. It's even better when made a day or two ahead of time.

Get

> 1 small head of red cabbage.

It will weigh around 2 pounds and go a long way. Remove the tough and wilted layer of outer leaves. Cut the cabbage downward into quarters.

Remove the white core at the base of each quarter and place the sections flat on a cutting board. With a long, sharp knife shred the cabbage as thinly as possible. Soak the shreddings in a large bowl of cold water for 1 hour. Drain in a colander and empty the water from the bowl. Replace it with

> ¼ cup vinegar
> ¼ cup dry red wine.

Stir in

> ½ teaspoon salt
> 2 teaspoons sugar.

Stir in the cabbage until the shreddings are well coated. Let it rest.

In a large, heavy casserole (don't use aluminum) sauté

> 2 strips lean bacon in
> 2 tablespoons butter.

When crisp, remove the bacon with a slotted spoon. (Save it for something else, or eat it!) To the butter and bacon fat add

> 1 medium-sized chopped onion.

Cook gently for 5 minutes. Add the cabbage mixture and cover the casserole tightly. Bring to a simmer. Meanwhile, core and slice thin

> 2 green cooking apples.

Add the sliced apples to the cabbage and replace the lid. Cook over the lowest possible heat for 1½ hours. Check every now and then to make sure it's not drying out. If it is, add a tablespoon of wine. Let cool completely before placing the casserole in the refrigerator for a day or two.

Before serving, reheat for 20 minutes over low heat. Then stir in

> ¼ cup currant or beachplum jelly.

Carrots

Carrots are a necessity as well as an embellishment for many soups, stews, roasts, and salads. I can't imagine a kitchen without a bunch on hand in the refrigerator. But as soon as I know that tiny new ones are available at the market in early April or in my garden at the beginning of July my taste buds are aroused. When carrots are 1 or 2 inches long and as thick as a pinky but no fatter than a thumb, they are ripe for the gods. With their green tops cut off and their dangling root removed, they only need to be lightly scrubbed with a rough cloth and rinsed in cold water and they're ready to go. They certainly shouldn't be scraped at this tender age.

BABY CARROTS (Serves 4 to 6)

Clean as described above

> 1 pound baby carrots.

Place in a saucepan with

> 1 cup water
> 2 tablespoons butter
> 1 teaspoon sugar
> a pinch of salt.

Cook covered tightly over medium-low heat 15 to 20 minutes. Add more water if needed. Drain and serve. The carrots can be garnished with more butter, chopped parsley, or chopped chives, but they're magnificent all by themselves.

GLAZED CARROTS (Serves 4 to 6)

All young carrots can be glazed, not just the tiny ones. Use big, fat older ones for other recipes. If they're babies, nip off tops and bottoms and wash, leaving them whole. Use your judgment about larger ones. They can be scraped and cut into pieces an inch or so long. Be sure the pieces are uniform in thickness.

Simmer

> 1 pound of cleaned carrots

in a heavy saucepan over medium-low heat with

> 1 cup beef stock or condensed beef bouillon
> 4 tablespoons butter
> 1½ tablespoons sugar.

Don't cover. Depending on the size of the carrots, cook 20 to 30 minutes. The liquid should reduce to a syrup. Use a wooden spoon to turn the carrots in the syrup till glazed. If the syrup is too thin when the carrots are tender, remove them with a slotted spoon and boil down the syrup till gooey. Return the carrots to the pan and turn them to coat with glaze.

Serve sprinkled with

> *salt and pepper*
> *chopped parsley.*

PURÉED CARROTS (Serves 4 to 6)

Obviously large and misshapen carrots can be used for this purpose.

> *1½ pounds carrots*

Scrape or peel with a vegetable peeler after tops and dangling root ends have been cut off. Wash and then slice them into 1-inch pieces. Boil in

> *2 cups lightly salted water with*
> *1 tablespoon butter*
> *1 teaspoon sugar.*

Cover the pan tightly and cook over medium-low heat for 30 minutes or until the carrots are very tender when pierced. Drain.

They can be puréed in two ways to serve different purposes. The first way produces a coarser mash for stuffing vegetables such as zucchini, or to surround meat when there's enough creamy stuff on the menu.

1) Press the tender carrots through a ricer or food mill, sprinkle with salt and pepper, and top with a little butter.

2) Put the carrots in the blender with

> *1 tablespoon cream*
> *1½ tablespoons butter*
> *salt, pepper, and nutmeg to taste.*

Blend 15 seconds till creamy. Serve in a bowl lovely enough to be worthy of the color, texture, and taste!

Cauliflower

Sometimes even *I* tend to forget this underrated vegetable unless I happen to pass near a head with lovely green leaves and no brown spots in the vegetable bin. It's delicious served steaming hot with sauce or buttered crumbs, and just as good cold with a mustard sauce or even raw in a salad or with a dip as an hors d'oeuvre. The cleaning and parboiling is the same for all recipes. You may balk at the idea of breaking apart the florets, but remember you want fairly small, uniform pieces to ensure tenderness in a minimum amount of cooking time.

PARBOILED CAULIFLOWER (Serves 4 to 6)

Get

1 small head of cauliflower.

First pull off and discard all green and whitish leaves. Cut out the center stem and the core. (Save for soup.) Cut apart the florets so that each "bunch" is not more than 2 inches in diameter. If the stem holding each little bunch together is thick, peel it and make a criss-cross slash in the bottom. Soak the cauliflower pieces for a few minutes in a bowl of water with a few teaspoons of lemon juice.

In a large kettle bring to a boil

4 quarts water
1–2 cups milk
1 tablespoon salt.

Drain the cauliflower and add it piece by piece, and cook uncovered from 8 to 10 minutes. Pierce or nibble a stem to see if it's tender, not mushy. Remove gently from the kettle to a colander using a slotted spoon. Don't bruise it. Let it drain. If you want to use it at once, it's now ready for sauce or seasoning. If you want to serve it later or serve it cold, put the colander under gently running cold water to refresh it. Then arrange the pieces side by side on toweling to dry. Place in the refrigerator in a covered bowl till needed.

To reheat, steam the florets in a metal colander over a pot of boiling water for 3 minutes. The pot should be large enough to hold the colander, but not allow the cauliflower to touch the water.

To Arrange and Serve

Be sure the dish you use is hot. Make a design with the florets. When using a flat dish, let the design be dictated by size and shape; the largest florets in the center, the smallest around the edge, criss-crossed diagonally by medium-sized ones, for instance. Or choose a bowl barely large enough to contain the florets snugly and mound them to simulate the original head of cauliflower. Parsley sprigs tucked around the edge add a nice touch. Do the arranging as quickly as possible, with spoons if the florets are too hot to handle, so the vegetable won't cool off. You're now ready to season it or pour on the sauce.

SAUCES FOR CAULIFLOWER

My favorite topping is Buttered Crumbs (page 47).
Lemon Butter (page 47) is speedy and excellent.
White or Cheese Sauce (pages 38–39) is always good.
So is Hollandaise (page 41)—naturally!

COLD CAULIFLOWER WITH MUSTARD SAUCE (Serves 4 to 6)

On a hot summer day, cold cauliflower is a terrific addition to a luncheon
or dinner. Shorten the parboiling (previous recipe) to 5 minutes to keep
the vegetable a little crunchier. After the cauliflower has been drained and
dried and arranged on a dish, refrigerate for at least 2 hours, covered with
a blend of

> ½ *cup mayonnaise*
> ¼ *cup sour cream*
> 3 *tablespoons Dijon mustard*
> 1 *teaspoon lemon juice.*

Add

> *salt and white pepper to taste.*

Sprinkle with chopped dill or parsley before serving.

Chestnuts

CHESTNUTS

Since I serve chestnuts primarily as a vegetable rather than as a dessert, I'm classifying them alphabetically in this chapter. (Also—I have no chapter called NUTS.) Once you get the hang of it, the chore of peeling and skinning them gets easier. They're rich, so you only need

24 chestnuts.

With a small, sharp knife make a slit or a criss-cross on the flattest side of each chestnut. Put the chestnuts into a pan covered with cold water. Bring the water to a boil and boil for 1 minute. Turn off the heat. Immediately fish out a few chestnuts at a time to peel while they're still hot. First cut off the tops and bottoms of the shells, then pull them off. Use the knife to pull off the brown skins under the shells. If the skins stick, put the nuts back into the hot water for a while. Proceed with the next few. It should take about 15 minutes to peel and skin them all.

BAKED CHESTNUTS (Serves 4 to 6)

Preheat the oven to 325°.

Choose a small casserole or baking dish into which

24 shelled and skinned chestnuts

will fit snugly in one layer. Arrange them and cover with

1 can condensed beef bouillon.

Make a smooth paste of

1 tablespoon arrowroot or cornstarch
2 tablespoons Madeira.

Stir the paste into the bouillon in the casserole and add

3 tablespoons butter.

If the chestnuts aren't covered by liquid, add a little water. Cover the dish with foil or a very tight lid and bring the contents to a simmer on the stove before transferring to the hot oven. Bake 50 to 60 minutes or until the chestnuts are tender when pierced. The liquid should be gooey; if it is not, remove the chestnuts with a slotted spoon and boil down the sauce until it gets syrupy. Return the chestnuts and roll them with a wooden spoon till glazed. Serve as a side dish or combine with Brussels Sprouts (page 229).

Corn

CORN ON THE COB

If I had lots of land, I'd reserve an acre just to plant corn. I've sometimes longed to devour a dozen ears all by myself, particularly the white, pearly kind called Silver Queen. Always pick (or buy) corn as close to cooking time as possible. If, for some reason, you have to shuck it ahead of time, wrap the ears at once individually in plastic wrap and refrigerate.

Fill a large kettle with water, add a tablespoon of salt, and bring it to a boil. Slide the ears into the water one by one. Don't crowd the pot—the ears should have plenty of room to bobble around while boiling. Do it in batches if you're serving lots of people. Rest the lid halfway across the top of the pot to catch steam and allow the water to return rapidly to a boil.

Five or 6 minutes after the corn has boiled briskly, remove and drain quickly in a colander. Bring it to the table with lots of butter, salt, pepper, and paprika so each person can slather up their ears the way they like!

CORNMEAL MUSH or POLENTA (Serves 4 to 6)

I believe I've finally learned to make Herbert's beloved polenta so that it's almost as "golden and good" as his mother used to make it.

The better the corn meal, the better the polenta. Ask a specialty grocer or health-food store for good ground meal with no additives.

In a bowl mix together

> 1 cup corn meal
> 1 cup water
> 1 teaspoon salt.

In the top section of a double boiler bring to a boil over direct heat

> 4 cups water.

Slowly stir in the cornmeal mixture, cooking and stirring for several minutes. Then set the pot over the bottom part of the double boiler, containing a few inches of hot water. Cover the corn meal and cook slowly over low heat for ½ hour. It should be very smooth and *very* thick. Stir in

> 2 *tablespoons butter*
> ¼ *teaspoon imported paprika.*

Serve at once. If any is left over, pour it into a buttered loaf pan and refrigerate at least 2 hours or until needed. Slice into strips or squares and fry in butter and oil. It makes a hearty breakfast or brunch accompanied by · sausages and fried eggs.

POLENTA WITH CHEESE

At the end of the cooking time, add the butter and paprika and stir in

> ½ *cup coarsely grated Swiss or cheddar cheese.*

Cook and stir for a minute till the cheese melts. Deeelicious.

Cucumbers

I think Herbert has a cucumber fetish. He could eat two a day every day of the year no matter how they're prepared. I grow them by the bushel in several varieties, and they certainly spoil you for the "store-boughten" kind. If you can't grow your own, ignore those horrid ones at the supermarket smeared with oil or wax and get them from a greengrocer.

GESCHMORRTE GURKEN (Serves 4 to 6)

These stewed cucumbers are delicious; especially when you call them by their hilarious German name.

Peel

> 2½–3 *pounds cucumbers (6 medium-sized ones).*

Slice them lengthwise into six sections and scoop out the seeds. Cut into 1-inch lengths. Toss them in a bowl in

> 1 *tablespoon white vinegar*
> 1 *tablespoon coarse salt.*

Let them stand for an hour before rinsing under cold water, draining, and drying with toweling.

In a large skillet or shallow casserole heat

>2 tablespoons butter.

When the foam subsides, add

>1 small chopped onion.

Cook until soft over low heat for 10 minutes. Over the onions sprinkle

>2 tablespoons quick-mix flour.

Cook and stir until the onions turn golden. Into the pan stir

>1¾ cup milk.

Turn the heat up a little and stir until the sauce thickens. Add the cucumbers and simmer uncovered for 10 minutes. Add

>¼ cup sour cream
>2 tablespoons chopped dill (or 1 teaspoon dill seeds).

Quickly blend the dill and sour cream into the sauce to heat through. Serve with a few gratings of pepper.

CUCUMBER SALAD (Serves 6)

Peel

>3 medium-large cucumbers.

Slice them paper thin and toss them in a bowl with salt and vinegar as for Geschmorrte Gurken (above). Follow the directions for rinsing and draining. Pat them dry and arrange in neat layers in a pretty glass bowl.

This will take a little time. Cover with a mixture of

>½ cup white wine vinegar
>1 tablespoon sugar
>½ teaspoon white pepper
>a pinch of dill seed.

Sprinkle the top with

>1 tablespoon chopped herbs (dill or chervil or parsley).

Chill at least 1 hour. Tip the bowl to drain off most of the liquid. (Reserve for another time.) Serve the salad as is or on a few lettuce leaves.

CUCUMBERS IN SOUR CREAM (Serves 6)

Peel and slice

> *3 to 4 cucumbers*

and follow the directions for steeping in salt and vinegar then rinsing, draining and drying for Geschmorrte Gurken (page 238). Whisk till smooth a mixture of

> *½ cup sour cream*
> *2 mashed hard-boiled egg yolks*
> *1 tablespoon Dijon mustard*
> *2 teaspoons white wine vinegar*
> *1 teaspoon lemon juice*
> *1 teaspoon sugar*
> *a pinch of white pepper.*

Gently stir the cucumber slices in the dressing till well coated. Chill for at least an hour before serving on fresh lettuce leaves.

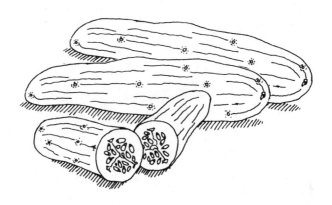

CUCUMBER ASPIC (Serves 6)

Make this summer delight a day or two ahead of time to allow the aspic to set firmly. It can be molded in six individual molds or in a 9-inch ring mold.

Peel

> *6–8 medium-sized cucumbers.*

Cut them in half lengthwise and scoop out the seeds with a spoon. Grate them coarsely. You should have about

> *4 cups, including the juice.*

Soften

> 2 envelopes gelatin in
> ¼ cup water.

Let rest for five minutes. Bring to a boil

> ¾ cup chicken stock or condensed canned broth.

Turn off the heat and add the softened gelatin. Stir till the gelatin has dissolved. To the gelatin and broth add

> 2 tablespoons grated onion
> ¼ cup lemon juice
> 1 teaspoon sugar
> a pinch of paprika
> a pinch of salt
> a few drops of green vegetable coloring
> the grated cucumbers.

Stir to blend the ingredients thoroughly before straining through a fine sieve. Rinse the mold or molds in very cold water. Shake them free of excess water. Pour the aspic into the molds and refrigerate 24 to 48 hours.

To unmold, follow the directions on page 20.

Be inventive with garnishes. Surround the mold with alternating slices of cukes and tomatoes and top with watercress. Set individual molds on slices of tomato or cuke. Surround the mold with cold Parboiled Cauliflower florets (page 234). Fill the center with Marinated Shrimp (page 72) or Mushrooms (page 63), etc. etc. It's also lovely all by itself.

CUCUMBER MOUSSE (Serves 6)

Beautiful, easy, and irresistible.

Soften

> 1 envelope gelatin in
> ¼ cup lemon juice.

After 5 minutes, dissolve the mixture in ¾ cup boiling water till clear. Let cool.

Peel, quarter lengthwise, and seed

> 3 or 4 medium-sized cucumbers.

Chop them coarsely till you have enough to equal 1 cup. Drain them in a sieve for 5 minutes.

In a bowl blend

> 1 cup sour cream
> the chopped cucumbers
> 2 tablespoons grated onion
> ½ teaspoon salt
> a pinch of white pepper.

Add the cool

> gelatin mixture.

Fold the ingredients together and pour into 1 lightly oiled 3-cup mold or into 6 oiled individual molds. Chill overnight before unmolding (page 20). Garnish with watercress.

Kasha

SASHA'S KASHA (Buckwheat Groats) (Serves 4 to 6)

Many years ago, I learned how to prepare this hearty brown grain from the great violinist and conductor Alexander Schneider. He brought the recipe from his birthplace, Vilna, and it's certainly not the only thing he cooks like a Maestro! Our family is as addicted to Kasha as to Sasha. Years ago the groats were hard to get but now they're available even at the super market. Try to buy the coarse variety at a fine grocery or a health-food store. It can be cooked plain or with mushrooms, onions, or both.

To coat the grain with egg, toss

> 1 cup buckwheat groats

in a bowl with

> 1 beaten egg

Turn into a large heavy casserole into

> 2 tablespoons hot butter.

Sauté over medium-high heat for 5 minutes stirring constantly till the grains separate and turn dry. Add

> 2 tablespoons butter
> 2 cups heated chicken stock (or 1 can condensed broth plus
>   ½ cup water)
> 1 teaspoon salt.

Stir briskly for a minute. Cover tightly, turn down the heat, and simmer 15 to 20 minutes until the liquid has been absorbed and the grains are loose and fluffy. Season with grated pepper and serve.

KASHA WITH ONIONS

Over low heat in a heavy casserole, sauté

> *1 large chopped onion in*
> *3 tablespoons butter.*

Stir

> *1 cup groats in*
> *a beaten egg*

and sauté in

> *2 tablespoons butter*

in a large skillet till toasty and dry. Then add it to the onions in the casserole and proceed with the previous recipe, adding the broth, etc.

KASHA WITH MUSHROOMS

Sauté

> *½ pound wiped, sliced mushrooms in*
> *2 tablespoons butter*
> *1 teaspoon oil.*

Cook a few minutes. When the Kasha has almost finished simmering, fold in the mushrooms. You'll be glad you did.

Lettuce

It's amazing how few people seem to know anything about lettuce beyond the iceberg and Boston varieties. They may occasionally buy a head of romaine, chickory, or escarole (all of which I stir-fry almost exclusively) but they seem unfamiliar with the many tender loose-leaf lettuces that send me into frenzies of delight. If you've ever examined a seed catalogue, you know how difficult it is to choose from so many. My selection is based on flavor, texture, appearance, and of course growing climate. In order of preference they are: buttercrunch, bibb, summer salad, and Tom Thumb. What fun to ask a guest to go into the garden to "pick a favorite salad." Then, to let them select from basil, thyme or rosemary, dill or mint, fennel or chervil for seasoning. In the city I rely on the greengrocer for available loose-leaf lettuces and fresh herbs. He also carries delights like field lettuce, Belgian endive, watercress, and rugola.

Cleaning lettuce is easy. If the head is laden with sand or grit, cut out the core, separate the leaves and swish them around in a sink full of water, shake the water from the leaves, and put into a salad basket. If it's only slightly gritty, cut out the center core and turn the head upside down, holding it under the faucet loosely with both hands to let the water wash through the core and into the leaves. Shake it before putting the whole head into the lettuce basket. Hold the basket out of the window and use a ball player's wind-up to whirl the basket around by the handle until no more water comes from the leaves. I usually do it a few hours before dinner and set the basket right into the refrigerator to give the lettuce time to crisp up. If I want to do it a day ahead of time, I remove the lettuce from the basket after twirling, wrap the leaves loosely in a clean towel to absorb more moisture, and then pop it, towel and all, into a large plastic bag.

Never put dressing on lettuce until you're about to serve it, and use it sparingly. Don't drown the lettuce. I like to "toss" it with my hands. Unless surrounded by intimate friends, I do it where I'm not seen. It's so much easier to use fingers instead of salad forks to make sure the leaves are evenly coated with dressing.

STIR-FRIED LETTUCE (Serves 4)

Use one head of escarole, chickory, romaine, mustard leaves, or iceberg lettuce. (Use up garden lettuce that has begun to go to seed or turned a little too bitter to eat raw.)

Coat the bottom of a large, heavy pot with

> 1 tablespoon peanut or light sesame oil.

Add

> 1 or 2 halved cloves garlic.

Cook the garlic until it browns, pressing down to extract flavor, then discard. Toss in the lettuce leaves. They will snap and crackle with a hell of a noise because of clinging water, but don't worry. Stir the leaves briskly until coated with oil. After a minute or so they will soften and wilt. Then sprinkle with salt, pepper, and lemon juice and serve at once.

LETTUCE PANCAKES (Serves 4)

These pancakes will flip you out.

Use

> *1 large head iceberg lettuce.*

Remove softened outer leaves and grate coarsely or shred very fine. Place in a colander over the sink and sprinkle with

> *1 tablespoon coarse salt.*

Let drain for 20 minutes and then put the gratings in the center of a clean linen towel, wrap tightly, and squeeze and twist as hard as you can until no more liquid escapes. In a bowl combine

> *2 beaten eggs*
> *1 small grated onion*
> *⅔ cup dry bread crumbs*
> *½ teaspoon salt*
> *a pinch of pepper.*

Fold in the grated lettuce. In a heavy skillet heat

> *½ cup peanut or vegetable oil to 365°.*

Use your deep-fry thermometer. Lower the batter into the oil by large spoonfuls. Don't crowd the pan; fry in batches if necessary. When the underside of the pancakes is golden, flip them over carefully and brown the other side. Remove with a slotted spoon and drain on toweling.

Orzo

Orzo is a Greek pasta that looks like very large-grained rice, and can be used wherever you might use noodles or rice. Its unique texture and flavor makes all who sample it rush out to a good Greek or Balkan store to buy their own supply. If you're unable to get imported Orzo, don't bother. An Italian-American company puts one out that can't hold a candle to the original.

I first had it at the charming gallery apartment of George Liamos; he works for I.B.M. which seems incongruous when you watch him roasting a spitted lamb in the fireplace or breaking into a wild Greek dance at the first sound of music.

GEORGIO'S ORZO (Serves 4)

Bring to a boil

4 quarts lightly salted water.

Slowly dribble in

1 cup raw orzo.

Cook for 20 minutes until the grains are tender and swollen. Drain in a colander, bouncing up and down to help moisture evaporate. Serve in a bowl with

4 tablespoons butter
⅓ cup grated Parmesan or crumbled feta cheese
1 tablespoon chopped parsley
salt and grated pepper to taste.

If you're serving it as a bed under fish or a beef stew, skip the cheese.

Peas

A tiny, sweet, green pea actually awes me. And I'm equally overwhelmed by delicate, transparent pods of snow peas, which the French call *Mange-tout.* Who wouldn't "eat-all" of these crisp green pearls in their shells?

I have only a few recipes for peas, because I don't bother with the mature ones that toughen up and need special tenderizing treatment. At the market I leave them on the counter and in the garden the peas are devoured long before they have a chance to reach maturity. The season for young peas is short; late March to mid June at the market and early June to early July in my garden. The snow-pea season is the same. Because I love peas, I compromise the rest of the year and buy the tiny variety of frozen peas, which are an acceptable substitute.

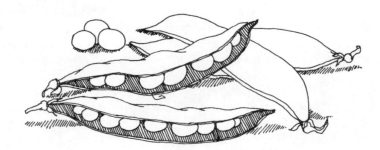

SHELLED YOUNG PEAS (Serves 4 to 6)

The pea pods should be light green and smooth, not lumpy, gray, or dry looking. If you're doubtful, cajole the salesman into telling you if they're truly young and have been freshly picked.

Two pounds of pea pods should yield about

>*2 cups shelled peas.*

The sound of peas plinking into a pot as they're being shelled always gives me a feeling of well-being. It's a cheerful task to do outdoors on a fresh spring or early summer day. Birds enjoy the sound and chirp their reply.

In a large pot bring to a boil

>*4 quarts water with*
>*1 teaspoon salt*
>*1 tablespoon sugar.*

Slowly dribble in

>*2 cups shelled peas.*

Cook uncovered over high heat for 5 to 10 minutes, depending on size. Taste to test. They should still be a little crisp. Drain in a colander. Heat a large dry skillet and roll the peas in it for 30 seconds until the moisture has evaporated, then add

>*2 tablespoons butter*
>*1 teaspoon sugar.*

Toss the pan until the peas are coated and serve at once.

MANGE-TOUT (Snow Peas) (Serves 4 to 6)

Buy or pick small, light green, smooth, and very thin pea pods. Treat them like green beans, nipping off tops and bottoms. If there are any strings at the sides, use the knife to pull them off. Wash thoroughly.

In a large pot bring to a brisk boil

>*4 quarts lightly salted water.*

A few at a time drop in

>*1 pound snow peas.*

Boil uncovered 6 to 10 minutes. Taste to test if they're nice and crunchy.

Drain in a colander and serve at once with butter, salt, and pepper.

Sometimes when I've harvested just a cupful, I put them in a skillet with only

½ cup boiling water
2 tablespoons butter
a pinch of salt and sugar

and cook them about 3 minutes. I drain them quickly and let Herbert eat them all by himself.

When snow peas are a little older and not as tender, they can be cut on the diagonal into 1-inch pieces and stir-fried over high heat in 2 teaspoons of peanut oil for a minute or so. Salt and pepper to taste and serve at once.

FROZEN PEAS

Use the tiny early peas. (I happen to prefer Le Sueur peas.) Cook them a shorter time than specified on the package. If you use those that come in a pouch, remove them from the pouch and put into a skillet, adding a dab of butter. Let them thaw in the skillet before cooking 3 or 4 minutes with

a pinch of salt
1 teaspoon sugar.

Garnish with chopped parsley.

MINTED PEAS

When the frozen peas above are almost cooked, or when freshly shelled peas are being tossed in the skillet with butter and sugar, add

1 tablespoon chopped mint leaves.

Finish the tossing and remove the peas to a bowl to serve. You'll think you've taken a quick trip to paradise

Potatoes

Twenty to thirty freshly dug and scrubbed and boiled little new potatoes, slathered with butter, sprinkled with salt and pepper and chopped parsley, can easily be devoured by four people in no time flat. They need almost no accompaniment. Well, maybe some buttered Baby Carrots (page 232), a bowl of newly picked string beans (page 220), a sliced beefsteak tomato with basil leaves, and some French-fried Zucchini (page 273). Then for dessert, a walk into the moors to pick a bowl of fresh blue- or blackberries.

Texture and flavor of newly dug home-grown potatoes are as different from market potatoes as freshly picked corn is from canned. It is easy to grow potatoes even if you have only a wee patch in your back yard. Since the potatoes you harvest will be the children of the ones you planted, be sure their parents are the best; lovely red-skinned ones, Idahoes, white and thin-skinned Oregon or California potatoes, or the delicious German fingerlings from Wisconsin. In early March, I begin a careful selection at the market and wait eagerly for the ones that will sprout. These are set aside in a paper bag and planted in early April. You can plant a whole potato that has sprouted or you can cut it up, making sure that each piece has at least two sprouted eyes. Just one piece will yield up to twenty potatoes. The soil should be turned over and loosened before setting a potato or piece of it an inch or two into the ground and about two feet apart. Cover with earth and forget about them. Leaves and blossoms of potato plants are pretty and will grace the corner of your garden visually as well. I wait two-and-one-half to three months from the time of planting to the first robbing of the cradle. Digging for them is like a treasure hunt, as they roll up where they're not expected.

BOILED NEW POTATOES

Scrub potatoes under running water and put them into a pot of lightly salted water. Cover the pot and bring the potatoes to a boil. Cook 15 to 20 minutes, depending on size. Pierce for tenderness. Drain, season with butter, salt, and pepper and freshly chopped parsley. Need I say more?

NEW POTATOES BRAISED IN BUTTER (Serves 6)

Scrub

>   20–30 small, new potatoes

and pat dry with toweling. In a heavy casserole with a lid, melt

>   1 stick butter (8 tablespoons).

Roll the potatoes in the butter till coated. Cover the casserole with foil, then with a lid, and cook over the lowest heat for about 40 minutes. Shake the pan every now and then so the potatoes won't stick. Season with the butter in the pan, salt and pepper, chopped parsley or chopped dill. You won't get enough of them

MASHED POTATOES WITH WHIPPED CREAM (Serves 4)

However I end up fixing mashed potatoes, after they've been boiled I like to put them through a ricer or a foodmill. They seem to come out fluffier this way. Use mealy, mature potatoes or regular baking potatoes, not your home-grown ones.

Peel, quarter, and wash

> *2 pounds potatoes.*

Cover them with lightly salted water and boil for ½ hour or until tender. Drain and bounce in a colander until completely dry. Put them through a ricer or foodmill.

Whip

> *½ cup heavy cream.*

Fold it into the riced potatoes. Season to taste with salt and pepper.

Cheese Variation When the potatoes have been folded with whipped cream, put them into a shallow buttered baking dish and top with

> *⅓ cup coarsely grated Swiss or cheddar cheese.*

Dot with

> *2 tablespoons butter.*

Place under the broiler for a few minutes until the cheese has melted and the potatoes are golden.

BAKED POTATOES

Use mature Idaho potatoes for light, fluffy baked potatoes. Scrub each potato, dry it, and rub with 1 teaspoon softened butter. Place on a rack in a preheated 425° oven for 30 minutes. Prick the skin once to allow steam to escape and continue baking another 10 to 20 minutes, depending on size. Pierce for tenderness. When done, cut criss-crossing slashes across the top. Squeeze the sides so the slashes open. Serve with butter or sour cream and garnish with chopped parsley or dill. Add salt and pepper to taste.

GERMAN-FRIED POTATOES (Serves 4)

Use leftover boiled potatoes or boil up a fresh pot.

Prepare and slice

> *2 cups boiled potatoes.*

In a heavy skillet melt

> *4 tablespoons butter.*

In the butter sauté

> *2 tablespoons grated onion.*

After a minute add the potatoes and turn up the heat. Cook until brown on both sides, turning with a flipper. Season with salt and pepper.

POMMES ANNA (Serves 6)

This fantastic, golden, molded potato "cake" is a classic. Thinly sliced potatoes are molded and the shape of the pot determines the shape of the "cake." I use a 3-quart iron casserole. Unless it's lined with Teflon or porcelain, spray it with the new nonstick, nonchemical vegetable spray. Buy potatoes that are uniform in circumference so the slices will be the same size.

Speed of the operation is important, so I organize equipment and ingredients before company comes.

Clarify (page 46)

> *2 sticks (1 cup) unsalted butter.*

Coat the bottom of the casserole with a little of the butter and keep the rest for later.

Peel

> *8 large boiling potatoes (about 3 pounds).*

Cover the peeled potatoes with cold water so they won't discolor.

Spread two clean kitchen towels on the counter, have a cutting board and a very sharp knife ready, and wait for the guests.

When you've served the hors d'oeuvres and your guests are having cocktails, ask the nicest one to help you slice the potatoes while you arrange them in the casserole.

Preheat the oven to 425°.

Slice the potatoes thinly into even pieces about ⅛ inch thick, no more. Spread the slices quickly side by side on a towel and use the other one to pat them dry. Turn on very low heat under the casserole and begin to arrange the slices across the bottom of the pot in circular overlapping layers. Sprinkle each successive layer with a little

> *salt, grated pepper, and dribblings of clarified butter.*

Some of the slices will be paper thin at one end. Save these to tuck upright around the side of the casserole, thin end down. The last layer will reach almost to the top of the pot. Sprinkle it, too, with salt and pepper and butter.

Now, rub some butter on the underside of a pot that is slightly smaller than the casserole. Press the buttered pot down firmly on the layered potatoes to compress the "cake" and help the slices stick together. This pressing-down process will be repeated, so set the buttered pot aside upside down.

Cover the casserole and set it in the hot oven for 20 minutes while you join your guests for a drink or serve the first course of your dinner. Remove the lid of the casserole, and press down on the potatoes again with the bottom of the buttered pot. Return the *uncovered* casserole to the oven and cook 25 minutes until the potatoes are golden. Press down on them with the buttered pot one last time. Replace the lid, leaving a little slit, and tip the casserole to pour off all butter that hasn't been absorbed. (Reserve this butter for other use.) Put a serving plate on top of the casserole and invert the whole thing. If necessary, give the casserole a sharp rap to release the molded Pommes Anna. Bring this golden beauty to the table and wait for applause! (If it collapses or has stuck to the pot, it will taste just as good, although it's never happened to me.)

POTATO PANCAKES (Serves 6)

These pancakes are a "must" with Sauerbraten, and delicious with roasts, broiled chicken, and breaded fish. As with Pommes Anna, the potatoes should be handled with speed so they won't discolor.

In a bowl make a batter of

> *2 beaten eggs*
> *2 tablespoons milk*
> *4 tablespoons flour*
> *1 tablespoon grated onion*
> *1 tablespoon chopped parsley*
> *1 teaspoon salt.*

Whisk till smooth, cover, and set aside. Then peel

> 6 large, mature potatoes.

Cover them with cold water until ready to grate.

At dinnertime, grate 2 potatoes at a time on the coarse side of the grater and put them in the center of a kitchen towel to twist and squeeze until no more liquid runs out. Stir them into the batter at once and proceed with the next two potatoes.

When the batter is finished, melt in a large heavy skillet over medium-high heat

> 1 tablespoon butter
> 1 tablespoon oil.

When the fat is hot, add a few spoonsful of batter to the pan, using about ¼ cup per pancake. Cook until golden on each side, using a flipper to turn them. Drain on toweling and keep them hot in a warm oven until completed. Add butter to the skillet between batches as needed. Serve at once.

POTATO PANCAKES WITH FRUIT

If you wish to serve potato pancakes topped with applesauce, blueberries, or blackberries and sour cream, follow preceding recipe, omitting the onions and parsley from the batter.

UTA'S POTATO SALAD (Serves 6)

A secret was taught to me a long time ago by that great violinist-conductor-chef, Alexander Schneider; peel and slice the potatoes while still hot, immediately sprinkle with wine, which is sopped up by the potatoes until almost dry again, *then* add dressing and seasoning.

Scrub and boil until just tender

> 8 large young potatoes in their jackets.

Avoid mealy, mature, baking potatoes, and get them uniformly shaped for even slices. Drain the potatoes. As soon as they can be handled, peel and slice about ¼-inch thick. Run the knife under the water every now and then to keep the potatoes from sticking to it. Arrange the slices in a large bowl and sprinkle each layer successively with

> dry white wine or dry vermouth (3 tablespoons wine in all).

Allow the potatoes to steep for 15 minutes. Then add

> ½ cup Uta's French Dressing (page 48).

Sprinkle with salt and pepper and add your favorite herbs such as

> 1 tablespoon chopped parsley
> 1 tablespoon chopped dill
> 2 tablespoons minced shallots or onion
>   or
> 2 tablespoons chopped basil leaves
>   or
> 2 tablespoons chopped tarragon.

Another pleasant option is to beat one or two egg yolks into the dressing before adding to the potatoes.

Coat the sliced potatoes with dressing and chopped herbs, using your hands or wooden spoons. Do it gently. Cover the salad with plastic wrap and let it rest at room temperature before serving. (Don't chill it.)

I think "risotto" sounds much more glamorous and flavorful than rice. I even cook it a l'Italiano in lots of boiling water. I use converted rice rather than the raw kind, which needs so much soaking and rinsing.

COOKED RICE (Serves 4)

In a large pot bring to a brisk boil

> *4 quarts lightly salted water with*
> *½ a squeezed lemon.*

Squeeze the juice right into the water and then drop the lemon, rind and all, into the pot slowly. Dribble in

> *1 cup converted rice*

so the boiling won't stop. After 20 minutes, taste a few kernels for the right degree of tenderness. Drain in a colander, bouncing it up and down to help moisture evaporate. Remove the lemon rind.

If you want to reheat the rice or keep it warm for any length of time, leave it in the metal colander, rinse under very hot tap water, and place the colander with the rice over a pot of simmering water till needed.

Garnish with dotted butter and paprika or chopped parsley. If you like it really lemony, add the grated rind of one lemon just before serving.

RISOTTO WITH POACHED EGG AND CHEESE

It's fabulous as a side dish with roast meat or fowl, but can also be a supper all by itself.

Poach the eggs ahead of time as described on page 26,

> *1 poached egg per person.*

Boil the rice as described above. Reheat the eggs just before draining the rice. Mound the rice on individual plates and make an indentation in the top of each mound. Gently place the drained egg in the indentation and sprinkle with

> *1 tablespoon grated Parmesan.*

Over each egg dribble

> *1–2 tablespoons Brown or Black Butter (page 46).*

Serve and sigh with pleasure.

RISI E BISI (Rice with Peas)

The way Herbert sighs for "risi e bisi" must mean his mother made it on special occasions. I don't know if this is the authentic Austro-Italian way of preparing it, but he's satisfied.

Boil the rice as described on page 255.

Meanwhile thaw one package frozen tiny early peas and cook them in a skillet for a few minutes. Drain the rice, put it in a bowl, and fluff it up with a few tablespoons of butter, using a fork. Fold in the cooked peas. Season to taste and serve sprinkled with chopped parsley.

RICE SALAD (Serves 4)

Leftover rice may be used for this, or boil up a fresh batch. If it's just been made, drain it and refresh under cold running water while it's still in the colander. Bounce it around and run your fingers through it to separate and loosen the grains.

Add

> 3 tablespoons *Uta's French Dressing (page 48)*
> or
> 3 tablespoons *mayonnaise (page 42).*

Garnish with chopped parsley or dill. Try a few halved cherry tomatoes in a ring around the salad.

Before adding the dressing, the cold rice can be mixed with diced cooked chicken, diced ham, poached shrimp, or marinated mushrooms. Serve on lettuce leaves if you like.

GREEN RICE SALAD (Serves 4)

Boil rice as described on page 255, refresh it under cold running water, and drain it well. In a bowl blend together

> *⅓ cup olive oil*
> *2 tablespoons minced parsley*
> *2 tablespoons minced chives*
> *1 tablespoon minced basil leaves*
> *1 tablespoon minced tarragon*
> *1 tablespoon minced dill*
> *salt and pepper to taste.*

Fold the mixture into the rice and serve.

PILAV (Serves 4)

There are almost as many pilav recipes as fish in the sea. Here's a dandy.

In a heavy casserole, sauté

> 1 chopped onion in
> 2 tablespoons butter.

In a bowl mix

> 1 cup converted rice in
> 1 beaten egg.

Stir until the rice is well coated. In a skillet heat

> 1 tablespoon butter.

Add the coated rice and stir over medium heat until the rice is toasty and a little dry. Add it to the onion mixture in the casserole. Pour in

> 2½ cups heated chicken stock or 1 can condensed broth plus
>   1 cup water.

Add

> ½ teaspoon salt
> ½ teaspoon sesame seeds (optional).

Cover the casserole and let the rice simmer over low heat 25 to 30 minutes until the broth has been absorbed and the rice is fluffy. At the last minute

add

> ½ cup slivered, toasted almonds.

(Toast the almonds in a skillet in a little peanut or sesame oil for a minute or two.) You can also add a handful of raisins at the last minute if you like.

Salads

Webster defines "salad" as 1) Any cold dish of meat, fruit, or vegetables served singly or in combination with mayonnaise or other dressings; 2) any green herb grown for salad. I describe salads in several sections of this book. In case you're referring to this title for ideas, I'll list them together.

Most leftover vegetables make a pleasant salad when chilled and doused with Uta's French Dressing (page 48) or mayonnaise (page 42). Combinations of lettuce and herbs are endless, but here are a few that may not have occurred to you:

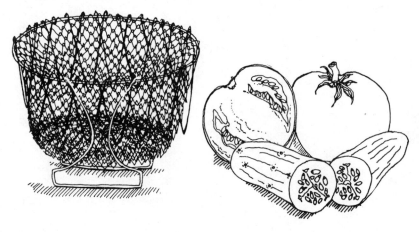

1) Thin slices of

> *cucumbers*
> *green peppers (seeded and deveined)*
> *scallions*
> *tomatoes.*

Arrange the vegetables in alternating circular layers and top with snippets of chives or dill. Add a little Uta's French Dressing (page 48) and sprinkle with salt and pepper.

2) Arrange attractively on lettuce leaves thin slices, strips, or cubes of

> *Münster or Swiss cheese*
> *boiled or Virginia ham.*

Sprinkle with Uta's French Dressing and a crumbled hard-boiled egg yolk.

WATERCRESS AND BELGIAN ENDIVE

Watercress is a snappy addition to many salads and a marvelous garnish for meat and poultry. It can also be a tasty salad all by itself when mixed with a little of Uta's French Dressing (page 48). Remove the largest stems and, if you wish, coarsely chop the leaves of one or two large bunches of washed watercress.

Those pale yellow, plump Belgian Endives with their nutty taste and crisp texture also make a delicious salad when served only with a little of my dressing. Quarter them with a sharp knife and sliver into thin strips before arranging nicely.

Endive mixed with diced raw apples is a delicious combination!

When I mix watercress leaves with strips of endive, I always make a hit with my guests.

Additions of sliced or chopped anchovies, a few drained capers, and crumbled hard-boiled egg yolks are always welcome.

NIÇOISE SALAD

My version of Niçoise is close to the classic recipe from the south of France. Arranging it carefully and beautifully is half the secret.

Cook the vegetables separately and let them cool before dousing with a little of Uta's French Dressing (page 48) in individual bowls. Then arrange as described.

Make

>   *2 cups Uta's Potato Salad (page 253), omitting the onion.*

Parboil 10 minutes

>   *½ pound green beans (page 220). Cool and coat with dressing.*

Parboil 5 minutes

>   *¾ cup broccoli (page 225). Cool and coat with dressing.*

Cut into wedges

>   *2 beefsteak tomatoes.*

Layer the potato slices around the bottom edge of a large salad bowl.

Evenly mound the string beans in the center. Sprinkle the cubed broccoli stems between potatoes and beans. Alternate tomato wedges with broccoli florets. Place

>   *6 to 8 anchovy filets*

in a pinwheel over the mound of beans. Sprinkle over everything

>   *2 crumbled hard-boiled egg yolks.*

Make a design with

>   *12 black Italian olives.*

Sprinkle

>   *2 additional tablespoons Uta's French Dressing (page 48)*

over everything, concentrating on the tomatoes. Tuck a few parsley sprigs around the edge. *Finis!*

Sauerkraut

MICKEY'S SAUERKRAUT (Serves 6)

Mickey Levy is one of those ladies who knows everything, finds anything, and does everything well. I can't imagine Kasseler Rippenspeer (page 213) without Mickey's Sauerkraut.

Wash

>   *2 pounds fresh sauerkraut*

and drain it in a colander. Soak in a bowl of water for 15 minutes and drain again.

Heat

> *2 tablespoons bacon grease (or rendered goose fat if you have it)*

in a large heavy skillet and add the sauerkraut. Cook over medium heat for a few minutes, stirring with a long-handled fork to keep the strands separate. Add a scant

> *2 cups dry white wine.*

Let it come almost to a boil, then lower the heat as far as possible. Cover the casserole and simmer for an hour or more, until the wine is almost absorbed. Add

> *2 teaspoons caraway seeds.*

Simmer another 5 or 10 minutes and serve at once. *Fabelhaft!*

Spinach

If I could afford the plot of land adjacent to mine, I'd have enough room to plant spinach and harvest it when crisp and young. It's available at a farmer's market or greengrocer's, and much better than the kind packed in plastic bags at the supermarket.

PREPARATION OF SPINACH

One pound of fresh spinach will serve 4 people. Buy the greenest, crispest leaves and discard yellowed or wilted ones. Pull off the stems at the base of the leaves. If the leaves are large, fold them in half, stem exposed, and pull upward toward the tip of each leaf. If the leaves tear in the process it doesn't matter. Wash all spinach, even the supposedly prewashed kind. It's no fun to bite into grains of grit or sand. Fill the bottom of the sink with cold water and swish the spinach around to let grit settle on the bottom. Lift out the leaves, empty the sink, and repeat the process. Drain in a colander.

If I'm using the spinach for salad, I put it in the salad basket and whirl it dry like lettuce leaves. Then I chill it right in the basket in the refrigerator. If I'm not using it the same day, I wrap the dried leaves loosely in a towel and then refrigerate.

SPINACH SALAD (Serves 6)

The possibilities for additions to one pound washed and crisped spinach leaves are almost limitless. Use the following singly or in combinations:

> ½ cup fresh bean sprouts
> 6 sliced water chestnuts
> 4 slices crumbled, cooked bacon
> ¼ pound raw sliced mushrooms
> 4 chopped anchovy filets
> 2 teaspoons drained capers
> ½ chopped Bermuda onion
> 1 crumbled hard-boiled egg yolk
> ½ tablespoon chopped fresh herbs
> a handful of pine nuts or chopped walnuts.

Anchovies, capers, and onions are the ingredients I use least often, because many people don't care for them. They certainly won't go well with the nuts!

I prefer John's Sweet Dressing (page 49) to any other on this salad.

BOILED SPINACH (Serves 4 to 6)

Prepare

> 2 pounds spinach (page 261).

Don't whirl it dry but lift it from the water with your hands, shaking it a little, and put it directly into a large pot. Sprinkle it with salt, cover the pot, and simmer for about 5 minutes until wilted. Stir it once in a while.

Drain in a colander and serve with butter. Season to taste.

STIR-FRIED SPINACH

Prepare the spinach as described on page 261, whirl dry, and cook exactly like stir-fried lettuce (page 244).

CREAMED SPINACH

Wash and remove stems from

> 1 pound fresh spinach.

Cook the leaves for 5 minutes in

> 2 cups boiling water.

Drain in a colander, pressing out most of the liquid with the back of a spoon. Place in an electric blender with

>   *¼ cup milk*
>   *1–2 tablespoons chopped onion*
>   *½ teaspoon grated lemon rind*
>   *½ teaspoon salt*
>   *a few gratings of nutmeg.*

Purée till smooth.

In a large skillet, heat

>   *2 tablespoons butter.*

Blend in

>   *1 tablespoon quick-mix flour.*

Cook for several minutes and add

>   *¼ cup cream*
>   *1 teaspoon sugar.*

When the sauce is smooth and thick, stir in the puréed spinach till well blended and cook for another minute until heated through.

>   *Note:* To save time, I sometimes serve the frozen creamed spinach that comes in a pouch and spruce it up with a few gratings of nutmeg and a little grated lemon rind. Remember that dishes labeled "Florentine" are food resting on a bed of creamed spinach.

Don't forget the Green Gnocchi or Bacci Di Caruso on page 112.

Squash (Winter)

Hard-shelled winter squash, such as Hubbard, acorn, and butternut, are terribly simple to bake and can be served in place of potatoes or rice. I get fairly small ones and serve ½ squash for person. Although there are many ways to prepare them and possibilities for endless stuffings, such as hash (chicken or beef), mushrooms, crabmeat, and even cranberries, I always end up doing them the simplest way.

Preheat oven to 375°.

Wash the squash, cut in half, and scoop out the seeds. Butter the skin and place the halves in a shallow baking dish, cavity side up. Sprinkle the rim of the flesh as well as the cavity with

> *a few teaspoons of brown sugar*
> *a pinch of salt*
> *several gratings of nutmeg.*

Dot with

> *1 tablespoon butter.*

Bake from 45 minutes to 1 hour, depending on size. Serve as is, or even better, fill each cavity with hot buttered peas.

Tomatoes

Once you've tasted a juicy, meaty, deep-red beefsteak tomato you're spoiled for anything less. Those pale disgusting cottony ones that come three to a box at the supermarket aren't good enough for the birds.

I grow too many of four different varieties and end up giving them away and inventing recipes even for the green ones just before frost. The four kinds are quite different from each other; deep red Big Boys, huge orange Jubilees, firm little cherry tomatoes, and yellow plum tomatoes that are good in salad and make terrific jam too.

PEELING TOMATOES

Drop a tomato into boiling water for 30 seconds. Remove with a slotted spoon, run under cold water for a second, nip out the stem, and slip off the skin. Done!

CHOPPING TOMATOES

After peeling, quarter the tomato and use a finger to push out seeds and watery membrane. Chop the remaining flesh.

STUFFED TOMATOES

Preparing Tomatoes and Cherry Tomatoes

Slice the top quarter from a large unpeeled tomato, scoop out the pulp, and sprinkle the cavity with a little salt. Invert the shell on a rack over bowl to drain for ½ hour. Finish by dabbing the inside lightly with toweling.

Wash cherry tomatoes. Slice a small section from the top of a cherry tomato leaving it attached at one end to open and close like a little cap. Retain the flattest end for standing. Stick your finger inside to force out seeds and pulp. Sprinkle the cavity with salt and invert to drain, or just dab dry with toweling.

STUFFING FOR LARGE TOMATOES:

Sometimes my ideas may seem a little presumptuous—you're probably ahead of me. But try:

>   Cold Chopped Vegetables Marinated in Dressing or Blended
>   with Mayonnaise
>   Marinated Shrimp or Crabmeat (page 72)
>   Marinated Mushrooms (page 63)
>   Cucumbers in Sour Cream (page 240)
>   Green Bean Salad (page 222)
>   Cottage Cheese with Chopped Herbs.

STUFFING FOR CHERRY TOMATOES:

>   Cream Cheese Blended with Chopped Herbs, Shallots, or Onions
>   Uta's Guacamole (page 56)
>   Tuna and Mayonnaise
>   Cottage Cheese with Minced Ham or Anchovies.

Garnish with paprika, curry powder, or dried herbs.

BAKED STUFFED CHERRY TOMATOES

Stuff each cherry tomato with

> ½ teaspoon Pesto or Pistou (pages 43–44)
> or
> ½ teaspoon cream cheese plus ½ teaspoon Duxelles (page 62).

Place the little lid of the tomato over the stuffing and arrange stuffed tomatoes in a lightly oiled baking dish. Drizzle a little oil over the tops, sprinkle with salt and pepper, and bake in a 350° oven for 5 or 10 minutes until heated.

SAUTÉED CHERRY TOMATOES

Wash and dry cherry tomatoes. In a heavy skillet sauté

> 1 peeled, halved clove garlic in
> 2 tablespoons olive oil.

Brown the garlic, pressing down with a spoon to extract flavor before discarding. Toss the tomatoes in the oil for a minute until hot. Serve with salt and pepper.

BAKED TOMATOES

Preheat the oven to 375°.

Remove 1 inch from the top of washed tomatoes, using

> 1 medium-sized tomato per person.

Sprinkle each one with

> 1 teaspoon brown sugar
> a pinch of salt
> a grating of nutmeg.

Cover the top with

> 1 tablespoon dry bread crumbs
> 1 tablespoon dotted butter.

Place side by side in a buttered baking dish in the hot oven for 15 minutes. If the bread crumbs haven't browned, run the dish under the broiler for a minute.

TOMATOES DIVINE (Serves 6)

They are!

Peel

> *6 beautiful tomatoes.*

Use a heavy Teflon- or porcelain-lined skillet to sauté

> *1 small finely chopped onion in*
> *4 tablespoons butter.*

Add the tomatoes and cook slowly over low heat for 10 minutes. Then add

> *2 tablespoons brown sugar*
> *1 teaspoon salt*
> *a few gratings of nutmeg.*

Stir the sauce around the tomatoes carefully and spoon it over them. If they break up a little, don't worry. Remove them to individual plates with a slotted spoon. To the juices in the skillet add

> *1 tablespoon quick-mix flour.*

Cook and stir, then add

> *½ cup heavy cream.*

Cook and stir over medium heat for another few minutes until the sauce thickens. Spoon it over the tomatoes and serve at once. Wow!

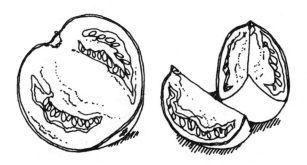

TOMATO SALAD

When beefsteak tomatoes are beautiful, they're best simply sliced, arranged in overlapping layers, drizzled with a fine olive oil and a few drops of lemon juice, and sprinkled with salt and pepper. Top with freshly chopped basil leaves. (Tomatoes and basil are an unbeatable combination; even for companion planting to keep the bugs away.)

TOMATO ASPIC

Like the cucumber aspic, due to acidity this aspic should be allowed to set till firm, at least 24 hours, in the refrigerator. Texture and flavor are superb and it looks gorgeous.

In a large, heavy saucepan melt

>   *3 tablespoons butter.*

Add and sauté over low heat

>   *¼ cup minced onions*
>   *¼ cup minced carrots*
>   *¼ cup minced celery stalk.*

When soft, add

>   *3 large ripe tomatoes, coarsely chopped*
>   *1 cup tomato juice*
>   *1 teaspoon tomato paste*
>   *1 teaspoon Worcestershire sauce*
>   *½ teaspoon salt*
>   *a pinch of sugar*
>   *a pinch of dried tarragon*
>   *a pinch of dried basil*
>   *a few gratings of pepper.*

Simmer the mixture 45 minutes.

Near the end of the cooking time, into a large bowl put

>   *½ cup strong chicken stock or canned condensed broth.*

Gently stir in

>   *2 packages gelatin.*

Let the broth and gelatin rest for 10 minutes.

When the tomato mixture has cooked 45 minutes, set a sieve over the bowl with the broth and gelatin and strain the hot tomato sauce through it into the bowl. Push down on the vegetables to extract juice and flavor. Discard the pulp and stir the aspic until the gelatin has dissolved completely.

Brush a 3-to-4-cup ring mold lightly with vegetable oil and pour in the aspic. Chill for a day or two and unmold (page 20). It can be filled and garnished like the cucumber aspic on page 240.

BAKED GREEN TOMATOES

Preheat the oven to 350°.

Butter a baking dish and in it arrange in layers

>*2 pounds sliced green tomatoes.*

Sprinkle each layer with

>*1 teaspoon brown sugar*
>*salt and pepper to taste.*

In a skillet heat

>*4 tablespoons butter*

and add

>*½ cup dry bread crumbs*
>*a pinch of thyme*
>*a pinch of basil.*

Brown the crumbs in the butter over medium heat, stirring constantly. Top the sliced tomatoes with the brown crumbs and sprinkle with

>*½ cup grated Parmesan.*

Dot with

>*2 tablespoons butter.*

Bake for 45 minutes and serve at once.

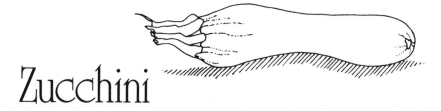

Zucchini

My garden overflows with them as they grow to gigantic proportions, sometimes shooting from 2 inches to 24 in a few days. I haven't decided whether it's really such a versatile vegetable or whether the quantity has forced versatility on it. (Yellow thin-skinned or crook-neck squash can be substituted for all of them.)

When zucchini are small and the seeds are tiny, they can be cooked whole or sliced without peeling. As they grow larger, I peel them with a vegetable peeler, slice them lengthwise, scoop out seeds and pith, and then slice, cube, dice, or cut strips for a given recipe.

SAUTÉED ZUCCHINI WITH WALNUTS
OR PINE NUTS (Serves 4)

Wash and nip the ends from

>   *1½ pounds small zucchini.*

Cut them into ½-inch slices and set aside while you slice

>   *¼ cup scallions (white parts only).*

Sauté them in a large skillet over medium heat for a few minutes in

>   *2 tablespoons butter*
>   *2 tablespoons oil.*

Add the sliced zucchini and cook and stir for 5 minutes. Then add

>   *¼ cup dry white wine or 2 tablespoons dry vermouth*
>   *1 tablespoon lemon juice.*

Simmer a few minutes longer and add

>   *½ cup pine nuts or coarsely chopped walnuts.*

Cook and stir another minute and serve at once, sprinkled with salt and pepper.

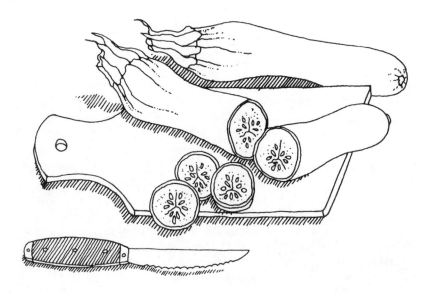

BAKED ZUCCHINI IN SOUR CREAM

Preheat oven to 375°.

Peel

>2 pounds medium-sized zucchini.

Cut slices ½-inch thick. Braise for 5 minutes in a little butter and water as in Braised Zucchini (below). Drain. In a heavy, shallow casserole melt together

>2 tablespoons butter
>½ cup sour cream
>½ cup grated Swiss or Parmesan cheese.

Add

>a pinch of salt
>¼ teaspoon paprika.

Cook over medium heat stirring constantly until the sauce is smooth. Turn off the heat. In a small bowl beat together

>1 egg yolk
>2 tablespoons sour cream.

Fold the egg-cream mixture into the sauce in the casserole and add the zucchini. Stir to coat the vegetable slices with sauce. Sprinkle the top with

>dry bread crumbs
>grated Parmesan

and dot with

>butter.

Heat through for 10 minutes in the preheated oven, then brown the crust quickly for a minute under the broiler.

BRAISED ZUCCHINI (Serves 4)

Wash and nip the ends from

>8 small zucchini.

Leave them whole or slice into

>1-inch pieces.

Put them in a saucepan with

> *2 tablespoons butter*
> *2 tablespoons water.*

Cover the pan and simmer for 10 minutes, until the vegetable is tender when pierced. Drain and serve with a little more butter and sprinkle with salt and pepper.

or

Top with

> *¼ cup sour cream.*

Garnish with chopped dill or parsley and sprinkle with paprika.

ZUCCHINI MIT DILL (Serves 6)

Straight from Austria, the thought of it makes my mouth water. The size of the zucchini is unimportant but you will need

> *2½ pounds zucchini.*

Make

> *zucchini strips.*

Peel the vegetables. Slice them lengthwise into 6 sections and scoop or cut out seeds and the pithy core. Discard. Cut the zucchini sections into even strips no more than ½-inch thick or 2 inches long. Place them in a colander sprinkled with 2 tablespoons coarse salt. Drain over the sink or a bowl for at least ½ hour to let the moisture run out. Rinse off the salt, drain quickly, and pat the strips dry with toweling.

In a shallow casserole melt

> *3 tablespoons butter.*

Toss in the drained zucchini strips and turn them with a wooden spoon until coated with butter. Cover the casserole and simmer over medium-low heat for 5 minutes.

Meanwhile, in a bowl mix together

> *3 tablespoons flour*
> *1 cup sour cream.*

When smooth, stir this paste into the zucchini and simmer for a few minutes until the sauce thickens. Add

> 2 teaspoons sugar
> 2 teaspoons white wine vinegar.

Simmer another minute and add

> 1 tablespoon chopped dill (or 1 teaspoon dill seeds).

Serve and eat hearty.

FRENCH-FRIED ZUCCHINI

Prepare zucchini strips, using 3 or 4 medium-large zucchini (page 272). After patting as dry as possible, put a handful at a time into a paper bag with

> ½ cup quick-mix flour
> ½ teaspoon salt
> generous grindings of pepper.

Shake the bag vigorously to coat the strips with seasoned flour. Lift them out and shake off excess flour. Fry by the handful in a deep skillet in

> 1 inch vegetable or peanut oil, heated to 375°.

After they turn golden, remove with a slotted spoon and drain on toweling. Sprinkle with more salt and pepper and serve with cocktails, or with anything where you might use French-fried potatoes. Like peanuts, no one ever gets enough.

BATTER-FRIED ZUCCHINI

Make zucchini strips (page 272) and dry them thoroughly. Dust them with flour and dip them in Uta's Fluffy Batter (page 118), and proceed with the deep-frying technique for French-fried zucchini.

MARINATED ZUCCHINI STRIPS

Use

> 1½–2 pounds large zucchini.

Make zucchini strips (page 272). They don't need to be dried. Cook the strips over low heat for 10 minutes in a saucepan with

> 3 tablespoons butter
> 1 teaspoon white vinegar
> a pinch of dill seeds
> a pinch of salt.

Drain the zucchini and arrange neatly in layers in a serving bowl. Cover with

> Uta's French Dressing (page 48)
> 2 teaspoons lemon juice.

Garnish with

> 1 tablespoon chopped parsley
> a few drained capers (optional).

Chill for several hours. Just before serving, tip the bowl to pour off most of the dressing. (Save it for another batch.) The strips can be served on lettuce leaves or alone. They'll keep for weeks covered with the dressing in a sealed jar in the refrigerator. I often make double the amount to have some on hand at a moment's notice.

NATALIE'S ZUCCHINI PUFFS (Serves 4 to 6)

Natalie Burns Cilona, an excellent actress, is also a cook who can teach me a thing or two. She gave me this recipe and it's always a hit.

Peel

> 1½ pounds zucchini
> 1 medium-sized onion.

Grate the vegetables coarsely and put them into the center of a kitchen towel to twist and squeeze until no more moisture runs out.

In a bowl beat together a batter of

> 2 eggs
> ½ cup milk
> 1 tablespoon olive oil
> ⅓ cup flour
> a pinch of salt and pepper.

Carefully fold the squeezed, grated zucchini and onion into the batter.

In a deep, heavy skillet heat

> 1 inch peanut or vegetable oil to 375°.

Drop the batter in by large spoonfuls and fry the puffs until golden on each side. Do it in batches. Don't crowd the pan. Remove the puffs with a slotted spoon and drain on toweling. Keep hot on a platter in a 200° oven until finished. Serve at once. I want some more.

STUFFED ZUCCHINI

I dreamed this up because I wanted to show off one of my enormous zucchini. This recipe can also be made with smaller ones, in which case use 1 per person. Use your judgment as to how many people you can serve with a giant. The same is true for the amount of stuffing.

Wash the zucchini and nip off the ends, but don't peel. Poach in barely simmering water. For very large ones use a fish poacher or covered roasting pan. In 10 minutes pierce the zucchini to see that it's barely tender. Drain it. Cut it in half lengthwise and scoop out seeds and pulp. You should now have a boat-shaped cavity in each zucchini half. Turn onto a rack, cavity side down, to drain for ½ hour. Dry with toweling and place the zucchini halves gently into a buttered baking dish or roasting pan, cavity side up. Fill the cavities with puréed carrots (page 233). Sprinkle with salt, nutmeg, pepper, and lots of grated Parmesan cheese. Dot with butter. Put it into a preheated 350° oven for 15 minutes or until the vegetables are heated through.

Present it to your guests and listen to delighted shrieks.

BAKED VEGETABLE POTPOURRI (Serves 6)

Preheat the oven to 350°.

In a heavy skillet melt

> *4 tablespoons butter.*

Over medium heat, gently sauté

> *½ cup finely sliced scallions (white part only)*
> *1 cup finely sliced green peppers (seeded and deveined)*
> *¼ cup minced parsley.*

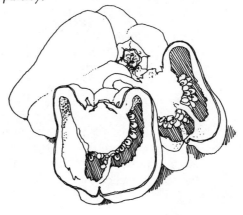

After 5 minutes add

> *1½ cups grated carrots.*

Continue to cook and stir. In 5 minutes add

> *6 small sliced, unpeeled zucchini*
> *1 tablespoon chopped basil (or a pinch of dried)*
> *1 teaspoon salt*
> *a few gratings of pepper.*

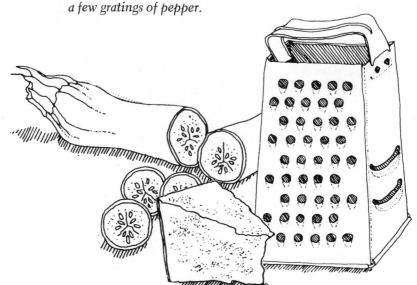

Saúté a few minutes longer and then stir in

> *1 cup sour cream*
> *½ cup grated Parmesan.*

Cook and stir a few minutes longer, then remove from heat. Place the vegetables in a buttered casserole and sprinkle the top with

> *¼ cup grated Parmesan*
> *2 tablespoons dotted butter.*

Bake for 30 minutes and serve at once.

Note: Good conservationists may want to know what to do with the water in which vegetables have cooked. Like meat and poultry stock, it's difficult to preserve without spoilage in our overheated homes, and the average freezer or refrigerator won't hold them all. But they can be used within a day or two as a base for broth, stews, or braised meat, poultry, and fish instead of plain water. They can also be reheated with the addition of green vegetable parings to be used as a base for soup.

XII. Bread

Baking bread is an act of love. It connects you with life. When you knead bread with your whole being, not just your hands, you are creating. Something breathes and rises through your efforts. Tension leaves you and a sense of peace and purpose settles in. While bread is baking, the aroma turns your house into a home.

A loaf of homemade bread served with cheese, sausage, or a simple stew with salad and a bottle of wine is a festival. Loaves resting on a sideboard or table transform the atmosphere. They don't rest there very long, of course. In our family, one loaf out of three usually disappears before it's cool.

Breadmaking seems clouded in mystery. "She bakes her own bread," is whispered in awesome tones, implying some secret skill or hidden knowledge. Yet once shown how, a twelve-year-old can make good bread. Even beginning efforts will produce better bread than the cottony, artificially aerated loaves piled high at the supermarket. The "store-bought" coarser type of "brick-oven-baked" bread is fine for many recipes to which bread is added or for making croutons, croustades, or bread crumbs. Many bakeries make beautiful hard-crusted bread or rye or pumpernickel. Otherwise, change your life and bake your own.

In primitive societies, bread is baked with flour, water, salt, and nothing more. It can be hearty and good. The things we add are embellishments: yeast, shortening, sweeteners, eggs, nuts, herbs, cheese, even fruit. If you become enchanted with breadmaking, there are marvelous books to help you with Swedish or French bread, braided loaves, black, rye, pumpernickel, and others. I'm going to stick to the few simple kinds I bake most often, with a fervent desire of influencing those who are convinced they can't do it or that it's not worth the effort. I want converts who will learn that breadmaking can change their lives.

THE INGREDIENTS

Flour. Use unbleached flour to bake white bread. Both Hecker's and King Arthur's are available at most supermarkets. Health or special food stores carry other excellent milled flour with none of the nasty additives or chemicals in the average all-purpose "enriched" flour. The same holds true for whole-wheat flour. Whole wheat behaves differently than white flour both when mixing and kneading. It's more difficult to handle, and the loaves are heavier. I mix it with white flour, sometimes as much as half and half.

Yeast is a living organism in a dormant state, brought to life by warm liquid and further activated by sweeteners. I use dry packaged yeast because it's readily available and keeps for months in the refrigerator before the expiration date stamped on each package. I have it on hand at all times to use when the breadmaking spirit moves me. (If you decide to use compressed yeast cakes, make sure they're fresh. One cake of compressed yeast is the equivalent of two packages of dry yeast and should be dissolved in liquid no more than 85° or the yeast will be killed. Remember this when measuring and activating it for recipes that stipulate dry yeast.)

Sweeteners add flavor and help to activate the yeast when added to warm water or milk. Most often used, in order of preference, are honey, brown sugar, molasses, and white sugar.

Salt should be used sparingly. Don't add it to the original yeast "sponge," or it will counteract the sweeteners' activation of the yeast. I prefer sea salt.

Shortening. In my opinion oil is the best: vegetable, peanut, or even olive. Butter, solid vegetable shortening, or lard also work, but must be melted first to incorporate them in the dough in the same manner as the oil.

Eggs and milk. These are bonus ingredients that enrich the bread.

THE TIME INVOLVED

Allow about five hours from the time you start organizing your materials until the bread pops out of the oven. During the long stretches when the sponge or dough is rising, you'll have time to do lots of other things. It's more a matter of being home to supervise the different stages. Work time is less than an hour, even for a novice.

WHITE BREAD [Whole-Wheat Bread]

Into a large bowl sift

> 8 *cups unbleached flour* [4 *cups whole wheat mixed with 3 cups white flour*]

As a perfect starter for the bread, make a "sponge."

Into a bowl pour

> 2 *cups hot water.*

Stir in

> 2 *tablespoons honey until dissolved.*

Whisk in

> ½ *cup dry powdered milk until dissolved.*

Whisk in

> 1 *egg.*

Whisk in

> *2 cups of the sifted flour.*

When the mixture is smooth, test with your finger to make sure it is just lukewarm, or no more than 110°, before sprinkling on

> *1 package dry yeast [1½ packages].*

Gently fold the yeast into the mixture. Cover the bowl with a towel lightly dampened in warm water.

Setting the Sponge (Rising Conditions)

When yeast has been activated by dissolving in lukewarm liquid, continued activation depends on correct temperature and a draft-free place: 75° to 85° is ideal. If you have an oven with a pilot light, your problem is solved. When the oven is turned off the pilot light provides the correct temperature, and the oven is draft free. Simply set the covered sponge in the middle, close the door, set your timer, and forget about it. If you don't have a pilot light, room temperature may suffice. Cooler temperature simply means slower rising. Or set the bowl on a warm—not hot—radiator. If there are drafts, surround the bowl with a shawl. It can also be set on a rack over a pan of hot water.

Allow the covered sponge to rest under these conditions for about 1 hour. It will puff up and bubble a little.

Mixing the Dough

To the sponge add

> *2 more cups of sifted flour*
> *2 teaspoons salt.*

Beat in the flour and salt briskly with a wooden spoon, using a lifting motion to aerate the dough. Every now and then stir the dough from the edge of the bowl toward the center.

After a few minutes of beating, pour

> *2 tablespoons peanut or vegetable oil*

in a thin ring around the dough at the edge of the bowl and fold it over and around the dough without cutting into it, until absorbed. Then add

> *2 more cups of the sifted flour.*

You won't be able to use the spoon much longer, as the dough stiffens. Then flour your hands and work the dough with a light pinching motion, using all fingers against the heel of your hands. Lift the dough a little as you pinch and toss it, always loosening it from the sides of the bowl. When you have a more or less compact mass, turn it out onto a floured board or table top. Scrape the remaining bits of dough out of the bowl to incorporate into the larger mass.

Kneading

Gluten in the flour is released through the motion and warmth of your hands. The kneading should proceed for at least 10 minutes. As the dough becomes sticky, work in more flour until it becomes smooth, silky, and elastic.

How much of the remaining flour is used depends on the flour itself, which can vary from bag to bag of the same brand. It also depends on temperature and humidity. I've specified a maximum amount.

With the dough in front of you on the floured surface, reflour your hands and push down and away on the lump with the heel of your hands, fingers loosely bent. Let the fingers curve around the dough to bring it up and over caressingly. Push down again with the heel of your hands. This kneading motion actually begins in the shoulders and rocks through the arms into the heel of the hands, ending with the soft grasp of curling fingers. The whole body can develop a rocking rhythm. I sometimes sing a nice slow Bach aria to accompany the motion—when no one can hear! Turn the dough around every third or fourth time and continue adding flour if it gets sticky. After 10 minutes or so, shape the dough into a round ball, drawing the seams of the mass together at the bottom. Let it rest while you wash out the bowl with hot water. Dry it and brush lightly with oil. Turn the ball of dough around in the bowl so it, too, will be coated with oil, then place it round side up and seam side down in the center of the bowl. Cover with a damp towel and set it to rise under the same conditions as the sponge (page 280).

Rising of the Dough

With the dough in a warm, draft-free place covered by a damp towel, set the timer for 1 hour. When the time is up, check to see that it has doubled in volume. If not, let it rise a little longer. (If it rises *too* long, it will swell so far that it will collapse.) Remove the towel and use your fist to punch down on the dough a few dozen times. (Now, if you want to knead it again for a few minutes, you may. It makes the texture of the bread finer.) After punching, form another ball, again drawing the seams together at the bottom. Replace the damp towel and let the dough rise another 40 to 60 minutes.

Shaping Loaves

This amount of dough will make 2 loaves in 2 4-by-8-inch loaf pans; 1 large and 1 small loaf in 5-by-9-inch and 3½-by-7½-inch pans respectively. You can bake the whole mass on a baking sheet not using a pan. You can even use clean, oiled clay flowerpots or ovenproof bowls. Whichever container you use, the dough should fill it from ½ to ¾ to leave room for final rising. Brush the containers with oil to prevent sticking. Make sure the dough touches the sides of the container to get support while rising.

Cut the dough into proportionate pieces and knead each piece to work out a little air. Then shape to the approximate width and length or circumference of the pan for which it's meant. After shaping and folding, make sure the seams will be at the bottom of the pan. Press the dough lightly into the containers and make three diagonal slits evenly spaced across the top of each loaf with a sharp knife. This allows steam to escape during baking and helps to spread the dough evenly in the pans. Let the pans rest and rise on top of the stove covered with a damp towel for 20 or 25 minutes. Preheat the oven to 375°.

Glazing, Baking, Cooling, and Storing

Brushing bread with a glaze is not necessary, but I love the look of a shiny crust. Melted butter brushed over the loaves just before baking is always nice. If you use an egg beaten together with 3 tablespoons of milk to brush over the tops, you'll have a shinier crust. If you want a hard crust, brush it with water and set a pan of boiling water into the oven under the bread while baking. Baking time depends on the size of the loaves and the containers you're using. In 40 minutes check to see if the bread has pulled slightly away from the sides of the pan. If it's in a metal pan, rap the bottom to see if it makes a hollow sound. One or both of these tests signal that it's done. Invert the containers to knock out the bread. If it sticks, loosen it at the edges with a knife. Place the loaves on a rack to cool.

When completely cool, wrap the bread in plastic or foil. Otherwise moisture may accumulate during storage to make it soggy, even moldy. It will keep in the breadbox for a day or two and in the refrigerator for a week. When well wrapped, bread will keep in the freezer for months. It thaws quickly and tastes very good, especially when wrapped in foil and warmed through in a 300° oven for 20 minutes before serving.

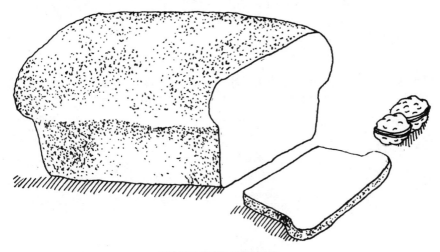

WALNUT BREAD

This is a hearty bread, not at all for dessert. Make whole-wheat bread, using the proportions given in brackets on page 279. When the dough has risen and you've punched it down with your fist, turn it onto a floured surface and flatten it to about 1 inch in thickness. Evenly distribute and press in

>*¾ cup chopped walnuts*
>*½ cup finely chopped onions (optional).*

Fold up the dough and knead for several minutes. Reshape it into a ball and place seam side down into the bowl for the second rising. Finish the basic recipe.

CHEESE BREAD

Make the recipe for white or whole-wheat bread on page 279, using the following substitutions:

In the sponge, use

> *2 tablespoons brown sugar instead of honey*
> *1½ packages yeast for white and 2 packages for whole-wheat bread.*

When mixing the dough, substitute

> *3 tablespoons melted butter for the oil.*

After the butter has been incorporated into the dough, beat in

> *1 cup coarsely grated cheddar or Swiss cheese.*

Complete the basic recipe.

DILL BREAD

The simple technique for mixing this bread differs from most others. The result is a delicious, coarse, almost crumbly loaf with a zing of tangy herbs.

The recipe will be enough for one nice-sized loaf.

Preheat the oven to 350°.

Into a bowl sprinkle

> *1 package dry yeast over*
> *¼ cup lukewarm water.*

Stir in

> *1 teaspoon light brown sugar.*

Let the mixture rest for 10 minutes until it puffs and bubbles a little.

Meanwhile, in a large saucepan combine

> *1 tablespoon melted butter*
> *1 cup cottage cheese*
> *1½ tablespoons light brown sugar*
> *1 tablespoon grated onion*
> *1 teaspoon salt*
> *¼ teaspoon baking soda.*

Set the pan over a very low flame and stir the mixture gently until it is lukewarm. Remove from heat and stir in the yeast mixture. Lightly fold in

> *2 teaspoons dill seeds.*

Stir in

> *2½ cups sifted unbleached flour.*

Beat briskly until it forms a stiff mass. Cover the dough in the saucepan with a lightly dampened warm towel and let it rise 1 hour (page 282).

Turn the dough out onto a lightly floured surface and knead gently for just a few minutes. Then turn it into an oiled 5-by-9-inch loaf pan. Let the dough rise in the pan from 30 to 40 minutes until it has risen above the edge of the pan. Bake for 45 minutes. Remove from the oven. Brush the top with melted butter and sprinkle with salt. Let the bread cool in the pan on a rack for 15 minutes before turning it out of the pan to finish cooling on the rack.

As a variation, use other herbs in place of the dill seeds: fennel or caraway seeds, 2 teaspoons of dry basil or sage, tarragon, or oregano. They all work.

STOLLEN (Christmas Bread)

When "You're baking me a Christmas stollen, aren't you?" first began to sound like a command, I stopped being flattered and balked. Now, instead of almost fifty of these beautiful loaves, I bake a round dozen and invite people to have a slice or two instead of sending them home with a loaf of their own.

Stollen batter is more like cake than bread dough, because less flour is used in relation to liquids and fat, so be set for a wetter consistency when kneading.

Sift and set aside

> *7 cups unbleached flour.*

Make a sponge in a large bowl by sprinkling

> *2 packages dry yeast over*
> *1½ cups lukewarm water.*

Stir in

> *½ cup powdered milk*
> *1 tablespoon honey.*

Fold in

> 1 cup of the sifted flour.

Cover the bowl with a damp towel and set to rise for 1 hour (page 282).

Meanwhile, in another bowl mix

> ½ pound blanched slivered almonds
> ¼ pound diced candied citron
> ¼ pound white or black seedless raisins
> ½ pound mixed, diced candied fruit.

Almonds are available at the supermarket in packages already blanched and slivered. Candied citron and mixed fruit also comes prepared in little jars, especially near holidays.

Sprinkle the fruit and nuts with ½ cup of the sifted flour and run your fingers through it to separate it and make sure it's evenly distributed. Set the bowl aside.

Make the batter in the large bowl of your electric mixer. First cream

> 3 sticks softened butter (1½ cups).

Little by little add

> ¾ cup superfine sugar.

Continue the beating in the mixer until the sugar has been absorbed. One at a time, add

> 3 eggs.

When each is absorbed, beat in

> 2 tablespoons grated lemon rind
> 2 tablespoons brandy
> a pinch of salt.

Remove the bowl from the electric mixer and gently fold in the yeast sponge. Use a wooden spoon to beat in all but ½ cup of the remaining flour. (Use the last ½ cup for flouring hands and board while kneading.)

The kneading motion employed for bread won't work here, because the dough is too soft. So, after beating the dough with about 100 lifting strokes with the spoon, let it remain in the bowl while you pinch it lightly. Use the thumb to press against the flattened fingers of each hand. Pull and lift the dough upwards and to the sides.

Lower and pinch, lift and pull again and again until the dough gets elastic and can be lifted from the bowl in one mass. Do it quickly. It should take only a few minutes. Turn the dough onto a floured surface. Flour your hands and continue to pinch, lift, and pull sideways for at least 5 minutes longer until the dough is smooth and elastic. Form it into a ball, like bread dough, seam side down, and place it in a lightly buttered bowl. Cover with a warm, damp cloth and let rise for 1½ hours or until doubled in bulk.

Again turn the dough onto a floured surface and flatten into a large oval slab about 1-inch thick. Distribute the floured fruit and nuts over the surface and push them into the dough. Roll up the dough and begin a proper kneading process (page 281). Nuts and fruit will roll out through little holes and air pockets, so keep kneading for about 5 minutes until the dough can be shaped into a ball with no loose nuts or fruit. Return the ball to the greased bowl, cover, and set to rise for another 1½ hours.

Preheat the oven to 350°.

Turn the dough onto a floured surface and divide it into the number of loaves you've decided on. To make presents, divide them equally between four 3½-by-7½-inch loaf pans. Or make two large ones for your family in 5-by-9-inch pans. Shape the pieces to the approximate size of the pans; they should fill the pans better than halfway. Let them rest while you generously butter the pans and then press in the loaves seam side down, making sure the dough touches the sides of the pans for support while rising. Cut 3 diagonal slashes, evenly spaced, across each loaf, and brush with melted butter. Set the pans on the stove for 45 minutes until the dough has risen above the brim.

The larger loaves should bake for 45 minutes and the smaller ones 35 minutes. They should have shrunken slightly from the sides of the pan and turned golden. Loosen them with a knife around the rim and turn out of the pans onto a rack to cool.

Make an easy glaze to brush over tops and sides of the cooled stollen.

In a bowl, stir till smooth

> 2 cups confectioner's sugar
> ¼ cup lemon juice
> 1 teaspoon vanilla
> ¼ teaspoon almond extract.

Brush the mixture on the loaves and let it harden.

To store, wrap in foil or plastic. Stollen will keep in the refrigerator for a week to 10 days. If you make them by the carload, as I used to, wrap the loaves in foil and freeze till time to give them away. After thawing, they lose a little in flavor and texture, but will perk up after ½ hour in a 300° oven while still wrapped in foil. (The glaze will run a little.)

Slice the loaves the way you would any homemade bread and serve smeared generously with sweet butter for breakfast, high tea, or a late snack.

Accompanied by a glass of wine, you'll become acutely aware that they are indeed Happy Holidays.

BAKING-POWDER FRUIT BREAD

Each of the following four fruit breads is strongly connected with a personal experience. The Date Nut Loaf (below) was the first bread I ever attempted, and since it was an immediate success, I've never stopped tossing it together when a goody was needed in a hurry.

I once gave a loaf of Banana Bread (page 291) to my passionate idol, Gérard Philipe, simply because it was the only homemade article available at our first encounter and I wanted to present him with an "offering." The sight of that incredibly gifted French actor standing tall and beautiful before me with the greasy loaf pan in his delicate hands will never leave me. He seemed dazed when I shoved it at him, but he *liked* the bread. Ever since, when I'm on the point of making a fool of myself, Herbert only has to whisper, "Banana bread!" and I get the message.

I was introduced to Cranberry Bread (page 292) by my dear friend Martha Greene and, almost in the same breath, to the cranberry bog where the fruit could be picked.

When my lovely friend Linda McGuire presented me with her Christmas loaf, I pleaded for the recipe. Now, near the holidays my friends divide into two camps: those who demand Stollen (page 285) and those who prefer the Christmas Loaf (page 290). From the cook's standpoint, the loaf is easier than the Stollen.

UTA'S DATE NUT LOAF

Preheat the oven to 325°.

Pit

> *1 pound dates.*

Sprinkle with flour for easier handling, and chop coarsely to equal

> *1 cup chopped dates.*

Set aside.

Into a bowl sift together

> 2 cups unbleached flour (or 1 cup white and 1 cup whole wheat)
> 2 teaspoons baking powder
> 1 teaspoon cinnamon
> ¼ teaspoon grated nutmeg
> ½ teaspoon salt.

Use the large bowl on the electric mixer to cream

> 6 tablespoons softened butter.

Gradually add

> ½ cup brown sugar.

One at a time beat in

> 2 eggs.

When everything is well mixed, remove the bowl and use a wooden spoon to beat in

> ½ cup milk alternating with
> a little of the flour mixture.

When everything has been added and stirred, fold in

> chopped dates
> ½ cup coarsely chopped walnuts or pecans
> 3 tablespoons grated orange rind.

Butter a 5-by-9-inch loaf pan and pour in the dough. Stud the loaf with some walnut or pecan halves and bake in the hot oven for 1¼ hours. Cool the bread in the pan about 15 minutes before turning it out on a rack to cool completely before slicing and gobbling up.

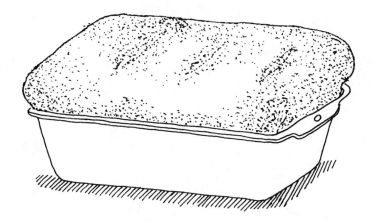

LINDA'S CHRISTMAS LOAF

Preheat the oven to 300°.

Into a bowl sift together

> 3⅔ cups unbleached flour
> 1 teaspoon baking powder
> ½ teaspoon salt.

In the large bowl on the electric mixer cream till fluffy

> 2 sticks softened butter (1 cup).

Little by little add

> 1 cup superfine sugar.

When well absorbed, beat in one at a time

> 4 eggs.

Remove the bowl from the machine.

Into a pitcher stir

> 1½ cups buttermilk with
> 1 teaspoon baking soda.

With a wooden spoon, beat a little of the flour mixture into the butter, sugar, and egg mixture and alternate it with a little of the buttermilk and soda until everything has been used up and is well blended.

Fold in

> grated rind of 2 thick-skinned oranges
> 1 teaspoon vanilla
> 1½ cups coarsely chopped pecans or walnuts
> 1 cup coarsely chopped dates.

Pour the batter into a large buttered tube pan and bake for 1 hour and 20 minutes. Or divide it between two buttered 4½-by-8¼-inch loaf pans and bake 1 hour and 10 minutes. Or divide it among three buttered 3½-by-7½-inch pans and bake for 1 hour.

The orange syrup is the final fillip.

Boil

> ½ cup orange juice with
> 1 cup sugar.

When the sugar has dissolved completely, turn off the heat and add

2 tablespoons Grand Marnier or other orange liqueur.

When the loaves have come hot from the oven, pour the syrup over them to be absorbed right in their tins. Set to cool completely on a rack before removing from the pans.

GÉRARD'S BANANA BREAD

Preheat the oven to 350°.

Into a bowl sift together

> *1¾ cups unbleached flour*
> *¼ cup wheat germ*
> *3 teaspoons baking powder*
> *¼ teaspoon grated nutmeg*
> *½ teaspoon salt.*

In the large bowl on the electric mixer beat

> *1 stick softened butter (8 tablespoons).*

Slowly add

> *⅔ cup superfine sugar*
> *1 egg.*

Beat till well absorbed.

Remove the bowl from the electric mixer and use a wooden spoon to beat in the sifted ingredients a little at a time, alternating with

> *1 cup mashed bananas (2–3 ripe bananas).*

When dry ingredients and bananas are all incorporated fold in

> *1 tablespoon vanilla*
> *1 teaspoon grated lemon rind*
> *½ cup coarsely chopped walnuts or pecans*
> *½ cup chopped dried apricots or dried raisins.*

Turn the dough into a well-buttered 5-by-9-inch loaf pan and stud with a handful of halved nuts. Bake for one hour. Let cool for 15 minutes in the pan before turning out onto a rack to cool.

MARTHA'S CRANBERRY NUT BREAD

Preheat the oven to 350°.

In the electric blender, a handful at a time, coarsely chop

1 cup fresh cranberries.

Mix with

¼ cup sugar.

Set aside.

Into a bowl sift together

3 cups unbleached flour
¾ cup sugar
4 teaspoons baking powder
1 teaspoon salt.

Into the sifted ingredients gradually beat

1 cup milk
1 beaten egg
2 tablespoons melted butter.

Blend well before folding in

½ cup coarsely chopped walnuts
1 tablespoon grated orange rind
chopped cranberries.

Generously butter a 5-by-9-inch loaf pan and turn in the dough. Bake for 1 hour. Let it cool in the pan for 15 minutes. Turn the loaf out on a rack to cool completely.

All three loaves are delicious when sliced and served plain or spread with sweet butter or cream cheese.

XIII. Tarts and Tortes and Other Desserts

Dessert at the end of a meal should be like the climax of a coronation, when the crown is put in place.

The tarts and pies I used to make were sometimes studded with jewels, but the base of the crown was cardboard. I had an enormous block about crusts until my friend Hal Holden not only removed my fears, but turned the making of crusts into such fun that I now have to resist making them too often.

Buy a pastry blender, a handled utensil with round cutting blades, which eliminates the old method of cutting shortening into flour with two knives. Tarts should be made in a 9-inch tart pan with a removable fluted rim. For pies I prefer a 9-inch Pyrex pie plate. Now all you need is a little courage and patience.

Tarts

TART CRUST

A tart crust is easier than a pie crust because it doesn't have to be as carefully handled or rolled out. It is simply pressed into the pan with the fingers. Flaky and slightly sweet, it's perfect for open-faced tarts filled with fruit, custard, or gelatin mixtures.

Preheat oven to 425°.

Into a bowl sift together

> 1 cup unbleached flour
> 2 tablespoons confectioner's sugar.

Bring almost to room temperature

> 1 stick butter (8 tablespoons).

Cut the butter into small pieces and sprinkle the pieces across the flour mixture. With the pastry blender, cut the butter into the flour, bobbing it up and down rapidly while turning the bowl with your left hand. When the dough is crumbly like coarse meal, work it together with your hands.

It shouldn't take too long. The warmth of your hands will help soften the butter so that the dough will hang together and form a ball. Put the ball on a board and push down on it a few times with the heel of your hand to fully incorporate the shortening. Smack it with the flat of your hand to flatten it. Put it into the center of the tart pan and use your fingertips to press it outward toward the rim all around the bottom and then up into the fluted edges. It should be approximately ⅛-inch thick and evenly distributed. If you are using a fairly dry filling like fresh berries, the crust is now ready for baking. If the filling is juicy or wet, before baking brush the crust with a mixture of

> 1 egg white, lightly beaten
> 1 teaspoon sugar.

(Use only the amount needed for a light glaze.)

Bake the crust for 10 minutes or until golden. Cool it in the pan on a rack.

CREAM CHEESE CRUST

An easy, tasty, flaky crust, it's not sweet and can be used for a quiche or for anything for which you might use a regular pie crust. It is also pressed into the pan with the fingers, rather than rolled out.

Preheat oven to 425°.

Sift together

> 1 cup unbleached flour
> ½ teaspoon salt.

Cut into small pieces

> 1 stick butter (8 tablespoons) at room temperature
> 1 3-ounce package cream cheese.

Sprinkle the pieces of butter and cheese over the flour and cut it in briskly with the pastry blender, turning the bowl with your other hand. When it's crumbly, looking like coarse meal, work the dough into a ball with your hands. Wrap it in wax paper and refrigerate for several hours, even overnight if you like. If, when ready to put into the pan, the dough is very hard, leave it in the wax paper while you whack it all over with the side of the rolling pin. It should soften up quickly for easy handling. Put the ball between two sheets of wax paper and flatten it a little with a rolling pin. Put the dough into the tart pan and press it from the center to the edges with your fingertips. Push it up into the fluted rim. The whole crust should have an even thickness of about ⅛ inch. If you're using a wet filling, glaze the bottom by brushing on a little frothy egg white.

Bake for 10 minutes or a little longer till the crust is golden. Cool in the pan on a rack.

PIE CRUST

Preheat oven to 425°.

For a single 9-inch pie shell, sift together

> 1 cup unbleached flour
> ½ teaspoon salt.

Pinch into small pieces

> 3½ tablespoons solid vegetable shortening
> 2 tablespoons butter

and sprinkle over the flour and use the pastry blender to cut it briskly into the flour. Keep rotating the bowl as you bounce the pastry blender up and down. Rub the mixture quickly between your fingers to break up remaining little balls of shortening. Over the mixture sprinkle

> 2 tablespoons very cold water.

Work it in with the back of a fork. Test the dough to see if it will hang together. If it still seems too dry, add

> 1 tablespoon cold water.

Work that in with the fork and test again with your fingers. Temperature and humidity affect the action of flour, fat, and water, so you have to work out the best mixture by feel. Just remember that too much water will make a soggy dough, and too much handling will make it heavy.

When you can work the dough into a ball, wrap it in wax paper and refrigerate from ½ to 1 hour.

To achieve the proper diameter for rolling out the dough, place it on two sheets of wax paper that slightly overlap and cover it with two more overlapping sheets of wax paper.

Always roll from the center outward, never back and forth. Press down with the rolling pin and roll out the dough in all directions, aiming for a large circle at least 2 inches larger in circumference than the pie plate itself and about ⅛ inch in thickness. Next, gently pull the wax paper from the top of the dough. (If the dough tears, it can be patched.) Take hold of the other piece of wax paper at the corners and lift it and the dough to the pie plate. Turn it over gently to lower the dough over the pie plate. Pull off the remaining paper. Ease the dough into the plate and press gently with your fingertips along the bottom edge. Use a scissors to cut off dangling dough around the rim, leaving *at least* a ½-inch overlap.

To make a raised, fluted edge, tuck under the ½-inch overlap along the rim of the plate. Flute the edge by pinching together the thumb and index finger of your left hand and placing it on the inside of the tuck at the rim. Use the index finger of your right hand to push the tuck into the two fingers of your left hand from the outside. Move all around the rim of the plate with this pushing-into-the-pinch. Or use the back of a fork to press a frill around the rim

As with the tart crust, if your filling is to be gooey or runny, brush the inside of the shell with a frothy egg white and a little sugar.

With many recipes the pie shell should be prebaked. To keep the flaky thing from blistering in the hot oven, cut a piece of foil to fit the pie plate, butter it, arrange it gently over the dough, and weight it down with raw rice, beans, or pebbles. (If you use rice or beans, keep them in a container to be used for the same purpose again and again.)

Bake the shell for 8 minutes. Remove the foil with filling. Turn down the heat to 350° and bake another 5 minutes or until the crust is golden.

Double Crust

If you feel like an upper crust, double the recipe for the pie shell. Divide the dough in half and refrigerate separately in wax paper. When the bottom crust has been made and filled, remove the other ball of dough from the refrigerator and roll it out as you did the first one, leaving a good ½-inch to dangle over the top of the rim. Place the dough over the filling and use the back of a fork to remove the excess dough around the rim of the plate as you press the top and bottom crusts together. Prick the crust with the tines of the fork to let steam escape while baking.

To make a latticed pie, roll out the top half of crust to the proper thickness and cut strips with a pastry wheel. Criss-cross the strips over the pie and trim the edges to fit using a scissors.

GRAHAM CRACKER CRUST

This crust is easy. My daughter used to make it when she was eight years old.

Place one row of graham crackers from the box between two sheets of wax paper. Crush with a rolling pin. Measure to make sure you have

¾ cup graham cracker crumbs.

Add

5 tablespoons melted butter
2 tablespoons grated semisweet chocolate (optional).

Blend the mixture thoroughly and press it evenly across the bottom of a pie plate or an 8-inch springform pan, depending on what you plan to use it for. If it needn't be prebaked, refrigerate for 2 to 3 hours before filling. Otherwise, bake at 300° for 15 minutes.

FRESH FRUIT TARTS

Easy, beautiful, and delicious, with endless possibilities for variation, fresh fruit arranged in a baked tart shell and glazed with fruit jelly is one of the most satisfying desserts. Topped with whipped cream and nuts it's even more special. My favorites should inspire you to invent your own combinations.

STRAWBERRY OR RASPBERRY TART

Use the 9-inch baked tart shell on page 294, still in the pan.

Wash and hull

3 cups strawberries
or
2 cups raspberries.

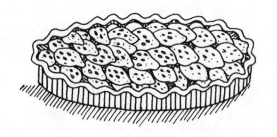

Gently pat the fruit dry before arranging it in circles inside the tart shell. Choose uniform berries or place the largest in the center and grade them downward, ending with a circle of the smallest berries around the edge.

Over low heat in a small saucepan melt

>*1 cup raspberry or apple jelly.*

Add

>*1 tablespoon Grand Marnier or orange liqueur.*

Let the jelly cool to thicken slightly and then spoon it evenly over the fruit. If you like, sprinkle with

>*¼ cup lightly toasted slivered almonds.*

(To toast blanched almonds, heat them in a skillet with a teaspoon peanut oil. Shake the pan until they turn golden and drain on toweling.)

Chill the tart at least ½ hour before serving. Just before serving, remove the rim of the tart pan. They look so pretty, it's a shame to cover the tarts with whipped cream, so I serve the cream in a separate bowl.

BLUEBERRY OR BLACKBERRY TART

Wash and pat dry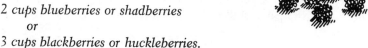

>*2 cups blueberries or shadberries*
>>*or*
>*3 cups blackberries or huckleberries.*

Arrange them evenly across the bottom of a 9-inch baked Tart Crust (page 294).

Melt

>*1 cup currant or damson plum jelly.*

Let it cool a little before spooning it over the fruit. Finish the recipe as described above. Sprinkle with

>*coarsely chopped pecans or walnuts*

and serve with a mixture of

>*1 cup whipped cream*
>*½ cup sour cream.*

Chill. Remove the rim of the pan just before serving.

PEACH TART

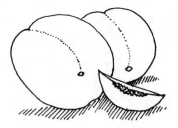

Peel and slice

> *2 pounds of rosy peaches.*

To do so, drop them in boiling water for 30 seconds and remove with a slotted spoon to run under cold water for a second. Slip off the skins.

Cut in half, remove the pits, and slice the peaches evenly. Immediately brush the slices with lemon juice so they won't discolor. Pat dry with toweling. Have ready a 9-inch glazed baked Tart Crust (page 294) and arrange the sliced peaches beautifully in overlapping circles or like a pinwheel across the bottom of the shell.

Melt

> *1 cup beachplum, quince, or currant jelly.*

Add

> *1 tablespoon orange liqueur, rum, or kirschwasser.*

When the jelly has cooled and thickened slightly, spoon it evenly over the fruit. Top with toasted slivered almonds or chopped pecans and remove the rim of the pan. Chill before serving with a separate bowl of whipped cream.

CUSTARD TART OR PIE

If you make this best of all custards, you can spoon it into a glazed baked Tart Crust (page 294) or Pie Crust (page 296). Serve with a little whipped cream. Or, layer the shell with ripe sliced bananas or fresh sliced berries and pour the custard over the fresh fruit. Any way you serve it, it's straight from heaven.

The Custard

Into a bowl sift together

> *5 tablespoons flour*
> *½ cup superfine sugar*
> *a pinch of salt.*

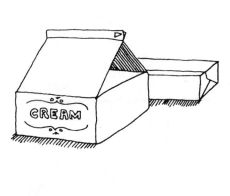

One at a time, beat in

> *3 egg yolks.*

In a saucepan heat

> *2 cups milk with*
> *2 tablespoons butter.*

When the milk starts to bubble around the edge of the pan and the butter has melted, dribble it slowly into the flour-and-egg mixture, whisking briskly as you do so.

Then whisk in

> *1 teaspoon vanilla*
> *2 tablespoons brandy or rum.*

Pour the mixture into a saucepan over medium-low heat and simmer and stir until smooth and thick. Let it cool.

Whip

> *½ cup heavy cream.*

Fold it into the *cool* custard. Pour the custard into the pastry shell and chill.

Graham Cracker Crust (page 298) can be used for this filling too.

HAL'S PECAN PIE

Every November Hal Holden's mama sends me a huge tin of fresh pecans from her own orchard in Mississippi. I put them to immediate use in her son's pie.

Prepare an unbaked Pie Crust (page 296). Prick the bottom and sides of the dough with the tines of a fork and refrigerate the shell until the filling is ready.

Preheat the oven to 350°.

In a large bowl beat until fluffy

>   *3 eggs.*

Beat in

>   *⅔ cup superfine sugar*
>   *a pinch of salt.*

Beat in

>   *1 cup dark corn syrup*
>   *⅓ cup melted butter.*

Fold in

>   *½ cup pecan halves.*

Pour the mixture into the pie shell.

Over the filling, arrange

>   *½ cup pecan halves.*

They may sink a little. Bake the pie about 50 minutes or until a knife or cake tester comes out clean. Cool and serve with a lattice of whipped cream piped over the top.

PEANUT PIE

This pie is similar in its cooking method to the pecan pie, but the flavor is quite different and should appeal to all peanut freaks like me.

Prepare an unbaked Pie Crust (page 296) and refrigerate until ready for filling.

Preheat the oven to 350°.

In a bowl stir together

> *½ cup smooth peanut butter*
> *1½ cups maple syrup*
> *½ cup superfine sugar*
> *6 tablespoons melted butter*
> *¼ teaspoon salt.*

Whisk in

> *3 lightly beaten eggs.*

Fold in

> *⅔ cup unsalted peanuts, coarsely chopped.*

If you're too lazy to husk and peel the skins from fresh peanuts before chopping, already shelled, skinned, and unsalted ones are available in jars.

Pour the filling into the unbaked pastry shell and bake from 50 to 55 minutes or until a toothpick comes out clean. Cool the pie and serve with a topping of whipped cream.

APPLE PIE

Prepare an unbaked Pie Crust (page 296) and refrigerate till needed.

Preheat the oven to 425°.

Peel, core, and thinly slice

> *4–5 large apples*

until you have

> *4 cups apple slices.*

Green apples are best to use, juicy ones are better than dry, and mealy ones *won't do*. As soon as they're sliced, drop them in a bowl of water with the juice of a lemon so they won't discolor.

In a bowl combine

> ⅔ cup sugar
> 1½ tablespoons cornstarch
> a pinch of salt
> a few gratings of nutmeg.

Dry the apple slices with toweling and toss them in the sugar mixture till coated. Then line the pie shell neatly with the slices, overlapping them in circles.

Sprinkle with

> 1 tablespoon lemon juice
> 2 tablespoons cream.

Top with

> 1 teaspoon grated lemon rind
> 2 tablespoons dotted butter.

Set the pie plate on a larger pan in the hot oven in case the juice runs over.

Bake for 15 minutes. Reduce the heat to 350° to bake another 30 minutes. If you want a double crust or latticed pie refer to page 297. It can be served with vanilla ice cream, but I don't think it needs it.

APPLE AND GREEN TOMATO PIE

As a nice variation, make the filling with

> 1 cup green tomato slices
> 3 cups apple slices.

Follow the preceding recipe but eliminate the cream.

JANIE'S BAKED PINEAPPLE (Serves 6)

Jane Eakin is one of my closest friends. She is a *great* painter, already recognized internationally but not yet sufficiently shouted about to suit me. She is also a fruit nut. When I asked her for her marvelous baked pineapple recipe, she wrote: "If you have a really handsome pineapple with a perfect crest, it's a shame to do anything except cut it, crest and all, into lengthwise wedges. It's elegant on a white or glass plate; the rough skin, the lovely yellow of the fruit with its green crest. Sprinkle it with salt and nothing else. Some people might like it sprinkled with a fruit liqueur; Framboise, for instance." Then she added another idea.

The crest can be removed from each piece before spreading the wedges with a good dollop of jam such as Uta's Peach Jam (page 343). Spread them side by side under the broiler on a baking dish for 10 minutes. Place on individual plates and replace the crest before serving. *But,* if your pineapple is less than perfect:

Preheat oven to 350°.

Cut top and bottom from a pineapple. Stand it upright and hold it firmly on a board to slice off the skin from top to bottom all the way around. Remove the brown eyes and any blemishes. Cut the pineapple lengthwise into 4 sections and slice and discard the core from each section. Then cut across the slices to form ½-inch wedges. Cut the wedges in half and arrange all pieces in 1 or 2 layers in a buttered baking dish. Sprinkle lightly with salt.

Over the sliced pineapple wedges pour

> *juice of one orange*
> *or*
> *¼ cup cranberry juice.*

The Top Crust

In a bowl crush about

> *1 dozen plain shortbread cookies.*

Put the crumbs in a bowl and mash them together with

> *4 tablespoons softened butter*
> *½ cup sugar*
> *½ cup chopped pecans or walnuts*
> *2 tablespoons shredded coconut (optional).*

Sprinkle the mixture over the fruit and press down firmly to form a crust.

Dot with

> *2 tablespoons butter.*

Bake for 30 minutes. Serve hot or cold, with or without whipped cream or vanilla ice cream.

PEAR OR APPLE CRISP (Serves 6)

I immediately borrowed the top crust (from the preceding pineapple) to press over sliced pears or apples and consequently discovered two more desserts.

Use

3 ripe but firm pears or 3 large green or juicy apples.

Peel, core, and slice them. Brush the slices with lemon juice and arrange them in the buttered baking dish. Cover with the fruit juice and proceed with the pineapple recipe, omitting the coconut in the crust. Beautiful.

APFEL STRUDEL

Before I leave apples alone, I must make you a present of this recipe. Carefully study the handling and stuffing of Strudel Dough (page 66). Use 2 sheets of strudel or fillo leaves per strudel. The stuffing will be sufficient to make 3 or 4 fat strudel, and each strudel will serve 2 or 3 people. I always make the entire recipe, bake the amount needed for dessert, and place the rest into the freezer in a pan covered with plastic wrap. They will keep for a month and can be thawed and returned to room temperature before baking for another party.

The Stuffing

Peel, core, and coarsely chop

6 green apples (they should equal 6 cups).

Combine them with

1 cup sugar
¼ cup crumbled almond paste (or ½ cup ground almonds)
¾ cup seedless raisins, preferably white ones
2 teaspoons cinnamon
1 tablespoon grated lemon rind
3 tablespoons melted butter.

Stir the mixture to distribute evenly.

Preheat oven to 375°.

Brush the first strudel leaf with melted butter, sprinkle with bread crumbs, cover with the second sheet, and brush with butter and sprinkle with crumbs. At one of the short ends of the top sheet spoon a fat, sausage-shaped roll of filling at least 1½ inches in diameter as described for Peggy's Mushroom Strudel (page 65). Roll up the strudel, flip it onto a buttered baking sheet, brush the top with butter, and proceed to the next strudel. When spooning out the stuffing, leave behind the liquid that will have accumulated at the bottom of the bowl.

Bake for 10 minutes, then lower the heat to 350° to bake another 15 minutes until the strudel are crisp and golden.

Serve plain or with cream or with vanilla ice cream.

Cakes

ZILLY DONOHUE'S LAMB CAKE

When this lamb sits on the table, it really looks like a charming wooly animal, and no one believes that I made it. Surrounded by colored eggs, candles, and a few fresh flowers, it's the very spirit of Easter.

Molds for these cakes are available at kitchen-supply stores and come in many shapes, not just lambs. They're made of two halves of heavy aluminum or iron that lock together. The back is punctured by a few small holes to allow steam to escape during baking. The instructions that come with the mold are explicit. The recipes however are rather boring. A Lady Baltimore cake is used most often, because it's firm and retains the shape of the mold without collapsing. One day, the mother of Nancy Donohue pulled me out of my dilemma with her Golden Cake recipe. Since Nancy is a marvelous actress plus being the very best greeting card artist, her mother, Zilly would obviously be creative too.

Brush both halves of the mold with vegetable oil and sprinkle with flour. Shake the mold to coat the inside evenly, then invert to knock out excess flour. Set aside.

Preheat the oven to 350°.

In the large bowl on the electric mixer, cream

>*1½ sticks softened butter (¾ cup).*

Gradually add

>*1¼ cups superfine sugar.*

Beat until pale and fluffy. One at a time, till well absorbed, beat in

>*8 egg yolks.*

Remove the bowl from the machine. Into a separate bowl sift together

>*2½ cups flour*
>*3 teaspoons baking powder*
>*¼ teaspoon salt.*

Stir the flour mixture slowly into the batter, alternating with

>   ¾ *cup milk.*

Then add

>   *1 teaspoon vanilla*
>   ½ *teaspoon almond or orange extract*
>   *1 teaspoon grated lemon rind.*

Pour the batter into the half mold containing the face, just up to the rim. (Pour any leftover batter into a small oiled and floured loaf pan to bake as a dividend along with the lamb.) Stick a toothpick down into the nose and place a toothpick across each ear to support the extremities when the cake in unmolded. Lock the back of the mold to the front and set the whole thing face down on a baking sheet into the oven for 45 minutes. Test the cake by inserting a toothpick or cake tester into an air vent. When it comes out clean, the cake is done. Cool the mold on a rack for 15 minutes before removing the top half. Let cool another 15 minutes. If necessary, run a knife around the edge of the cake to loosen it, then turn it out on its back to cool on a rack. Don't set it upright until you ice it.

Icing and Decorating the Lamb

Into the top section of a double boiler over boiling water put

>   *2 unbeaten egg whites*
>   *a pinch of cream of tartar.*

Beat in

>   1½ *cups superfine sugar,*

alternating with

>   *5 tablespoons cold water*
>   *2 teaspoons light corn syrup.*

Use an electric, rotary beater if you have one. Otherwise use brisk wrist action with a wire whisk and beat for 7 minutes. Remove the pan from the boiling water and add

>   *1 teaspoon vanilla.*

Continue beating or whisking until the icing cools and thickens enough to spread.

Set the lamb upright on a pretty platter and spread the icing over it with a spatula. Try not to disguise the molded shape of the animal too much.

Before the icing sets, press in

> ½–¾ *cup shredded coconut.*

It should look wooly. Leave the face fairly clear and press two raisins into the eyes or stick them in with broken toothpick ends. Do the same at the side of the mouth with a sliver of maraschino cherry as if the tongue were sticking out. Tie a ribbon around the neck and surround the base of the lamb with colored or chocolate eggs or jelly beans. Place it in the center of the table with yellow candles and a bunch of daffodils. Now it's Easter.

Cheesecakes

A really fine cheesecake is more American than apple pie. After much hunting, I came up with these corkers.

MARGOT'S CHEESECAKE

Margot Breier, one of my gifted students, gave me this recipe for a very firm and special cheesecake.

Line the bottom of an 8-inch cheesecake springform pan with the simple Graham Cracker Crust (page 298). Omit the grated chocolate and bake it for 15 minutes at 350°. Set it aside. Leave the oven at 350°.

In the large bowl on the electric mixer cream till soft and fluffy

> *2 8-ounce packages softened cream cheese.*

Gradually add

> *¾ cup superfine sugar.*

One at a time until each is absorbed, beat in

> *5 eggs.*

Add

> *2 teaspoons vanilla.*

Pour the mixture over the crumb crust and smooth off the top. Bake for 30 minutes. Cool, then refrigerate at least 4 hours. Remove the side of the springform pan before serving. It needs no embellishments.

CHOCOLATE CHEESECAKE

Perfection!

Make the Graham Cracker Crust with grated chocolate (page 298). Press it firmly into the bottom of the 8-inch springform pan. Refrigerate the crust. (Don't bake it yet.)

Preheat the oven to 350°.

In the small bowl on the electric mixer beat until fluffy

>   *3 eggs.*

Gradually add

>   *1 cup superfine sugar.*

Continue beating until the mixture is thick and light yellow. Remove the bowl from the machine. Wash and replace the beaters. In the large bowl on the mixer beat

>   *3 8-ounce packages of softened cream cheese.*

When fluffy, remove the bowl from the machine and beat in the sugar-egg mixture by hand.

Over simmering water in the top of a double boiler put

>   *12 ounces (1 package) semisweet chocolate bits*
>   *1½ sticks unsalted butter*
>   *1 cup sour cream*
>   *2 teaspoons vanilla.*

Stir occasionally until the butter and chocolate have melted and the mixture is smooth. Then fold it into the cream-cheese mixture. Fold in

¾ cup chopped pecans or walnuts.

Pour the batter over the crumb crust in the pan and bake for 1¼ hours. Cool it in the pan in the oven with the heat off and the door ajar. Then refrigerate overnight before removing it from the pan. It can be topped with whipped cream.

NUTTY CREAM-CHEESE CAKE

Place on a baking sheet into a 400° oven for 10 minutes

½ pound shelled hazelnuts or blanched almonds.

Stir them a few times and remove when toasted and golden. Grind them in the blender, or even better in a Mouli grater for fluffier texture. You should have

1½ cups ground, roasted nuts.

Set them aside.

Butter the inside of an 8-inch springform pan. Sprinkle it with

¼ cup graham cracker crumbs.

Shake the pan around to coat the bottom and especially the sides of the pan. Then press the Graham Cracker Crust (page 298) into the bottom of the pan. Refrigerate till needed.

Preheat the oven to 325°.

In the large bowl on the electric mixer beat

3 8-ounce packages softened cream cheese.

When fluffy, gradually add

1 ¾ cups superfine sugar.

Beat till the sugar is absorbed and then, one at a time until each is absorbed, beat in

4 eggs.

Dribble in while beating

½ cup heavy cream
2 teaspoons vanilla.

Remove the bowl from the machine and fold in the ground nuts. Pour the mixture over the crust in the pan and bake the cake for 1¼ hours. Cool in the oven with the heat off and the door ajar. Refrigerate at least 6 hours. Unmold. Serve. Eat your hearts out.

Tortes

Once you try these divinities, you'll never bake another "cake." They're bound by ground nuts and sometimes a few bread crumbs, using little or no flour.

HAZELNUT TORTE

This torte can be baked in one 8-inch springform pan and cut in half, filled, and reassembled. It's beautifully crumbly, so I prefer baking it in two pans to eliminate the cutting.

Preheat the oven to 275°.

Butter 2 8-ounce springform pans and sprinkle with

> *a few tablespoons quick-mix flour.*

Shake, tilt, and turn the pans till completely coated with flour. Invert to knock out excess. Set the pans aside.

Into the large bowl on the electric mixer put

> *6 egg whites (from extra-large or jumbo eggs).*

Beat the whites till almost stiff and then gradually, 1 tablespoon at a time, beat in

> *½ cup superfine sugar.*

When the whites are very stiff and the sugar has been absorbed, remove the bowl and set aside. Don't wash the beaters. Into the small bowl on the mixer put

> *6 egg yolks.*

Beat until pale yellow. Then, 1 tablespoon at a time, beat in

> *½ cup superfine sugar.*

When the yolk mixture is thick, remove the bowl from the machine and use a spoon to beat in

> *1½ cups ground hazelnuts (ground with the Mouli grater or in the blender).*

Stir in

> *⅓ cup fine bread crumbs.*

The batter should be thick. Beat in ¼ of the stiff whites to lighten the batter. Pour it into a larger bowl and over the top of the batter sprinkle

> 2 tablespoons quick-mix flour.

Carefully fold in the remaining egg whites until no white lumps are visible, but don't overfold.

Divide the batter between the two springform pans, smooth off the tops, and bake for 35 minutes. Unless the torte has shrunk slightly from the sides of the pan, bake another five minutes. Set the pans to cool on a rack and remove the sides of the pan. (Loosen from the pans with a knife, if needed.) Cool completely before filling.

Filling and Assembling

Beat until stiff

> 1½ cups heavy cream.

Fold in

> 3 tablespoons sifted confectioner's sugar
> 2 teaspoons vanilla.

Place one torte on a platter and cover with at least ½ inch of filling. Place the other torte on the filling and use the remaining cream to mask top and sides of the completed *Haselnuss Torte*, as we say in Vienna.

Sprinkle with

> ¼ cup ground hazelnuts.

Refrigerate for about 1 hour and serve. *Schön!*

CHOCOLATE NUT TORTE

By special request I just baked this torte again for Herbert's birthday.

Preheat the oven to 350°.

Butter two 8-inch springform pans. Sprinkle with a tablespoon or so of quick-mix flour, shake, tilt, and turn to coat with flour, then invert to knock out the excess. Set to one side.

Preferably in the Mouli grater, otherwise in the electric blender, grind

> ½ pound shelled pecans or walnuts.

You should set aside

> 1½ cups ground nuts.

Separate

> *7 jumbo or extra-large eggs.*

Stir, don't beat, the yolks together with

> *¾ cup superfine sugar.*

When the sugar has dissolved set the mixture aside to rest. Into the top part of a double boiler over simmering water put

> *8 ounces semisweet chocolate bits*
> *1 stick plus 2 tablespoons butter (10 tablespoons).*

Stir occasionally until smooth. Blend the chocolate mixture into the egg-yolk mixture.

Remove one cup of the butter-chocolate-yolk-sugar mixture and set aside to cool to be used later for the icing.

Into the remaining mixture fold the ground nuts.

In the large bowl on the electric mixer, beat the egg whites with a pinch of salt until stiff. Then beat ¼ of the whites into the chocolate mixture to lighten it. Fold in the remaining whites gently and quickly until no lumps are visible.

Divide the batter equally between the two prepared pans and smooth out the tops.

Bake for 45 minutes. The tortes are done when they have pulled slightly away from the sides of the pan and are springy when you press the tops.

Set to cool on a rack, loosening the sides with a sharp knife. When completely cool, remove the side of the springform pans. Use a long knife to loosen one torte from its tin bottom and slide it onto a cake platter. Spread the top with

> *½–¾ cup apricot jam.*

Remove the other torte from its tin bottom and place it over the jam on the first one.

If the icing that has been set aside isn't thick enough to spread, refrigerate it for ½ hour, then spread evenly over the top and sides of the assembled Chocolate Nut Torte. Chop

> *½ cup pecans or walnuts coarsely.*

Press them into the icing around the sides of the torte.

> Even better the next day.

MANDEL TORTE (Almond Torte)

Preheat the oven to 300°.

Into a bowl crumble

>*4 ounces almond paste (½ package or can.)*

Work it through with your fingers until as soft as possible.

Into the large bowl on the electric mixer put

>*4 egg whites (from extra-large or jumbo eggs).*

Beat until almost stiff. One tablespoon at a time, beat in

>*¼ cup superfine sugar*
>*a pinch of salt.*

When quite stiff, remove the bowl from the machine, and set aside. Don't wash the beaters. In the small bowl on the electric mixer cream

>*1 stick softened butter (8 tablespoons).*

Gradually beat in

>*¼ cup superfine sugar.*

One at a time until each is absorbed, beat in

>*4 egg yolks.*

Remove the bowl from the machine and use a wooden spoon to beat in the crumbled almond paste until the batter is fairly smooth. Then fold in

>*½ cup ground blanched almonds*
>*⅓ cup fine dry bread crumbs.*

Beat in ¼ of the stiff egg whites to lighten the batter. Pour the batter into a larger bowl and gently fold in the remaining whites. Don't overfold. Pour the batter into a buttered 8-inch springform pan and bake for 45 minutes or until the sides shrink slightly from the edge of the pan. Cool on a rack and immediately remove the side of the springform pan.

The torte can be served sprinkled with confectioner's sugar and dotted with toasted slivered almonds. It can also be brushed with this lovely glaze:

In a bowl combine

>*2 cups confectioner's sugar*
>*1 frothily beaten egg white*
>*1½ tablespoons rum or brandy*
>*1 teaspoon lemon juice.*

Stir till smooth and brush the glaze over the top and sides of the torte. Sprinkle with toasted slivered almonds. Refrigerate before serving. Sometimes I think it's even better the next day.

Meringues

Because many recipes call for just egg yolks, the whites have a way of accumulating. I keep them in a covered jar in the refrigerator, adding to them as I go along, so that whenever I feel down in the dumps, I can whip up a batch of meringues to cheer myself up. Meringues conjure up images of my mother in our cozy kitchen, of licking spoons and pans, of waiting by the oven to get a taste of a kiss even before it had cooled. *Küsschen* or Little Kisses are appropriately named: gentle, airy, sweet, and slightly crunchy before melting in your mouth. Of course meringues can be made in many forms. They retain the exact shape given them when placed in the oven because they don't rise, sink, or spread while baking. They're a challenge to artistic skill with spoon, spatula, or pastry tube.

Use an electric beater, otherwise it will take long, tedious beating by hand. If you remember to add the sugar little by little after the eggs have begun to stiffen, they won't deflate. Remember to bake meringues in a very low oven and you will always have success.

BASIC MERINGUE BATTER

Because the size of eggs is so variable, measure the whites. It usually takes

> *4 egg whites to equal ½ a cup.*

Let the whites come to room temperature for easier whipping.

Sift

> *¾ cup confectioner's sugar with*
> *½ cup superfine sugar*
> *a pinch of salt.*

Beat the whites in the large bowl on the mixer. When they're frothy, add

> *⅛ teaspoon cream of tartar.*

Continue beating. When they begin to stiffen add

> *1 tablespoon of the sifted sugar.*

Continue adding it by the tablespoon every 20 to 30 seconds as the beating continues. The entire operation should take 5 to 10 minutes. Halfway through add

> ½ teaspoon vanilla.

At the end add another

> ½ teaspoon vanilla.

Place the meringue, in whatever form, on a lightly oiled and floured baking sheet. Preheat the oven from 180° to 200° and you'll be ready for many things.

KISSES

If meringues are new to you, kisses are nice to start with. They're easy to shape, can be stored for weeks in a closed tin in the refrigerator, and are pleasant to have on hand for young or old surprise visitors.

Place dollops of basic meringue batter, the size of a lemon, on a lightly greased and flowered baking sheet. Slide them from a spoon with your finger. Space them so they won't touch each other. They don't need anything else, but it's fun to top each one with an almond, hazelnut, pecan, or walnut. You can also sprinkle them with colored sugar nonpareils or chocolate beads.

Leave them in the oven for 45 minutes. They should remain white but be firm to touch. Let them cool in the oven with the door ajar and the heat turned off for another hour.

Serve at once or store in sealed tins or plastic bags. They improve with age. They are a nice accompaniment to fruit desserts, with a mousse or pudding.

Variations

1) Pinch two kisses together with a layer of ice cream in between. Place them on their sides on a plate and cover with chocolate sauce.

2) Chocolate Kisses. When the meringue batter is completed, fold in

> 2 tablespoons sifted, unsweetened cocoa.

Place these kisses about 1½ inches apart because they may flatten out while baking.

3) Nut Kisses. Add

> ⅓ cup superfine sugar

to the basic batter while beating it. When completed, fold in

> ¾ cup ground nuts.

Hazelnuts are my favorites. Also space these kisses further apart on the baking sheet in case they flatten out.

ZEPHYR TORTE (Serves 8)

A huge decorated meringue shell filled with fruit and cream, it will get you an ovation when you bring it to the table. Once you understand how the torte is fluted out in rings and "glued" together with meringue batter, you can invent your own shapes and shells to fill with ice cream, mousse, or custard.

To make this torte, double the ingredients for the Basic Meringue Batter (page 316).

Lightly grease 2 large baking sheets and sprinkle both with flour. Shake them to distribute the flour. Invert to knock off the excess.

To make a visible ring, press the rim of an 8-inch cake pan into the flour. Place another ring near it without touching the first ring. Press the pan onto the second baking sheet to make two more visible rings. If you're planning to make a lid for the torte, make a fifth ring.

Fill a pastry bag with the batter. (Handling a pastry bag is described on page 19.) Pipe a circle just inside of the first ring and keep going in circles toward the center until the ring is filled in and you have a solid layer about ½-inch high. Smooth the top of this ring with a spatula; it will be the base of the torte. Inside three other rings pipe single circles, each one as high as possible. These will be for the sides of the torte. Now, if you're planning a lid, make another solid circle the way you did for the base. Wherever you find free space within the single circles, pipe out a few rosettes with the star nozzle, about 24 in all. (Make a cluster of rosettes on the center of the lid and stud the edges with evenly spaced rosettes.) Reserve leftover meringue batter for later.

Bake in the lowest possible oven heat for 1 hour.

To assemble, slip the bottom disc from the baking sheet and place it on an ovenproof platter. Dot it every ½ inch around the edge with a dab of the reserve meringue batter and "glue" one of the single rings to the base. Proceed with the next two rings, gluing them one on top of the other with dabs of unbaked batter. Remove the rosettes from the baking sheet and dab batter on the back to stick them around the sides of the torte in a pretty design and (if you're not making a lid) stick them all around the top of the last ring, evenly spaced. Replace the assembled shell in the oven for 15 minutes. Turn off the heat and let the shell dry out for another hour with the door ajar.

To make the simplest filling, beat until stiff

> *1½ cups heavy cream.*

Fold in

> *2 tablespoons sifted confectioner's sugar*
> *2 tablespoons brandy*
> *2 cups fresh strawberries or sliced peaches.*

It really isn't complicated for something so special.

FILLED MERINGUE TART (Serves 6)

Lightly butter an ovenproof platter and sprinkle with a little flour. Shake the platter to coat it and then invert to knock off excess flour.

Preheat the oven to 200°.

Make the Basic Meringue Batter (page 316) and mound the batter into a high circular ring with a hole for the filling in the center. Use a spatula to smooth it off, swirling or fluting the sides. Put it in the warm oven for 1¼ hours until quite firm to the touch. Turn off the oven and leave the door ajar and let the meringue rest in the oven another hour or so.

Fill the center with fresh or drained frozen fruit folded into a cup of whipped cream.

Sauce Sublime (page 334) really sets this off, but it's not a must.

CHOCOLATE NUT MERINGUE (Serves 6)

Three layers of nut meringue piled on top of each other filled with layers of chocolate mousse. Need I say more?

Much of the procedure is the same as Zephyr Torte (preceding recipe).

Butter and flour 1 or 2 baking sheets and press the rim of 8-inch cake pans into the floured surface to make 3 visible rings and set them aside. (If you can fit 3 rings on one sheet, fine.)

Use a Mouli grater or the blender to grind

> *1½ cups blanched almonds.*

Mix the grated nuts in a bowl with

> *1 cup superfine sugar.*

Stir nuts and sugar till there are no lumps. Over the nuts and sugar sift

> 1½ tablespoons cornstarch.

Stir again and set aside.

Preheat the oven to 225°.

Make a meringue batter in the large bowl on the electric mixer by beating till frothy

> 6 egg whites (¾ cup).

Add

> a pinch of salt
> ⅛ teaspoon cream of tartar.

Beat till quite stiff before adding, one at a time

> 6 tablespoons superfine sugar.

When the sugar is well incorporated remove the bowl from the machine.

Fold in

> 1 teaspoon vanilla
> ⅛ teaspoon almond extract.

Fold the sugared nuts into the meringue about ¼ of the amount at a time.

Use the largest round nozzle of your pastry bag or just the hole of the bag without a nozzle so the nuts can pass through. Fill the bag with batter and pipe it in circles inside the markers on the baking sheet. Work from the outside in to form 3 solid discs. When all 3 circles are complete (about ½ inch thick), bake them for 45 minutes.

Turn off the heat and leave the door ajar while they rest another ½ hour. Then cool on a rack before filling and icing with Chocolate Mousse (page 322). Spread the mousse between the layers of meringue and use it to ice the top and sides of this assembled wonder. Sprinkle with toasted almonds.

SCHAUMTORTE (Serves 6)

In German, *Schaum* means froth, and this is certainly a frothy delight; meringues and cake baked at the same time and filled with fruit and cream. Bake it the day before you serve it and fill it an hour before bringing it to the table.

Butter 2 8-inch springform pans and sprinkle with flour. Shake the pans to coat bottoms and sides, invert to knock out excess flour, and set aside.

Preheat the oven to 300°.

In the large bowl on the electric mixer cream

> ½ *stick softened butter (4 tablespoons).*

Add gradually

> ½ *cup superfine sugar.*

When well absorbed, continue beating while you add, one at a time till each is absorbed,

> *4 egg yolks.*

Add

> *1 teaspoon vanilla.*

Into another bowl sift

> *1 cup cake flour*
> *1 teaspoon baking powder*
> *a pinch of salt.*

Remove the bowl from the machine and use a wooden spoon to stir the flour mixture into the batter a little at a time, alternating with

> *6 tablespoons heavy cream.*

When the batter is smooth, divide it equally between the 2 buttered pans.

Wash out the bowl of the mixer and the beaters to make the Basic Meringue Batter (page 316), using 6 tablespoons instead of ¼ cup of the *superfine* sugar. When very thick, divide the batter in half and pile it in each pan directly over the cake batter. Smooth off the tops. Sprinkle one of the meringue toppings with

> ¼ *cup blanched, shredded almonds.*

Bake the 2 cakes for 45 minutes. Remove them from the oven to cool in their pans on a rack. Cover the pans with plastic and refrigerate till the next day. Should the meringue sink or crack while cooling or assembling, don't worry. They'll be masked with cream and the taste will be unaltered.

Filling and Assembling

Whip till stiff

> *1 cup heavy cream.*

Fold in

> 2 tablespoons sifted confectioner's sugar
> 2 tablespoons brandy or orange liqueur.

Into the sweetened cream fold

> 1 cup drained, mashed pineapple
> > or
> 1 cup mashed, drained peaches.

Remove the cakes from the springform pans. Take the one without the slivered almonds and put it on a cake plate, meringue side *down*. Spread the cream filling over the cake about ½ inch thick. Place the second cake on the filling, meringue and almond side *up*. Use the remaining cream and fruit to swirl over the top and sides of the assembled Schaumtorte and refrigerate for at least ½ hour before serving.

Mousse

I don't think anything can top the speed, ease, or deliciousness of a chocolate mousse. It's not only good served all by itself, but can be used as filling in tarts, pies, and cakes. So can lemon mousse. As with most classic dishes, the ingredients and methods of preparation vary a good deal, and I've experimented to produce my favorites.

UTA'S TEN-MINUTE CHOCOLATE MOUSSE (Serves 4)

Divide

> 4 eggs, jumbo or extra large.

Put the yolks in the small bowl and the whites in the large bowl on the electric mixer.

Into a Pyrex measuring cup put

> 4 ounces semisweet chocolate bits.

Just cover the chocolate with boiling water and let stand for 5 minutes.

Meanwhile, beat the egg whites with a pinch of salt till stiff. Remove the bowl (don't change the beaters) and replace it with the small bowl. Beat the yolks till lemon colored, then gradually add

⅓ cup superfine sugar.

When the yolk mixture is thick, tip the Pyrex cup to pour off all the water, holding back the chocolate with a rubber scraper. Turn the melted chocolate into the yolk mixture and beat till well blended. Remove the bowl from the machine and fold in

1–2 tablespoons Grand Marnier.

Beat in ¼ of the beaten egg whites to lighten the mousse. Then quickly but carefully fold in the remaining whites until no lumps are visible. Pour the mousse into a pretty bowl and refrigerate at least one hour before serving with cream or whipped cream. *Et voilà!*

Before chilling, the mousse can be sprinkled with toasted, slivered almonds.

When using it for icing or filling, spread it on *before* chilling while still soft.

MOUSSE TORTE (Serves 6)

It works! It's easy! It's *formidable!*

Preheat the oven to 350°.

Make double the recipe for Chocolate Mousse.

Butter a 9 inch Pyrex pie plate and sprinkle with

1½–2 tablespoons fine dry bread crumbs.

Toss and turn the plate till coated with crumbs and knock out the excess.

Fill the plate just to the rim with some of the completed chocolate mousse. Smooth off the top.

Bake for 25 minutes and cool on a rack for at least 1 hour. It will sink to form a thick crust in the plate as it cools. Pour the remaining mousse, which will have rested at room temperature, into the cool crust. Smooth off the top and sprinkle with toasted slivered almonds. (Toast them in a skillet in a teaspoon of peanut oil for a few minutes, shaking the skillet vigorously.)

Chill the mousse torte for at least 3 hours. Pipe a lattice of whipped cream over the top and bring it to the table while the guests sing the Halleluja chorus.

MOCHA MOUSSE (Serves 4)

Make the Ten-Minute Chocolate Mousse (page 322), adding

> *2 tablespoons instant powdered or granulated coffee*

to the chocolate bits before covering with boiling water. Finish the recipe.

LEMON MOUSSE (Serves 6)

Grate the rind of two lemons.

Set the gratings aside and squeeze the juice of both lemons into a small bowl. Sprinkle

> *1 envelope gelatin over*
> *¼ cup lemon juice.*

Let the gelatin soften 5 minutes. Separate

> *4 extra-large eggs.*

Put the yolks into the small bowl and the whites into the large bowl of the mixer. Beat the whites till stiff with a pinch of salt. Then *gradually* beat in

> *¼ cup superfine sugar.*

Set the whites aside. Don't change the beaters. Beat the yolks until lemon colored. Slowly beat in until quite thick

> *½ cup superfine sugar*
> *grated lemon rind.*

Remove the bowl from the machine.

In a small saucepan, heat the lemon juice and gelatin and stir until dissolved. (Don't let it boil.) Trickle it into the yolk mixture whisking all the while.

In a separate bowl whip till stiff

> *¾ cup heavy cream.*

Be sure the yolk mixture is quite cool before folding in the whipped cream.

Finally, fold in the beaten egg whites.

Pour the mixture into a pretty bowl or individual bowls. Sprinkle the top with toasted slivered almonds and refrigerate for at least 3 hours. Serve with a dollop of whipped cream. It'll melt in your mouth.

BRAZILIAN MOUSSE MARCUS (Serves 4)

My good friend Jim Marcus once made me this incredibly easy dessert. I believed neither the procedure nor the splendid results until I made it myself. He learned it from his children's Brazilian nanny.

Use

> 1 14-ounce can of sweetened condensed milk.

Put the *unopened* can into a large pot and cover it by several inches with water. Cover the pot and simmer 4 to 5 hours. Check every now and then to see that the bubbling water still covers the can. Remove the can and let it cool before opening both top and bottom with a can opener. Slip the solid mass of caramelly "mousse" onto a serving plate. It can be topped with shredded coconut, served with cream, whipped cream, or vanilla ice cream. If you're mean don't tell how it was made. If you're nice, do tell— no one will believe you.

Other Desserts

ZABAGLIONE, OR WEIN SCHAUM (Serves 4)

My mother used to make me this warm, creamy dessert when I was sick. I have no idea what its medicinal purpose could have been, but I remember it always cheered me up and made me feel pampered.

In the small bowl on the electric mixer beat

> 4 egg yolks.

Beat for three minutes until very thick while slowly adding

> ⅔ cup confectioner's sugar.

Set the bowl with the sugar-yolk mixture over a pot of boiling water, making sure the bowl doesn't touch the water. Continue beating with a wire whisk or an electric hand-held beater while dribbling in

> ¼ cup dry marsala, sherry, or Rose Hip Wine (page 360).

Beat 5 minutes longer. The zabaglione will thicken and increase in bulk. When you lift the beater, if it forms peaks, it's done. Serve at once in glass bowls or goblets.

COLD ZABAGLIONE (Serves 4 to 6)

I prefer cold zabaglione to hot, because I can make it a day ahead of time and don't need to work in the kitchen just before the dessert.

In the small bowl on the mixer beat

> *4 egg yolks.*

Gradually add

> *⅔ cup confectioner's sugar*
> *the peel of half a lemon.*

When the mixture is very thick, remove the bowl from the machine and fish out the lemon peel. If all the pieces are hard to find, continue fishing them out as they surface during further whisking.

Place the bowl over, not touching, a pot of boiling water as for hot zabaglione and whisk for 5 minutes, slowly adding

> *¼ cup dry marsala or sherry.*

When the beaten yolks form peaks as the beater is lifted, set the bowl aside.

In a small bowl soften

> *1 teaspoon gelatin (⅓ of an envelope) in*
> *1½ tablespoons brandy.*

After 5 minutes pour in 1½ tablespoons boiling water and stir till the gelatin is dissolved. Trickle this mixture into the zabaglione. When completely cool, fold in

> *1 cup heavy cream whipped till stiff.*

Pour the mixture into pretty bowls or one large one and chill at least 4 hours. Serve with an extra dollop of whipped cream.

LINDA'S UNBELIEVABLY GOOD AND EASY CHOCOLATE SOUFFLÉ (Serves 4 to 6)

Linda Urmy McGuire is not just a lovely actress but her culinary skills are such that she even *teaches* cooking. She made me this chocolate dream one evening and I've been copying her ever since.

Preheat the oven to 375°.

Butter a standard soufflé dish or a deep round casserole. Sprinkle the dish with

> *2 tablespoons sugar.*

Shake, turn, and tip it until thoroughly coated. Knock out the excess.

Melt

> *6 ounces semisweet chocolate bits*

using my trick (page 21).

Make the cream sauce for the base of the soufflé in your largest heavy skillet by melting

> *3 tablespoons butter*

and blending in

> *3 tablespoons quick-mix flour.*

Add

> *1 cup hot milk*

and whisk the sauce until it thickens and turns smooth. Still using the whisk, blend in

> *⅓ cup superfine sugar*
> *2 tablespoons coffee*
> *the melted chocolate*
> *1 tablespoon vanilla.*

Whisk till smooth and thick before removing from the heat.

Separate

> *6 eggs.*

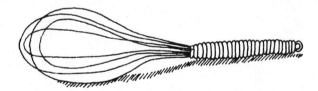

Whisk the yolks into the sauce one at a time until each one is absorbed. In a separate bowl beat the egg whites with a pinch of salt until they form stiff peaks. Beat ¼ of the stiff whites into the chocolate mixture to lighten it. Then gently pour the chocolate mixture into the bowl with the remaining whites and fold in the whites.

Turn the soufflé into the buttered, sugared dish and bake for 30 minutes. Serve it with

> *1 pint of softened vanilla ice cream.*

You'll think you're in heaven!

RØDE GRØDE MED FLØDE

The literal translation is mundane for something that tastes as though it had come from the garden of Eden. It means "red gruel with cream." It used to be quite a production when my Danish mom made it in the days before the electric blender. Now it takes just a few minutes to prepare. I sometimes wonder if my guests ask for it because they love it, or because they love to hear me pronounce it. You have to pucker your mouth forward fish-fashion to make the Ø sound. My good friend Thomas Tryon once wrote it out phonetically: Erreurdagrreuedamedfluerda. This pronunciation clearly has an American accent. In any event, whip up a batch. Then all *your* friends will ask you for the recipe.

The classic Danish dish is made of fresh raspberries, but you can use fresh or frozen raspberries, strawberries, even blackberries, or make combinations.

Wash and hull

> *1½ pounds fresh berries*
> *or thaw*
> *2 10-ounce packages frozen berries.*

Place the fruit in the blender and purée 15 seconds. Strain the fruit through a fine sieve into a large saucepan. Take a few minutes to stir briskly and push down on the fruit till nothing remains in the sieve except seeds.

Into the fruit in the saucepan stir

> *½ cup superfine sugar.*

Bring the mixture to a boil, stirring all the while. Turn down the heat and simmer another few minutes. Skim off the foam.

If you want clear gruel, use arrowroot to thicken; if you don't care that the gruel is a little cloudy, use cornstarch. Make a smooth paste of

> *2 tablespoons arrowroot (or cornstarch)*
> *2 tablespoons cold water.*

Stir the paste into the simmering fruit. As soon as it starts to thicken, remove from heat.

Pour into small glass bowls or one large one and refrigerate for at least 3 hours before serving. Then pass around a pitcher of cold heavy cream to let each person help himself.

STUFFED PEACHES (Serves 6)

I sometimes dream of this dessert during the months when fresh peaches aren't available. When they are—watch out!

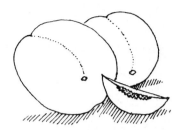

Preheat the oven to 350°.

Select

> 6 ripe peaches with rosy cheeks.

Dip the fruit into boiling water for 30 seconds to slip off the skins. Cut them in half and remove the pits. Rub the peaches with lemon juice so they won't discolor. With a knife or sharp-edged spoon, scoop out the cavity (about ⅓ the peach half). Put the peach pulp you've removed into the electric blender.

In a shallow buttered baking dish arrange 12 peach halves side by side, cavity side up.

To the pulp in the blender, add

> 4 tablespoons softened butter
> 2 egg yolks
> 2 tablespoons sugar
> 1 tablespoon vanilla
> ¼ cup crumbled, softened almond paste.

If you can't get almond paste in a can or package, substitute 6 small, stale, crumbled almond macaroons.

Blend the mixture till quite smooth and divide it among the peach cavities. Dot generously with butter and bake 20 to 30 minutes or until the stuffing is golden. Remove the dish from the oven and baste the peaches with the juice in the dish. Serve hot accompanied by heavy cream. Or let the peaches cool, then cover with plastic and refrigerate for at least 4 hours. Serve with cream. Wow!

Note: When making only 4 peaches, I make the same amount of stuffing. Whatever is left I freeze in a sealed jar. The next time I make the peaches, I thaw the stuffing, replace it in the blender with the pulp from the new peaches, and have enough stuffing for a fresh batch.

THOMAS TRYON'S STUFFED PEARS (Serves 4)

Tom, who wrote the only movie I ever made, along with many best-selling novels, put me up to these pears. (In fact, that gorgeous man put me up to this cookbook too.)

With a vegetable peeler, peel

> *4 firm but ripe pears.*

Cut them in half, allowing the stem to stay attached to one half. Scoop out the core and a little of the pulp, leaving a smooth round cavity. Brush the pears with lemon juice so they won't discolor. Beat till soft

> *2 ounces roquefort, blue, or (if you can stand Tom's favorite) Gorgonzola cheese*
> *2 tablespoons butter.*

When the butter and cheese are blended together and quite fluffy, stuff the cavities of the pears. Press the pear halves together. The cheese will make them stick.

In the blender grind

> *a handful of walnuts.*

Spread the nuts on wax paper and roll the pears in the nuts until well coated. Arrange on a plate and refrigerate for 2 hours or more before serving.

The topper is that Tom likes his with a side dish of vanilla ice cream. I don't!

HOMEMADE APPLESAUCE

Wash and quarter no less than 2 quarts of apples. (Of course applesauce can be made in much larger batches.) They don't need peeling or coring. Put them in a kettle and barely cover with water. Let them come to a boil, lower the heat, and simmer till tender (15 to 30 minutes). Put them through a food mill or mash through a coarse sieve. Place the purée into a saucepan and stir in enough sugar to taste. (Apples vary in sweetness.)

Add

> *1–2 tablespoons lemon juice to taste.*

That's it.

APPLESAUCE PUDDING (Serves 4 to 6)

A simple but comforting dessert to serve in fall or winter after roast pork or chicken or after sausages in lentil soup. If you've just been given some newly picked apples or crab apples, you may want to use

> *1 quart fresh applesauce (preceding page).*

Otherwise use

> *1 16-ounce can or jar of applesauce.*

Pour it into a deep baking dish or casserole and stir in

> *2 egg yolks*
> *2–4 tablespoons brown sugar*
> *½ teaspoon cinnamon*
> *½ teaspoon nutmeg*
> *1 tablespoon melted butter*
> *1 teaspoon vanilla or ¼ teaspoon almond extract*
> *½ teaspoon grated lemon rind.*

Preheat the oven to 325°.

Make a light meringue topping by beating till stiff

> *2 egg whites with*
> *a pinch of cream of tartar.*

Slowly beat in

> *6 tablespoons sifted confectioner's sugar.*

Fold in

> *½ teaspoon vanilla.*

Pile this topping over the applesauce pudding, swirling it attractively. Sprinkle the meringue with ½ teaspoon grated lemon rind. Bake for 30 minutes and serve at once. Or cool before refrigerating to serve when you like.

GLAZED ORANGES (Serves 6)

Gorgeous looking, cool, and delicious, this is a marvelous dessert after a heavy meal.

Use

> *6 large navel eating oranges.*

Peel the skins with a vegetable peeler so you'll have only the orange skin and none of the white membrane underneath. Chop the peelings coarsely or, if you want to be elegant, cut them into 1-inch-long strips less than ⅛ inch wide. Place the chopped or sliced peel into a saucepan with a little water and a pinch of baking soda and simmer for 10 minutes until tender. Drain in a sieve and rinse under cold water. Pat dry with toweling and place in a small bowl with

> *2 tablespoons Grand Marnier or orange liqueur.*

Stir to coat with liqueur and set aside.

Slice the remaining rind from the bottom of each orange, then cut out the navel core at the top. Make 6 evenly spaced slits from top to bottom just the thickness of the rind and pull off the sections of rind and discard. Pull off or peel as much of the remaining white membrane as possible so the fruit will be sleek and smooth. If the orange won't stand upright, slice off a little more of the bottom.

In a saucepan over low heat melt

> *1 8-ounce jar of orange marmalade (or raspberry jelly).*

Add

> *2 tablespoons Grand Marnier or orange liqueur.*

Stir 3 tablespoons of this mixture into the bowl of orange peel. Then roll each orange separately in the melted jelly, so it will be a little sticky, and place it upright on a pretty plate. While the remaining jelly is cooling a little, cut small petal shapes from

> *a few red maraschino cherries*

and leaves from

> *a few green maraschino cherries.*

Arrange a little red flower with green leaves over the navel core of each orange. Divide the remaining jelly among the 6 oranges, drizzling it carefully over the top to let run down the sides.

Chill for several hours. Just before serving, spoon the orange peel and liqueur around the base of the oranges. Serve with a fork and sharp knife.

HAL'S BANANAS FLAMBÉ (Serves 2)

Another of Hal Holden's southern treats!

If you have a chafing dish, these bananas are fun to make at the table for two people at a time. If not, use a large skillet on the stove. The given recipe is for two and can be made in batches, but I sometimes double it and make it for four people at a time.

Stir over medium heat till well blended.

> *2 tablespoons butter with*
> *4 tablespoons brown sugar.*

Add

> *1 peeled, sliced, or halved ripe banana.*

Turn up the heat and sauté till well coated by butter and sugar. Then add

> *a pinch of cinnamon*
> *1 ounce banana liqueur*
> *2 ounces rum.*

Light a match to the contents of the skillet. (Invite the guests to watch the flambéing, it's half the fun.) Swoosh the pan till the flames have subsided and pour the contents into individual bowls over scoops of vanilla ice cream.

BILL'S FRUIT POTPOURRI WITH CHAMPAGNE (Serves 8 to 10)

That brilliant actor Bill Herndon, who is so little kitchen-oriented that he eats his breakfast at a restaurant, sometimes gives dinner parties with a little outside help. I showed him how to make this effortless but gala dessert.

In a pretty bowl combine 6 packages frozen fruit. For instance:

> *2 packages frozen raspberries*
> *2 packages frozen peaches*
> *2 packages frozen pineapple chunks.*

(*Don't* use already combined fruit packages containing grapes and melon balls!)

Let the fruit thaw and sprinkle with

> *½ cup brandy*
> *¼ cup white mint liqueur (optional).*

As it thaws, turn the fruit now and then to combine with the liquor. At dinnertime, ladle it into individual bowls and fill each bowl with foaming iced champagne!

TWO SAUCES FROM THE RIDICULOUS
TO THE SUBLIME

SAUCE RIDICULOUS

One weekend after having done more than my share of cooking, I sat back in my chair after dinner and asked Hal Holden to invent a dessert at once —because I had a bad sweet tooth. He disappeared in the kitchen and returned in ten minutes with a bowl of ice cream from the freezer and something hot, aromatic, and velvety brown in a pitcher. We poured this poem over the ice cream and ate with childlike pleasure.

He had poured ¼ cup milk in the top part of the double boiler, set it over boiling water, and in the milk melted five Milky Way bars. He stirred until the mixture was glistening and smooth. (If anyone wants the sauce with nuts, melt Snickers!)

SAUCE SUBLIME

I once saved a dreary steamed pudding with this sauce. It would save anything. Try it once instead of the whipped cream filling and icing on the Schaumtorte (page 320), over Meringue Tart (page 319) or over a slightly stale cake, or on a pudding or mousse.

In a small bowl on the electric mixer beat

>*4 egg yolks.*

When pale yellow, add

>*½ cup superfine sugar.*

Beat until very thick. Set the bowl over (not in) a pan of boiling water and continue beating with an electric or hand rotary beater for 5 minutes. Remove the mixture from the hot water and fold in

>*¼ cup Grand Marnier or orange liqueur.*

Let it cool for an hour. Then whip till stiff

>*1 cup heavy cream*

and fold in

>*2 tablespoons confectioner's sugar.*

Fold the sweetened whipped cream into the cold sauce, adding

>*2 more tablespoons orange liqueur.*

Pour over anything—and be happy!

XIV. Putting Up with UTA

(PRESERVING FRUIT AND VEGETABLES)

Two years ago on another vibrating September day, I was sitting on the opposite sundeck in a state of euphoria as the sea reflected a soft blue sky, a few gulls hovered in the air to catch the right current for an effortless hover, and the pines and flowers dazzled me with their colors and scents. The experience had to be written down, almost as an expression of gratitude, and so I was led into the introduction for this book.

Today as I approach the end of my cooking diary, I have a different view. The ocean carries sparkles of diamonds on a deeper blue. The reeds on the moors have opened into feathery plumes. Purple joe-pye weed has faded and the goldenrod is at its peak. Field daisies are having a late summer revival. In the distance I can see wild grapes awaiting greedy paws. I know the beachplums have been stripped and are nicely preserved on my pantry shelves. Although the cranberries in their bog are out of sight, I remember they must be picked next week. In the vegetable garden below me, the weight of the tomatoes has almost pulled the vines from their stakes while the bluish leaves of the Brussels sprouts conceal pearly heads. Many orange zucchini blossoms promise other meals. The shiny green pepper patch looks almost tropical, and behind it, faded sunflower heads droop on the tall fence. Their seeds and the brown dill seeds haven't been completely harvested, so chickadees, towhees, robins, and kinglets are having a feast. The September clematis, planted only a few years ago, has climbed right up the house to cluster at my feet with fragrant star-shaped flowers that tremble with bees and butterflies.

The joy I feel for the subject of this chapter is similar to that I feel for vegetables and bread baking. All three are at the heart of nature, from planting to harvesting the yields of the garden and fields to the activation of yeast. The cycles of life become specific when waiting for fruit and vegetables to reach their peak. Insensitivity, dullness, or superficial distractions that make many people immune to these wonders sadden me. I give thanks for the intensity with which I feel the miracles around me and

send up fervent prayers that we *stay* aware as we participate in creation and that we don't destroy these sources on earth or in ourselves.

I want to lead you through a summer of preserving fruit and vegetables to share my pleasure and convince you how easy it is. You don't need special knowledge or skill for the things I turn out, and you'll end up with many jars of goodies for your family and your friends.

If you don't have a garden or live near fertile fields, pretend you do, while you keep an eagle eye on fruit and vegetable markets for seasonal abundance and lowest prices.

Note: Any cook already experienced in preservation methods can scan this chapter for asterisk (*) recipes which may be of interest to them.

BASIC METHODS FOR JELLY, JAM, AND PRESERVES

Jelly is clear and transparent, made just from the juice of the fruit. Jam and marmalade include the fruit pulp in a mashed or ground state. Preserves and conserves attempt to keep the fruit as much in its original shape as possible.

Don't yell—but in most of the fruit recipes I use commercially made pectin to insure proper jelling. I'm at odds with all the experts who advocate the "natural, old-fashioned" method of boiling down fruit until jelling occurs by itself. God knows I've tried, and ended up with a runny mess or something resembling rock candy that couldn't be pried out of the jar with a chisel. I also find it hard to believe that flavor and nutritional value aren't higher after boiling fruit only *one* minute when the pectin is added, than after the half-hour or more needed without it. The commercial pectin is colorless, tasteless, and odorless, so the quality of the jam or preserve depends solely on the fruit.

Every bottle of Certo comes wrapped with a recipe booklet. (I use many of the recipes [not the ones for uncooked frozen fruit] and sometimes make changes or additions, which I'll specify. The booklet does not contain some of the recipes I can't imagine doing without.) You can put up a batch or two of any fruit in a few hours, so don't be dissuaded by images of Grandma sweating away her summer days in the kitchen. Many of my friends have adopted "Uta's putting-up habits" after they've watched how easy it is.

ORGANIZATION AND EQUIPMENT

1) Wash and prepare fresh fruit as soon as possible after you get it home for maximum flavor and texture and to prevent spoilage.

2) Clear and clean the stove, sink, drainboard, and counter space for ease of operation.

3) Set out your *largest* pot, 2-to-4-gallon capacity. (I use my 4-gallon lobster pot because I often double the recipe and the fruit must boil up very high.)

4) Put a *wooden spoon* next to the pot for stirring without bruising fruit. Place a long-handled *ladle* next to it for skimming foam and ladling fruit into jars (preferably with a crook-neck handle to hang on the rim of the pot between distributions).

5) A potato masher comes in handy if fruit is to be crushed. Otherwise use the back of a spoon.

6) Get out sugar and a *large measuring cup*. I use a 2-quart size because of large amounts of sugar.

7) Put a bar of *paraffin wax* (available at the supermarket) into a *metal cup* or *coffee tin* or in the top of a double boiler. The melted wax is for sealing the final product. I like to use the metal cup set in a small saucepan of water. I use it only for this purpose, don't have to remove old wax, and simply add to it for the next round of jam making.

8) Put your *jars* in the sink, more than you think you'll need. Don't buy stock jelly jars but recycle pickle, mayonnaise, and peanut butter jars. Once you start saving them, you'll see how quickly they accumulate in all shapes and sizes. For gifts the sides and lids can be decorated. For tiny gifts, baby-food jars are excellent! When making some of the preserves that have a thinner, less jellied syrup which can't be sealed with wax, you'll need *Mason jars* with self-sealing metal lids and screw tops. I use pint or half-pint sizes most often.

Wash the jars in sudsy water and rinse thoroughly. Drain and then set them upright in the sink to sterilize them. My tap water runs scalding hot so I simply fill each jar and let it stand till needed, when the jam has boiled. At the last minute, I pour off the water. The jar will still be hot when I ladle in the fruit. I put the washed lids into a colander and scald them at the last moment. If your tap water doesn't run hot enough, have boiling water ready in a teakettle.

9) Fancy *labels* are fun and can be ordered from the Certo company, but they're not necessary. Gummed plain labels are available at any dime store.

10) For tender hands that can't deal with hot jars, use *tongs* or *heavy pot holders*.

11) You'll probably be squeezing lemons, so set out your *juicer*.

12) A *jelly bag* or clean *pillowcase* isn't necessary for jam or preserves —obviously. But for all that lovely jelly you should know how to use it. Jelly bags are hard to come by except through a kitchen catalogue. They come with a stand that clamps on the bowl and supports the bag while juice drips through. I prefer filling a pillowcase with fruit when it's draped over a large bowl. Then I tie it to the handle of an overhead kitchen cabinet with strong twine and set a bowl underneath to catch the juice. Afterwards, I clean out the dregs, wash the case, and use it over and over again.

EXPLANATION OF A FEW TERMS AND METHODS

A *rolling boil* confused me until I understood that it didn't mean just the visual effect of the fruit rolling high in the pot, but that the high boil should be difficult to stir down again. It's important so you won't have an under-cooked jam.

Skimming the foam from jam, jelly, or preserves takes a little time. Use the tilted edge of the ladle to remove the bubbly lumps and foam from the surface of the cooked fruit. (The foam creates air bubbles, which will produce spoilage in the jars.) Draw the ladle lightly across the center of the fruit toward the edge of the pot, then all around the edge where the foam concentrates. Stir and skim again. Avoid scooping out pieces of fruit. (Reserve the foam to spread on bread the same day.)

When making jelly, let the juice drip for a long time (overnight, for instance) and don't hurry up the process by squeezing the bag, or your jelly will be cloudy.

When making preserves, I allow the fruit to stand whole, layered in the pot with the correct amount of sugar overnight, and then cook it the next morning.

When the fruit has been filled into the jars, use the tip of a spoon to break the little bubbles that have formed around the edges. Immediately spoon a thin layer of melted paraffin wax over the top. Tilt the jars to distribute the wax evenly and make sure they're airtight. Let the jars cool on a rack or board. Wipe them with a hot, damp sponge to remove all possible stickiness before sealing them with their lids. Paste on labels and they're ready for storage.

They can be stored for a year or two on shelves or in closets where they won't get too hot or freeze.

A Summer Adventure With Fruit

JUNE FRUIT

Strawberries are usually abundant around the middle of June. Washing and hulling them takes little time, so they're a marvelous beginning if "jamming" is new to you. I follow the recipe in the Certo booklet to make several batches of jam and one or two of the preserves.

Soon after the strawberries, the cherries are at the market, fabulous and ridiculously expensive. If you know someone with a black cherry tree or want to splurge, make the following:

*BLACK CHERRY PRESERVE

Use the Certo booklet but:

Allow the cherries to stand in the sugar overnight or for a minimum of 6 hours before cooking. When filling ½-pint Mason jars with fruit, to each one add

>   1 tablespoon brandy or kirsch.

Seal with sterilized metal lids and screw tops.

Don't use this preserve exclusively on bread, but try it on crêpes, pancakes, or ice cream.

JULY FRUIT

Soon there will be apricots and peaches from the South. I try to be patient and wait for the local ones in August.

Now come the raspberries, a fruit for the gods, particularly as they seem to become scarcer and more expensive all the time. If you have them in your back yard or live near wild raspberry bushes, make as many batches as possible straight from the recipe in the Certo booklet.

Like raspberries, currants seem to be disappearing. Early in July they used to be available in quart boxes at every market. Now I often have to make do with the yield from a few bushes in my garden. Currant jelly is used in sauces for meat and poultry, for glazes on cakes and tarts, and I never seem to have enough. I end up supplementing it with commercially produced jars. Do splurge and buy a few quarts of these fresh currants to make this very special jam.

*BAR LE DUC

Pick out and discard shriveled or rotten berries from

2 quarts currants.

A few underripe berries add flavor to the jam. Wash the fruit and gently run your fingers down the stems to remove the currants. Discard the stems. Set 2 pots on the stove and use the heaviest one to *slowly* heat

4 cups sugar.

Spread a layer of fruit on the bottom of the other pot and crush well. Throw the remaining currants on top of the crushed ones. Bring the fruit to a boil (don't add any liquid). Turn down the heat and simmer a few minutes. Add the hot sugar to the fruit and stir and simmer for 5 minutes. Slowly stir in

½ cup heated honey.

Simmer 5 minutes longer and quickly ladle the jam into hot sterilized jars. Seal with paraffin, allow to cool, clean the jars, label, and store. What a treat!

Note: Currants are rich in *natural* pectin.

*GOOSEBERRY PRESERVE

Gooseberries are getting as scarce as currants. They ripen at about the same time. Try to beg, borrow, or steal at least 1 quart of them to make a small amount of the preserve which is so *fabelhaft* with a roast lamb or pork.

Nip stems and blossom ends, wash, and discard shriveled or rotten goose-berries. Include a few underripe berries for extra tang. To each

>1 quart gooseberries

add

>1 quart plus ½ cup sugar.

Place the fruit and sugar into a heavy pot and stir them together gently with a wooden spoon. Cover the pot with plastic wrap and let stand at room temperature overnight.

In the morning, remove the plastic and bring the mixture to a boil. Simmer uncovered over very low heat for 20 minutes. Ladle the preserve into sterilized Mason jars and seal with sterilized lids and screw tops. Cool, label, store—and hoard!

MINT JELLY

In the middle of July, herbs reach their peak before flowering. I started with one little potted spearmint plant in my garden and it turned out to be a "rank weed" as it spread to come up even in the lawn. But I'm grateful for the Mint Jelly (the easiest of all jellies, you don't even need a jelly bag). Other uses in tea, juleps, salad, and with vegetables are bonuses. I also have peppermint, apple, and lemon mint. From the moors I gather the best of all—wild peppermint. The grayish-green sparse and spiky leaves don't seem related to the other mints, and the aroma is so pungent you could almost use it for a scent on your body. Whichever mint you use, the procedure for making jelly is the same. Wash the mint and strip the leaves from the stems. Discard the stems. When you have packed them down you should have

>1½ cups leaves.

Mash them in a kettle with a potato masher or the back of a spoon until bruised.

Cover with

>2¼ cups water.

Bring it to a boil. Turn off the heat and let it steep, covered, for 10 minutes to make a mint "infusion." Strain through a fine sieve and follow the recipe in the Certo booklet to make your jelly.

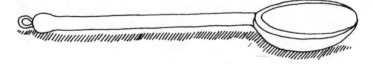

AUGUST FRUIT

You may find other fruit to put up in July, but I'm heading for August to check the fields for ripe blueberries and blackberries. Theoretically, you're supposed to know that they're ripe when bird droppings splash dark blue or purple on the flagstones or terrace. I'm always in a quandary whether to go berry-picking alone or to share the excitement with a friend. When you're all by yourself and you surprise a rabbit or flush a quail while harvesting, when the only other sound comes from humming insects, the movement of grass and bushes as you proceed with the hunt, you experience nature so intensely that you know why you've been put on earth.

Picking blueberries or their cousin, shadberries, takes a long time because they're so small. If you don't have enough for jam, make a pie or a tart or serve them in a bowl with fresh cream. Blackberries, on the other hand, are so big that when you find a good bush you can stand in one spot to fill a pail. As soon as you get home, pick them over to discard unripe or shriveled fruit and remove any stems still stuck to them. Do this chore outside, while sipping a drink. Wash and drain either kind of berry and make the jam from the Certo booklet.

*APRICOT OR PEACH PRESERVE

From mid to late August start to scour the environs for local apricots and peaches. I must put in a plug for the Long Island *white* peach. It's truly white with rosy cheeks and I'll stack it against the most exotic fruit in the world. When you find it, make jam and preserves by the peck.

I make lots of apricot jam, using the Certo recipe booklet. The jam is needed for fillings in tortes and over desserts, as well as being delectable with bread or pancakes. Both peach and apricot preserves are marvelous slathered over ice cream, crêpes, and pancakes.

Peel peaches or apricots by dipping in boiling water for 20 seconds. Remove with a slotted spoon and slip off the skins. A bad spot or two may need help with a knife. Cut in half and remove the pits. Free-stone peaches are easy, cling-stone peaches need a knife to remove the pits. Slice the fruit evenly (apricots can be left halved if you like). Save one pit for each jar.

You won't need your enormous pot because the fruit must simmer rather than boil. Measure the sliced or halved fruit and use

> ¾ cup sugar to
> 1 cup sliced fruit.

Layer the fruit in the pot with the sugar, cover with plastic wrap, and allow it to rest overnight at room temperature, or for a minimum of 4 hours.

Uncover the pot and stir in

2 tablespoons lemon juice per cup of fruit.

Bring to a boil, lower the heat, and simmer uncovered for 30 minutes or until the fruit turns translucent.

Use a nutcracker or hammer to crack the reserve pits and place one in each sterilized hot Mason jar. Remove the sliced or halved fruit from the pot with a slotted spoon and almost fill the jars. In the uncovered pot, boil down the syrup until it thickens a little and ladle it over the fruit in the jars. Seal immediately with sterile lids and screw tops. Cool, label, and store.

Peaches are juicier than apricots and you may have leftover syrup. Ladle this syrup while hot into sterile Mason jars and add a few tablespoons of brandy. Seal at once.

*HAL'S GREEN PEPPER JELLY

At the end of August my green pepper plants produce in such abundance that I begin making endless jars. Hal is already "peppered" throughout the book so I won't talk about him again, just his fabulous jelly. Serve it as a relish like mint jelly, or smear on a slab of dark bread along with a little sweet butter.

As with the mint jelly, you won't need a jelly bag.

Cut up

3–4 large, meaty green peppers.

Slice out the white veins and remove seeds. Grind coarsely in the electric blender. Including the juice, you should have at least

2 cups of ground peppers.

Hal gives you the option of adding

1 ground hot pepper.

I don't like such spicy things. Now, in the large pot, heat

1½ cups white vinegar with
6½ cups sugar.

Stir and simmer until the sugar has dissolved. Add the ground pepper and bring the jelly to the famous "rolling boil."

Then stir in *1 bottle Certo.*

Continue stirring over high heat for 3 minutes. Skim off the foam and then ladle into sterilized hot jars. Seal with paraffin. Cool, label, and store. You should have 9 or 10 half-pints.

SEPTEMBER FRUIT

*BEACHPLUM JELLY

September rolls around and I'm ready for more adventures in the fields as rose hips and beachplums start to ripen. Beachplums are native to America's Atlantic seacoast, a good reason for living there. In size and appearance they're somewhere between a Concord grape and a Bing cherry. When ripe they're lavender blue. When red or green, leave on the bush. You can pick a few red ones to add to a batch of fully ripe ones for more flavor in the jelly. A bountiful year means easy picking as they hang in grapelike clusters under their leaves. Gather more than you need because they keep for a year in their raw state in the freezer. As soon as you get home, pick through them to discard shriveled or rotten fruit, leaves, or remaining stems. Wash and dry thoroughly. Store in plastic bags in the refrigerator (or freezer for long periods) until you have time to make the jelly. Be generous and give some to city friends who may have fun putting up their own.

To make 8 half-pints of jelly wash

> *2 quarts whole beachplums.*

They don't need to be pitted, just crushed with a potato masher or your hands. Put them into a pot with

> *1½ cups water.*

Cover and simmer for ½ hour till soft and mushy. Put the fruit in a jelly bag or pillowcase and allow the juice to drip into a bowl overnight. You should end up with

> *3 cups juice.*

If there's a little extra juice, include it. Pour it into the huge pot over

> *6 cups sugar.*

Stir the mixture till blended and immediately stir in

> *½ bottle of Certo.*

Bring to a full rolling boil which can't be stirred down and boil 1 minute longer. Turn off the heat, skim the foam from the jelly, and ladle into sterilized jars. Seal with paraffin, cool, label, and store.

This jelly can be used in many sauces and glazes and also as a substitute in recipes calling for currant jelly. The flavor is difficult to describe. It's unique. Some people like to eat the plums raw. To me their magic comes out only in the cooking.

If you have patience and want to make jam, you have to cut or squeeze out pits.

BEACHPLUM JAM

Add

4 cups sugar to each
1 quart washed and pitted beachplums.

In the large pot, stir and bring to a rolling boil. Immediately pour in

½ bottle Certo.

Stir and boil hard for 1 minute. Turn off the heat and skim off the foam.

Stir another 5 minutes to prevent floating fruit. Ladle into sterilized jars, seal with paraffin, cool, label, and store.

Try beachplums with a pot roast or braised beef. When you first sauté the onions and carrots in butter in the casserole, add a cup of uncooked, pitted beachplums just before adding the browned beef and liquid. Delicious!

*ROSE HIP JELLY

The wonders of rose hips! When roses are left to wither on the stalk, they form seed pods or rose hips. The gardens and fields near the sea are rampant with wild roses. In autumn they are dotted with the red hips or seed pods. They come in many varieties, but the most useful for cooking come from the Rugosa rose, whose pod is the size and color of a ripe cherry tomato. They're richer in vitamin C than any other fruit or vegetable.

I don't agree with the theory that they're best after having been nipped by the first frost. By then, most of them have dried or shriveled up. In September pick the biggest and reddest you can find (making sure to avoid those that may have been chemically sprayed by a garden fiend).

To make about 6 pints of jelly you will need

2 quarts firm rose hips.

Pick through them to discard shriveled or rotten ones. Nip off stems and blossom ends and wash thoroughly. Cut them up or mash them with your hands. Don't be surprised at their dryness or the countless seeds in each pod. Put fruit and seeds into a pot and barely cover with water (about 1¼ quarts). Cover the pot and simmer about half an hour or until the fruit is tender. Pour the contents into a jelly bag to drip into a bowl overnight.

You should have at least

4 cups clear juice.

Pour the juice into your large pot and stir in

7 cups sugar
½ cup lemon juice.

Bring the jelly to a rolling boil and boil for 2 minutes before stirring in

1 bottle Certo.

Turn off the heat and skim the foam from the jelly. Ladle into sterilized jars. Seal with paraffin, cool, label, and store. The taste is rather like an exotic honey.

*CRAB APPLE JELLY

Connie and Martha Greene, my very dear friends, have the biggest gnarled old crab apple tree in Montauk. In spring, it's covered with fragrant white blossoms and in September it's laden with golden fruit. They let me help myself in return for some of the delicious jelly I make for them.

Nip off the stems and blossom ends and wash the apples. Cut them in half. They don't need to be peeled or cored. Place the fruit into a pot and pour water over them until it's barely visible under the top layer of apples. Simmer for ½ hour or until the fruit is soft and mushy. Ladle everything into a jelly bag to drip into a bowl overnight.

Next morning, measure the golden juice. You should use

1 cup sugar for each .
1 cup juice.

Mix juice and sugar in a pot and stir well. Bring it to a normal boil and boil for 15 minutes. Apples are high in natural pectin, so none need be added. Test it by placing a spoonful on a saucer in the refrigerator for a minute or so. If a skin has formed on the jelly it's done. If not, keep boiling for a few minutes.

Skim off the foam and ladle the jelly into sterilized jars. Seal with paraffin, cool, label, and store.

*APPLE MINT JELLY

If your garden is still rampant with mint, pick and wash a few sprigs. Place a few mint leaves in the bottom of each sterilized jar before ladling in the apple jelly. Nice?

*SECKEL PEAR PRESERVE

Anne Kaufman Schneider is not only famous because she's George Kaufman's daughter and the wife of the brilliant producer Irving Schneider, or because she's the wittiest of all my friends, *but* because she has a terrific Seckel pear tree. She shares both the pears and her recipe with me.

Pick the nicest of available pears and nip off blossom ends but retain the stems. Wash them carefully and prick the skin of each pear in half a dozen spots with a needle.

You'll need

>   6–7 *pounds pears.*

Make a syrup of

>   6 *cups white wine vinegar*
>   8 *cups brown sugar.*

Into a square cut from several layers of cheesecloth, put

>   1 *cinnamon stick*
>   2 *tablespoons allspice*
>   2 *tablespoons whole cloves.*

Tie the spices securely and drop the spice bag into simmering syrup. Cook about 10 minutes. Use a spoon to lower the pears into the syrup. Cover and cook over medium low heat for 20 minutes. Pierce a pear to see if it's tender. Cook longer if needed.

Use a slotted spoon to fill sterilized Mason jars with pears to within an inch of the tops (7 to 8 Mason jars in the pint size will do).

To the remaining syrup in the pot, add

>   *a few pieces of candied ginger (optional).*

Bring the syrup to a boil and lower the heat to simmer uncovered for 5 or 10 minutes. Spoon it over the pears in the jars to within ½ inch of the top. Seal at once with sterile metal lids and screw tops. Cool, label, and store.

Surround a roast with these pears and it will always be a holiday!

GRAPE JELLY

The end of September ushers in wild grapes. On a still, sunny day, drive slowly down country roads with the car windows open until you catch a whiff of warm, ripe grapes. Get out of the car, follow your nose and you'll find them clustered under the leaves of the vines, fat, juicy, and sun-warmed.

To make one batch, or about 7 cups, of grape jelly, you'll need

   3 pounds of grapes.

Follow the recipe in the Certo booklet.

*GRAPE JUICE

When I get carried away and pick baskets full of the luscious things, I make grape juice. Kids love it. Adults love it over ice cubes with a little vodka and a lemon wedge.

Remove the stems, discard imperfect fruit, and wash the grapes. Put them in a pot and *just* cover them with boiling water. Simmer for ½ hour or until grapes are soft and mushy. Strain them overnight in the jelly bag or pillowcase, letting the juice drip into a bowl. Next morning put the juice into the refrigerator and leave it for several days. Then strain the juice again through several layers of cheesecloth and pour it into a pot. Bring it to a simmer with

   ⅔ cup sugar to each
   1 quart grape juice.

Remove from heat after 15 minutes. Let it cool and refrigerate again for at least 1 hour before serving.

*CRANBERRY JUICE

Summer is officially over on September 21, but mine doesn't end until the last berry-picking expedition into the cranberry bogs, usually on Columbus Day. Connie Greene and I celebrate by settling down peacefully among the low, scraggly shrubs in our blue jeans while we run our fingers under the tiny leaves to pluck the hard red berries. You can't pick too many.

Cranberries will keep in their raw state for months and months in open boxes in a cool, dry place. If you have a surplus try something delicious and totally unlike its commercial counterpart.

Wash

> *2 cups cranberries.*

Boil in a pot with

> *2 cups water.*

After a few minutes, when the skins have popped, strain the juice in a colander lined with several thicknesses of cheesecloth. Set the colander over a bowl to drip for a few hours. Then boil up the juice with

> *½ cup sugar.*

Let cool and stir in

> *½ cup fresh orange juice*
> *1 tablespoon lemon juice.*

Chill, serve, and tingle. Or try it at a Twelfth Night celebration, heated and served in a mug with a shot of vodka or brandy, spiced with nutmeg and a piece of cinnamon stick.

*CRANBERRY NUT JAM

Into a pot put

> *4 cups washed cranberries*
> *1½ cups water.*

Boil for 5 minutes until the skins pop. Stir in until dissolved

> *3 cups sugar.*

Stir and simmer a few minutes. Then add

> *¾ cup crushed pineapple*
> *¼ cup seedless raisins or dried currants*
> *1 peeled, chopped orange, minus seeds.*

Simmer 20 minutes and stir in

> *½ cup chopped pecans or walnuts.*

Turn off the heat. Ladle the jam into sterilized Mason jars and seal with metal lids and screw tops.

Try it on pancakes, as a sauce with roast poultry or meat and, of course, on fresh buttered bread.

CRANBERRY SAUCE

So many people buy this in a can, not realizing they can make it at home in 10 minutes.

In a saucepan boil up a syrup of

> *2 cups water*
> *2 cups sugar.*

After 5 minutes, add

> *4 cups cranberries.*

Cook another 5 minutes until the skins pop. Pour into a bowl and cool. Makes 1 quart.

*CANDIED CRANBERRIES

Enlist a few friends to help. They'll be glad they did.

Wash

> *1 cup cranberries.*

Prick each berry with a needle a few times.

In a saucepan make a syrup of

> *1 cup sugar*
> *1 cup water.*

Let the syrup cook to the soft ball stage, 238° on your candy or deep fry thermometer. Remove the syrup from heat and stir in the cranberries. Leave them in the syrup for 5 minutes until translucent. Remove with a slotted spoon and spread on wax paper to cool. When they are *almost* dry, roll them in granulated sugar on another piece of wax paper. After the cranberries are well coated with sugar, chill them at least an hour. Serve like candy or as a dessert in a small bowl for each person. Sensational!

My fruity summer is at an end and I won't return to the fields till Christmas when the holly berries have reddened and I'll gather sprigs of it to bring a festive air inside the house. But let me turn back the clock and return to the vegetable garden, where surplus will be used for winter surprises.

Vegetables

There's no question of my preserving carrots, beans, Brussels sprouts, or potatoes, because they're eaten as fast as I can grow them. Tomatoes, peppers, squash or zucchini, and cucumbers are a different story. Their huge quantities have made invention a necessity.

TOMATO JUICE

This recipe will make about 2 quarts and will keep fresh in the refrigerator for at least a week. Wash and cut up

>   *12 to 16 medium-sized tomatoes.*

Use up misshapen ones. Put the tomatoes in a kettle with

>   *¼ cup water*
>   *½ a sliced onion*
>   *1 chopped celery stalk with leaves*
>   *a few parsley sprigs.*

Cover the pot and simmer about 30 minutes. Strain through a fine sieve, pushing down on the vegetables to extract all goodness. Season the juice with

>   *1 teaspoon salt*
>   *1 teaspoon sugar*
>   *½ teaspoon paprika.*

Pour into bottles and chill before serving. What a Bloody Mary this makes!

TOMATO PASTE

I put tomato paste into sterilized baby-food jars sealed tightly and keep it for up to a year in the freezer. It's a great present.

Wash and cut up

> 12 *large tomatoes.*

In a large, heavy pot melt

> 4 *tablespoons butter.*

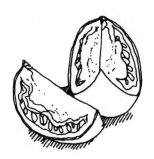

Add the tomatoes and stir in

> ¼ *cup dark brown sugar*
> 1 *tablespoon paprika*
> 2 *teaspoons salt.*

Cook over very low heat for several hours, stirring occasionally to make sure nothing is sticking. Lower the heat even more or set the pot on an asbestos pad and simmer several hours longer. When the mixture is very thick with little remaining moisture, push it through a strainer, leaving behind just a small dry mass to discard. Spoon into sterile jars, cover, and store in the freezer. This amount produces only a few baby-food jars full, but a teaspoon is all that is needed to flavor meat or sauce.

TOMATO RELISH

There must be as many recipes for this as cooks in the world. Here's my favorite.

You'll need

> 16–20 *large tomatoes*
> 3–4 *peeled, diced onions*
> 6 *hard pears, peeled, cored, and diced*
> 3 *green peppers, veins and seeds removed, thinly sliced*
> ¼ *cup pickling spice mix (comes in a box)*
> 1 *tablespoon salt*
> 3 *cups brown sugar*
> 1 *cup malt vinegar.*

Slip the skins from the tomatoes after dipping in boiling water for 10 seconds. Cut into evenly shaped small hunks and put them in a large pot with the other vegetables and spices—except the sugar. Simmer 15 minutes. Stir in the sugar and simmer 15 minutes longer. Ladle the fruit and vegetables into sterilized Mason jars, using a slotted spoon. Pour in enough juice to cover the vegetables and seal the jars with sterile self-sealing lids and screw tops. Cool, store, and relish.

YELLOW PLUM TOMATO JAM

The tomatoes don't need peeling, just washing before cooking in a heavy pot.

In the pot to each

>   *1 quart yellow plum tomatoes*

add

>   *1 lemon thinly sliced, seeds removed*
>   *1 peeled orange, thinly sliced, slices halved and seeds removed*
>   *¾ cup sugar*
>   *¾ cup brown sugar.*

Stir the mixture gently with a wooden spoon to blend well. Cover the pot with plastic and allow to rest overnight or at least 8 hours at room temperature.

Bring the mixture to a boil uncovered. Turn the heat down as far as possible or set the pot on an asbestos pad to simmer for 1 hour or until the mixture is thick. Stir occasionally. Spoon into sterilized Mason jars and seal with metal lids and screw tops. Cool, label, and store.

ANNE'S APPLE-TOMATO CHUTNEY

This is Anne Schneider's recipe.

Use about

>   *2½ pounds ripe tomatoes.*

Dip in boiling water and slip off the skins. Slice them and place in a large bowl.

Peel

>   *2 pounds green cooking apples.*

Remove the cores, slice them, and add to the tomatoes in the bowl.

Peel and slice

>   *3 small onions.*

Add them to the bowl. Cover fruit and vegetables with

>   *2 cups malt vinegar.*

Sprinkle with

> 1 tablespoon powdered ginger
> 1 tablespoon crushed, dried red pepper
> 1 teaspoon salt.

Stir the contents of the bowl and cover with plastic wrap to let stand overnight at room temperature.

Put the mixture into a large pot and stir in

> 1 cup brown sugar
> ½ cup seedless raisins.

Into a square of cheesecloth cut from several thicknesses, put

> 2 teaspoons mustard seeds.

Tie up the cheesecloth and drop the little bag into the pot. Bring the mixture to a boil, then lower the heat, and simmer uncovered until it's thick and most of the liquid has evaporated. Remove and discard the bag of mustard seeds. Spoon the chutney into sterilized Mason jars and seal with lids and screw tops. Cool, label, and store. Let the chutney rest for several weeks before using it.

UTA'S ZUCCHINI RELISH

This relish is a true *pièce de résistance* and draws bravos and encores!

Wash, peel, and dice into ¼-inch pieces

> 8 large zucchini, to equal 6 cups
> 4 large onions, to equal 3 cups
> 3–4 celery stalks, to equal 1½ cups.

Let the vegetables stand overnight in a large bowl sprinkled with

> ½ cup coarse salt.

In the morning, wash in a colander under cold running water and then drain. Make a syrup in a large pot using

> 3½ cups brown sugar
> 3 cups cider vinegar
> 2 teaspoons celery seeds
> 2 teaspoons mustard seeds
> 2 teaspoons turmeric
> 1 teaspoon whole cloves.

Bring it to a boil and add the drained vegetables. Stir for a minute, turn off the heat, and let the mixture rest for a few hours. Return it to a boil, lower the heat, and simmer for 5 minutes before spooning the relish into sterilized

Mason jars. About 8 half-pint jars should suffice. Let cool, label, and store for future happiness.

PICKLED GREEN TOMATOES

When frost threatens, I run outside to gather the large green tomatoes still hanging on the vine and make this recipe, which worms its way into the hearts of all.

Wash and thinly slice

>*2 dozen large green tomatoes, to equal 2 quarts sliced tomatoes.*

Peel and slice

>*4 large onions, to equal 1 quart sliced onions.*

Put the vegetables in a large bowl and sprinkle with

>*1 cup coarse salt.*

Let them rest overnight covered with plastic wrap. The next day, rinse them in a colander under cold, running water and allow to drain. In a large heavy pot put

>*2 cups white vinegar and 1 cup malt vinegar or 3 cups cider vinegar*
>*4 deveined and seeded, thinly sliced green peppers*
>*2 large pressed garlic cloves*
>*3 cups brown sugar*
>*2 teaspoons dry mustard*
>*1 cinnamon stick*
>*1 teaspoon whole cloves*
>*1 teaspoon powdered ginger*
>*1 teaspoon celery seed*
>*1 teaspoon salt.*

When the mixture has begun to boil, add the vegetables and stir well. Return to a boil before lowering the heat to allow the pickled tomatoes to simmer uncovered for 1 hour. Use a slotted spoon to fill sterilized Mason jars with the hot vegetables (about 8 half-pint jars). Remove the cinnamon stick from the syrup in the pot. Bring it to a boil once more and ladle it over the vegetables, filling the jars within ½ inch from the top. Seal with sterilized lids and screw tops. Cool, label, and store.

The next three recipes need a "boiling water bath" for long preservation. This is a cumbersome method requiring special equipment or difficult-to-manage improvised equipment. I've solved it by storing a few jars in the refrigerator up to a month and giving the rest to friends with a warning to eat it up quickly or store in the refrigerator for just a few weeks. Anyone interested in serious canning of vegetables should buy a proper book covering only this subject.

BASIL CHERRY TOMATOES

Remove the little green core from cherry tomatoes with the point of a knife.

Dip them in boiling water for 10 seconds to facilitate slipping off the skins. Pack the peeled tomatoes at once into sterilized Mason jars, leaving about 1 inch of space at the top. When you've packed as many jars as you want, boil tomato juice for a few minutes and fill each jar with it just to cover the tomatoes. Add to each jar

> 2 tablespoons olive oil
> a few fresh basil leaves
> a pinch of salt.

Seal with metal lids and screw tops. Cool and refrigerate. Use soon or give away. They can be used in any recipe where tomatoes are called for or as a garnish around roasts or poultry. They're delicious in a salad.

SENFGURKEN (Mustard Pickles)

If you aren't using your own cucumbers, be sure to buy the kind that haven't been waxed or oiled because they won't be peeled. Slice them about ¼ inch thick.

You will need

> 6 cups sliced cucumbers
> 4 cups onions, thinly sliced
> 4 large green peppers thinly sliced, veins and seeds removed.

Put the vegetables into a large bowl and sprinkle with

> ¾ cup coarse salt.

Cover with plastic wrap and let stand overnight.

The next day rinse the vegetables in a colander under cold running water and then drain. In a large pot mix together

> 1 cup brown sugar
> ½ cup dry mustard
> 2½ cups white vinegar and 2 cups malt vinegar or 4½ cups cider
> vinegar.

Into a cut-out square of several layers of cheesecloth put

> *1 teaspoon celery seeds*
> *1 tablespoon whole allspice.*

Tie the cheesecloth together tightly and add it to the pot. Bring the syrup to a boil and add the drained vegetables. Return it to a boil, lower the heat, and simmer 10 minutes until the vegetables are tender, yet crisp. In a small bowl mix together

> *¼ cup quick-mix flour*
> *1 teaspoon turmeric*
> *⅓ cup cold water.*

Make a smooth paste and stir it into the pickles to simmer another 5 minutes until the syrup thickens a little. Remove from heat and discard the spice bag. Pack about 10 sterilized half-pint Mason jars with pickles and sauce to within ½ inch of the tops. Seal at once with sterile lids and screw tops. Cool, label, and refrigerate. Don't store longer than 1 month.

BREAD AND BUTTER PICKLES

The cucumbers should be sliced almost paper thin. These pickles are quite different in flavor and texture than the Senfgurken.

Select

> *24–30 small-to-medium-sized cucumbers.*

Use unwaxed, unoiled cucumbers ideally with the smallest and least seeds. Put the thinly sliced cucumbers into a large bowl with

> *6 medium-sized onions, thinly sliced*
> *2 green peppers, seeded, deveined and thinly sliced.*

Over the vegetables sprinkle

> *½ cup coarse salt.*

Let stand overnight covered with plastic wrap. The next morning, wash the vegetables in a colander under cold, running water and drain them. Make a syrup in a large pot, using

> *3 cups cider vinegar*
> *3 cups brown sugar*
> *2 teaspoons salt.*

Cut a square from several layers of cheesecloth and into the center put

> 1 teaspoon whole allspice
> 1 teaspoon celery seeds
> 1 tablespoon mixed pickling spice (comes ready in a box)
> 1 tablespoon mustard seeds.

Tie the cheesecloth together and add the bag to the syrup in the pot. Bring it to a boil. Add the vegetables and let it return to a boil, cook for 5 minutes. Remove from heat and ladle the pickles into sterilized half-pint Mason jars to within ½ inch from the top. (Discard the spice bag.) Seal the jars with sterile lids and screw tops. Cool, label, and refrigerate. Use up within a month.

(Should there be large amounts of syrup left over, bottle it and save it for another batch.)

Homemade Liquors

These bottled "preserves" are unusual, fabulous treats about which I have no modesty.

JENNIFER'S VODKA SUPREME

Jennifer Scanlon, a member of the José Limon dance company, learned how to prepare this vodka from some Russian colleagues. She generously passed the recipe on to me. Jennifer doesn't need a sip of it to sparkle like the star she is.

Use a bottle of

> imported Russian vodka.

Remove ¼ cup of vodka. Save it—or sip it at once. Carefully peel

> the rind of 3 lemons.

Stuff the rind into the bottle and add

> 1–2 teaspoons sugar
> a pinch of salt
> 4–5 drops glycerine (available at any drugstore).

Recap the bottle and shake the contents. Refrigerate one week. Before serving, place the bottle in the freezer for 3 hours. Pour into chilled liqueur glasses. Pow!

MITCH'S KAHLUA

Mitchell Erickson, who has acted, directed and stage managed throughout our fifty United States, picked up this marvel from some little old ladies in Hawaii who seem to whip up a batch at the slightest provocation. I like it better than the commercially bottled liqueur, and it costs a fraction as much when you make it yourself. The most expensive ingredient, relatively speaking, is a vanilla bean or two.

In a large pot, boil till clear

> *2 cups water*
> *2 cups sugar.*

Remove from heat while you *slowly* add and stir in

> *1 small jar very good instant coffee.*

(Don't put the coffee in all at once or you'll have a congealed ball of it in the syrup.) When the coffee has been completely dissolved by stirring, return the pot to the stove, and simmer over lowest heat for 5 minutes. Remove from heat and stir in

> *a fifth of bourbon.*

The liquor can be a cheap brand, because it turns smooth and velvety with the blend of coffee, sugar, and vanilla bean.

Divide the Kahlua among two or three pretty, washed, and recycled bottles. Add a vanilla bean to each bottle, cork or seal it, and put away for at least 2 months to steep and blend.

Serve it in liqueur glasses with dollops of whipped cream or ice cream. As a dessert, pour it over scoops of ice cream. Serve it over shaved ice. All terrific.

ROSE HIP WINE

Read about rose hips on page 346.

Making this wine has become an annual ritual. Siphoning it from the barrel a year later has become a regular festival. The recipe was passed on to me by a little Southampton lady. The color is clear gold, the texture is satin, the aroma reminds you of blossoming fields, and the aftereffects are a glowing buzz.

When first following the crude instructions, I did everything wrong and got excellent results anyway. Since then, I've learned more and achieved even better results.

(Legally, you're allowed to make 200 gallons of wine annually which you promise not to sell. I make from 5 to 10 gallons. If you get serious about winemaking, get a book on the subject. Special equipment can be obtained at the Milan Laboratories, 57 Spring St., New York, N.Y., 10012.)

Nip off both ends and wash

> 2 quarts tightly packed rose hips.

Put them into a large crock or plastic pail. (*Don't* use metal.) Cover the rose hips with

> 8 pounds sugar.

Stir well and pour on

> 2 gallons boiling water.

Allow the mixture to become lukewarm or to cool almost to room temperature. The hips will float to the top. Crush them thoroughly with your hands, in the water. This takes a little time. Then dissolve

> 2 packages dry yeast in
> ½ cup lukewarm water.

Let the yeast mixture rest for 10 minutes before stirring it into the crock. Cover loosely and set aside to ferment for about 2 weeks. Stir twice a day until no more scum rises to the surface.

Strain everything through a pillowcase in 3 or 4 batches and pour it back into the cleaned crock or pail. Cover tightly with a lid or plastic wrap to rest undisturbed for about 6 weeks in a warm place (65° to 70°). By that time it should have stopped actively fermenting. Now "fine the wine." The first time I read that, I hadn't the foggiest notion what it meant; it's a process by which the sediment in the wine is made to sink so the clear wine can be siphoned off. Like this:

For the entire amount of wine in this recipe, lightly beat

> 1 egg white into
> 2 cups of the wine.

Pour this mixture back into the remaining liquid and whisk gently for 30 seconds. Let the wine stand covered for another day or so. Place the crock or pail on a counter and put a long, plastic tube into the top of the wine. Have ready clean empty wine bottles (or, ideally, a wooden wine cask). Suck on the tube till the wine comes into your mouth and then quickly insert the tube into a bottle to let it flow and fill up. You may get tiddly doing this, but it's fun. Leave behind any and all sediment at the bottom of the crock or pail. Seal the bottles snugly with corks. The best are obviously new ones that come with a wooden corker and complete instructions. But the first few years, I used the kind that are on screw tops from old liqueur bottles with excellent results. (At first I made rose hip wine in plastic gallon jugs sealed with screw caps, and even that worked.)

Label the bottles, date included, and keep in a cool place for one year. The result should resemble a jaunt to Eden.

(If a bottle stays cloudy, I use it for cooking and in recipes calling for Madeira or Masala. It's better than either.)

XV. Menus
for all Seasons

JANUARY

FEBRUARY

MARCH

APRIL

MAY

JUNE

JULY

AUGUST

SEPTEMBER

OCTOBER

NOVEMBER

DECEMBER

January

EASY, SHOWY NEW YEAR'S DINNER

Liptauer 75 on thin black bread

Baked Ham 211 with Apricot Glaze
  with Pineapple 212
Jazzy Canned Baked Beans 222
Brussels Sprouts in Butter 228

Boston Lettuce and Watercress

Lemon Mousse 324

Jennifer's Vodka
  Supreme 359

Vin Rosé

Champagne

SUPPER FOR A BLUSTERY NIGHT

Cheese Croustades 76

Lentil Soup with Sausages 89
Cheese Bread 284
Spinach Salad (with Mushrooms and
  Bean Sprouts) 262

Janie's Baked Pineapple 304

Imported Beer

ANNIVERSARY GALA

Miniature Quiches 81

Oysters on the Half Shell 70

Roast Filet of Beef 180
Pommes Anna 251
Puréed Broccoli 227
Baked Stuffed Cherry Tomatoes (with
  Duxelles) 266

Watercress and Belgian Endive Salad 259

Zephyr Torte 318

Champagne-Orange 54

Moselle White Wine

Red Bordeaux

Liqueur

RUSSIAN WINTER

Caviar Beets   58   and Water Chestnuts
  with Bacon   61

Chicken Cutlets Kiev   163
Kasha with Mushrooms   243
Green Beans   220
Carrots   230

Glazed Oranges   332

Imported Vodka

Burgundy Red Wine

February

GERMAN HOLIDAY

Raw Cauliflower with Red Caviar and
  Sour Cream Dip   55

Kasseler Rippenspeer   213
Mickey's Sauerkraut   260
Boiled Potatoes   249
Red Cabbage   230
Green Beans   220

Hazelnut Torte   312

Cocktails

Red Rhine Wine

PRESIDENT'S DINNER

Shrimp Puffs

Consommé with Avocado   86

Tafelspitz   182   with Schnittlauch Sauce
  186
Mashed Potatoes   250
Brussels Sprouts   227
Bake Stuffed Cherry Tomatoes   266

Bill's Fruit Potpourri with Champagne   333
Meringue Kisses   317

Cocktails

Red Bordeaux

HOMEY GET-TOGETHER

Tony's Greek Cheese Balls   78

Iranian Stew   194   Vin du Pays
Walnut Bread   283

Mixed Green Salad

Applesauce Pudding   331

LEAP YEAR HOP

Tony's Own Paté   60   Cocktails

Braised Duckling in Red Cabbage   166   Vin Rosé
Risi e Bisi   255

Green Bean Salad   222

Apfel Strudel   306

March

PASTA FESTA

Prosciutto with Melon   72   Italian Vermouth on Ice

Fettuccine   102   Red Chianti

Sacher Schnitzel   198   White Soave
Broccoli   225

Mixed Green Salad

Mandel Torte   315   Anise Liqueur with a
                                             Floating Coffee Bean

PATRICK'S PARTY

Stuffed Cucumbers   59   and Marinated
    Mushrooms   63   Cocktails

Beinfleisch   186   with Horseradish
    Dressing   49   Red Rhône Wine

Boiled New Potatoes   249
Cauliflower   234   with Buttered Crumbs
  47   surrounded by
Peas   247   and Carrots   231–233

Janie's Baked Pineapple   304   Green Crême de Menthe

AWAKENING OF SPRING

Peanut Butter Sticks   56   Cocktails

Artichokes Stuffed with Mushrooms   74

Broiled Chicken   145   Alsatian Traminer Wine
Snow Peas   247
Baby Carrots   232
New Potatoes Braised in Butter   249

Asparagus   219   with Uta's French
  Dressing   48

Chocolate Nut Meringue   319

END OF MONTH QUICKIE

Cheese Puffs   Cocktails

Filet of Sole in Brown Butter (with
  Almonds)   124
Georgio's Orzo   246   Chablis
Snow Peas   247

Hal's Bananas Flambé   333

April

EASTER FEASTER

Caviar Eggs   57   Champagne with Cran-
Roulades   58   berry Ice Cubes   54

Mushrooms Divine   64

Roast Leg of Lamb   203   Red Bordeaux
Polenta   237
Green Beans   220
Puréed Carrot   233

Boston Lettuce and Rugola

Zilly Donohue's Lamb Cake   307   Mitch's Kahlua   360

FIRST CATCH DINNER

Mushroom Caps a la Pennie   61   Cocktails

Poached Blue Fish   130   on a bed of
   Rice   255   Chablis

Asparagus   219

Pear Crisp   305

COMING OF THE GREEN

Raw Vegetable Strips with Mustard Sauce   41

Bacci di Caruso   112

Veal Cordon Bleu   200   Vin Rosé
Sautéed Mushrooms   62
Tomato Salad   267   on Lettuce Leaves

Cold Zabaglione   326

SHOWERY NIGHT DINNER

Cold Flounder in Vodka Sauce   128   Dry Vermouth on the
                                                Rocks

Haskel's Pot Roast   189   Red Rhine Wine
Boiled New Potatoes   249
Glazed Carrots   232

Spinach Salad   262

Peanut Pie   302

May

MAY DAY

Peggy's Mushroom Strudel 65	Champagne
Straciatella 88	
Backhendl 153	Austrian Red or
New Potatoes Braised in Butter 249	White Wine
Broccoli in Butter and Lemon 226	
Snow Peas 247	
Nutty Cream-Cheese Cake 311	

EASY COME, EASY GO

Water Chestnuts with Bacon 61	Cocktails
Gourmet's Shrimp Delight 119	Grâves
Georgio's Orzo (without Cheese) 246	
Asparagus 219	
Fresh Pineapple Liquored	

STEAK OR POTPOURRI PARTY

Suisse Toast 78	White Wine on Ice
Steak 176 or Mixed Grill 214	Burgundy Red Wine
Baked Potatoes 250	
Creamed Spinach 262	
Mixed Green Salad with Grated Carrots	
Stuffed Pears 329	

MEMORIAL DAY

Marinated Shrimp 72	Cocktails
Vegetable Consommé 86	
Manicotti Lotsa Cheese 106	Italian Red Wine
Green Bean Salad 222	
Fresh Fruit	

June

FAMILY GET-TOGETHER

Conventional Appetizer 54–55   Cocktails

Mitch's Gazpacho 96

Carole's Quiche 80   California Red Wine

Mixed Green Salad

Strawberries and Cream

UTA'S BIRTHDAY

Uta's Guacamole 56 Rice Wafers   Cocktails

Fettuccine Verde 104

Escargots (Snails in Shells) 69   Pouilly Fuissé
Minted Peas 248
French Bread

Last of the Asparagus 219

Schaumtorte 320   Champagne

FATHER'S DAY

Smoked Salmon on Thin Black Bread
  with Cream Cheese   Cocktails

Braised Leg of Lamb 207   Red Bordeaux
Boiled New Potatoes (with Parsley) 249
June Peas 247
Carrots 231–233

Cucumber Salad on Lettuce Leaves 239

Chocolate Mousse Torte 323

FIRST DAY OF SUMMER

Cheese and Crackers   Cocktails

Borscht Gazpacho 97

Cold Roast Chicken   142
Uta's Potato Salad   253
Broccoli Braised in Butter   226

Strawberry Tart   298

Chilled Red Burgundy

July

THE FOURTH

Caviar Potatoes   57

Champagne with Cranberry Ice Cubes   54

Oeufs en Gelée   68

Cold Roast Beef   181
Green Rice Salad   256
Green Beans   220

Château Neuf du Pâpe

Tomato Salad (with Basil Leaves)   267

Apple Pie   303   and Ice Cream

FISH FRY

Steamed Clams   70

Baby Fish, Battered and Deep Fried   124
Zucchini Puffs   274
Peas   247 · and Carrots   231–233

Chablis

Loose-Leaf Lettuce with Herbs

Blueberry Tart   299

HEAT WAVE GALA

Poached Shrimp   71   with Seafood
   Dip   71

Filetto Tonnato   191
Cold Rice (with Lemon)   255

Cocktails

Iced Vin Rosé

Platter of Halved Cherry Tomatoes,
  Marinated Zucchini Strips   273,   and
  Green Bean Salad   222
  (Platter Garnished with Watercress Leaves)

Stuffed Peaches   328

LOBSTER PARTY

Jellied Cucumber Soup   98

Boiled Lobster   120   with Lemon
  Butter   47   Champagne
French Bread

Niçoise Salad   259

Røde Grøde med Fløde   328
Meringue Kisses   317

August

MIDSUMMER'S NIGHT DREAM

Prosciutto with Pears   72   Iced Sweet Vermouth

Green Gazpacho   97

Suprême Chaud-froid garnished with
  Tarragon   159   Champagne
Cold New Potatoes   249
Green Beans   220

Hazelnut Torte   312

VEGETABLE HARVEST

French-fried Zucchini   273   and Roast
  Peppers   74   Cocktails

Marinated Roast Leg of Lamb, Hot or   Beaujolais
  Cold   205

Boiled New Potatoes (with Parsley)   249
Garden Green Beans   220
Baby Carrots   232

Tomato Salad   267

Peach Tart (white peaches)   300

GARDEN PARTY

Cold Zucchini Soup in Mugs   92   Iced Vin du Pays

Cold Polish Ham   211
Uta's Potato Salad   253
Tomato Aspic (filled with peas)   267

Blackberry Tart   299

CRISP WEATHER SUPPER

Roulades   58   Cocktails

Tomatoes Divine   267

Battered Shrimp   119   Austrian White Wine
Corn on the Cob   237
Baked Zucchini   275   stuffed with Puréed
   Carrot   233

Herbed Green Salad

Chocolate Mousse   322

September

PISTOU PARTY

Cheese Bombes   77

Vegetable Soup with Basil Sauce   90   German White Wine
Dill Bread   284

Apple Crisp   305

LABOR DAY SWELTER

Cold Shrimp Avocado   72   Cocktails

Cold Chicken Poached in White   White Moselle Wine
   Wine   150
Green Rice Salad   256
Cucumber Aspic   240   filled with
   Marinated Mushrooms   63

Fruit Filled Meringue Tart   319

HERBERT'S BIRTHDAY DINNER

Stuffed Cucumbers   59   Cocktails

Snails in Mushroom Caps   69

Wiener Schnitzel   198   Italian Red Wine
Risi e Bisi   255
Green Beans   220

Chocolate Nut Torte (with candles)   313   Champagne

END OF SUMMER

Cheese Croustades   76   Cocktails

Steak Tartar   178   Red Bordeaux
Zucchini mit Dill   272
Dill Bread   284

Zabaglione   325

October

OKTOBER FEST

Herring in Sour Cream on Thin Black Bread

Beef Carbonnade   195   on a bed of   German Beer
   Fettuccine   102

French Bread

Large Green Salad

Apfel Strudel   306

FALL FONDU GATHERING

Prosciutto with Pears   72

Cheese Fondu   82
French Bread

Spinach Salad   262

Røde Grøde med Fløde   328

Cocktails

Dry Swiss White Wine

COLUMBUS DAY

Smoked Fish on Crackers with Anchovies

Steak   176
Pommes Anna   251
Baked Green Tomatoes   269

Boston Lettuce with Rugola

Chocolate Cheesecake   310

Cocktails

California Cabernet
  Sauvignon

HALLOWEEN

Nut and Sunflower Seed Nibbles

Casserole Roast Pork with Prunes and
  Apples   209
Baked Potatoes   250
Brussels Sprouts   227

Watercress and Belgian Endive   259

Stuffed Peaches   328

Homemade Grape Juice
  349   with Vodka

Vin Rosé

November

COZY TIME

Water Chestnuts with Bacon   61

Coq au Vin   148   Beaujolais
Rice   255
Carrots   231–233
Green Beans   220

Lemon Mousse   324

MEATLESS ARMISTICE

Artichokes Stuffed with Sautéed Mushrooms
   and garnished with Shrimp   74

Ravioli di Bacci   111   Italian Red Wine
Broccoli   225–227

Lettuce and Tomatoes

Hal's Bananas Flambé   333

PORK PARTY

Celery Stuffed with Liptauer   75   Cocktails

Roast Loin of Pork   209   Dry White or Red Wine
Relishes, Zucchini   269–275   and Green
   Pepper Jelly   344
Connie's Grits Soufflé   36
Baked Zucchini in Sour Cream   271

Boston Lettuce Salad

Apple Crisp   305

THANKSGIVING

Margaret's Roast Peppers   74   Homemade Cranberry
Tony's Own Paté with Crackers   60   Juice   350   with
   Vodka

Steamed Clams 70	Chablis
French Bread	

Roast Duckling   164   with Orange Sauce   166   Red Rhône Wine
Sechel Pear Preserve   348
Kasha with Mushrooms   243
Peas   247   and Glazed Carrots   232

Watercress and Belgian Endive (with Diced
   Apples)   259

Hal's Pecan Pie 302	Mitch's Kahlua 360

December

EASY COMFORT

Cheese Croustades 76	Cocktails
Uta's Hungarian Goulash 196	Austrian Red Wine
Boiled New Potatoes 249	
Carrots 231–233	
Green Beans 220	

Applesauce Pudding   331

ADVENT DINNER

Black and Red Caviar on Thin Black Bread	
with Cream Cheese	Cocktails
Sauerbraten 187	Red Rhine Wine
Potato Pancakes 252	
Red Cabbage 230	
Stir-fried Spinach 262	

Chocolate Nut Meringue   319

PREHOLIDAY QUICKIE

Conventional Appetizers 54–55	Cocktails

Hot Cucumber Soup   93
French Bread

Cheater's Sole Florentine   128   Chablis
Georgio's Orzo (without cheese)   246

Green Salad

Ice Cream topped with Kahlua

MERRY CHRISTMAS

Margaret's Roast Peppers   74
Goose Liver on Toast Rounds   172   Champagne

Cold Salmon Mousse   135   White Rhine Wine

Christmas Goose   171   with Homemade
   Relishes   Sparkling Burgundy
Riced Potatoes   250
Red Cabbage   230
Brussels Sprouts Braised with Chestnuts   229

Watercress and Belgian Endive Salad   259

Schaumtorte   320   More Champagne

   Breakfasts can be planned from Chapter III and many luncheons can be found in Chapters III and V.

FINAL HINTS

Tragi-comedies could be written about the early days when at midday I would decide to have a dinner party that same evening. A few phone calls took care of the invitations. Then, after leafing through a few cookbooks for ideas, I'd get enthusiastic about some grande cuisine menu, run to the store for supplies, and return to losing battle maneuvers in the kitchen. Sometimes I didn't even have the correct utensils, or I'd prepare two different dishes for the oven before realizing that one needed 350° heat and the other 425°. There never seemed to be enough burners on the stove. There wasn't time to complete complicated desserts. I'd forget the salad. While completing the hors d'oeuvres, I'd suddenly remember that one of the guests was allergic to caviar, another hated eggs, or one was squeamish about mushrooms. When the company arrived, they often spent the evening wiping away my tears.

I eventually learned to conceive all menus a week in advance. Somehow, when written down, I could see errors and make corrections. I could make sure they were varied from night to night. Texture, even color is important within a single menu, not just the kinds of food. Now I try to watch that they don't get unbalanced with my weakness for sauces, starches, and fats. And I always check out preferences of family and guests.

Before marketing, I check the individual recipes of the menus to make a list of all ingredients not on hand. I try to stay flexible in case an unexpected special sale greets me at the market. Unless you're experienced, plan just one fancy meal a week and try out an elaborate dish on your family or truly close friends first.

Getting everything on the table at the right time seems to frighten beginners more than anything else. Use my favorite trick of preparing as many things as possible in advance. Many hors d'oeuvres, soups, stews, casseroles, parboiled vegetables, salads without dressing, and most desserts can be fixed hours and sometimes days before dinner is to be served. I've stressed what and when throughout the book.

For each meal I usually write out an exact timetable, when what food goes in the oven or on the stove, including the time when food previously cooked must be reheated. I jot it down on a washable slate and keep my timers set.

If you acquire these habits, you'll present beautiful meals with grace while you yourself stay as cool as a cucumber.

Addendum:
The Seven Deadly
Kitchen Sins

When I was eight years old I had the shattering experience of seeing my mother weep. It was on a lovely spring evening in Madison, Wisconsin, and she was walking arm in arm with my father down the alleys in back of the frame houses to admire the color and fragrance of blossoming fruit trees. I dawdled behind as they took an occasional closer peek into the backyards. Suddenly my father stopped to take my mother into his arms. Her tears streamed as she echoed the refrain of everyone who has known hunger: "It's awful! I could feed a hundred people with the food from these garbage pails!"

Having emigrated from Germany only a few years earlier, we had survived not only the raging inflation that followed World War I, but a degree of starvation that made it possible to buy a house for a dozen eggs. My parents were staggered by the bounties of the United States and deeply grateful, too, but it seemed impossible to accept such waste. Until my mother died in 1938, she saved every ounce of fat to make her own soap, she turned tough old pea pods into delicacies, she used coffee grounds over again without their ever seeming bitter. Each bone was boiled down to extract flavor and nutrition while vegetable tops or parings were used for flavoring, for soup, for broth. Yet each meal was served like a feast. These things influenced me only much later and now I can't bear to watch a monster scraping pats of butter or portions of uneaten food into the garbage pail. Throughout the book I've tried to stress the total use of food, but I really wish I'd learned how to incorporate all of my mother's salvaging techniques.

There was a time when I was actually proud of the "well-stocked" pantry or refrigerator that led to having to throw out moldy cottage cheese, sour milk or cream, spoiled meat or poultry, and wilted or dried-out vegetables. Finally I hung my head in shame when I realized that this was the result of greed, improper organization of grocery lists, and inadequately planned menus. *Overbuying* didn't only mean I'd thrown my money away, but that I'd taken the food from someone else's mouth. *Overeating* is not just bad for your own body when you learn that if all of us in the United States ate just six ounces of beef less per *week*, we could free enough grain used for fattening cattle to feed the starving nations.

It doesn't do a bit of good to play ostrich about our changing way of life. World food shortages *will* worsen. The wilderness *is* threatened and diminishing, and the list of endangered species of wildlife *is* increasing. Natural resources are being exhausted with horrendous speed. Water pollution reaches to the centers of our oceans while the problems of our air extend to the very layer of ozone protecting our planet. The population continues to explode by the billion, and each new person is not only a consumer but a polluter! To ignore the mind-boggling facts presented us by scientists and educators, or to accuse them of perpetrating doomsday philosophies, or to assume we're not individually responsible only assures a quicker trip down the path leading to the catastrophes they've warned us about.

The more information you get about these problems, the more passionate you become. I've been guilty of most ecological abuses, which is probably why I'm so adamant about reforming. I'm not ready to become a saint or a martyr in order to help solve these earth-shaking dilemmas, but I have made practical changes of habits that seem individually unimportant but add up collectively as they lead from the store to the kitchen, into the dining room and back again—the areas in which the homemaker is the biggest polluter. I try hard to:

> plan menus in detail and make considered shopping lists
> use up leftovers within a day or two
> remember that serving overly generous portions turns me into a food "pusher"
> serve at least one meatless meal a week
> fast once in a while and send the money I'd have spent on food to CARE.

Perhaps most important, it becomes an obligation never to treat food carelessly, but to prepare it beautifully and to eat with reverence and thanks.

Not just the food we prepare and eat, but almost everything used for preparation, clean-up, and disposal influences the ecology. I think Rachel Carson first opened my eyes to man's destruction of the environment so that I was forced to concern myself more and more with things like the death of rivers and lakes from wastes and detergents, the poisoning of animals, fish and birds by pesticides, the depletion of natural resources—all of which seemed to arise not only from the producer's greed for higher profits but from the consumer's greed for more energy and all conveniences. Now it seems as if both producers and consumers may be on the road to being consumed. The day my grandchild was born, a summation of this knowledge affected me powerfully. What kind of a world would we have given her by the time she reached twenty?

You're probably as attuned to a change in life style as I am, but if you want more and continuing information, join organizations such as Friends of the Earth.

Meanwhile I'll pass on some specific conservation habits that I attempt to practice.

PAPER

Knowing that an entire tree is destroyed to produce only a few tons of paper, I take a string or canvas bag to market and flatly turn down the endless paper bags they seem so anxious to foist off on you. I complain loudly about excess packaging. I make newspaper logs for my fireplace and use crumbled newspaper to wash windows. The rest I take to a recycling center.

Paper toweling is an unquestionable "convenience," but its expendability can turn it into a scandalously wasteful item. Throughout the book I've specified uses for "toweling" when dealing with certain foods and have deliberately avoided the word "paper." Use it only for draining very greasy things or where cloth wouldn't do. I have a drawer for squares of worn and torn sheets, terry toweling, old dish towels, even old table linen. These squares are clean and ready to use in cooking until they're stained and worn beyond retrieving. Even when paper towels are necessary, they're often used excessively. I try to go easy on paper napkins and table accessories, one of my great weaknesses.

PLASTIC

In today's kitchens this stuff is almost as useful as toweling but it is also a terrible polluter, giving off noxious fumes when burned. It has a petroleum base as well. Except for plastic wrap, which I use to preserve and store food, I almost never buy a plastic bag. So many items come wrapped in them that once you get the habit of rinsing them out and hanging them up to dry for reuse, you'll find there are always plenty on hand.

Whenever you have a choice between buying something in a plastic container or one made of cardboard or glass (such as scouring powder, ammonia, window cleaner, etc.) settle for glass or cardboard. Plastic containers will not break down or rot on the garbage dump and must be burned, adding to air pollution. Recycle the ones you have for other uses. The tops can be cut off and the remainder used as containers in a workroom, garage, or for gardening purposes. (Even egg cartons can be used to plant seedlings.)

ALUMINUM

Cans or foil made of aluminum will not rust or decompose and so they become yet another disposal problem. Sometimes I dream that we'll all be buried under garbage. Wash out cans and take them to a recycling center along with empty bottles or glassware. Use aluminum foil, that marvelous kitchen aid, sparingly. It's also easily washed and dried for reuse.

AEROSOL CANS

Freon, the chemical used to propel the liquids from cans, may be seriously damaging the layer of ozone protecting our planet from too much sun. When you read this, aerosol cans may already be banned. Otherwise, cut down on the use of all spray cans you feel you can't live without. Often there's a choice of getting the identical product in a can or bottle from which the liquid pours or just sprays by means of a plunger rather than a Freon propellent.

DETERGENTS

Soon detergents may be outlawed everywhere, not just in isolated sections of the country. Cleanliness may be next to godliness, but not once you've seen rivers rushing along piled high with suds that won't dissolve or lakes that have "died" from the algae produced by phosphates from detergents. Good old biodegradable soap is still the best and leaves everything as white and sparkling as I once imagined my detergent did.

(Certain ironies crop up. Here in Montauk where our septic tanks clogged up and our drinking water was threatened, they've banned detergents, but they still allow a dishwasher detergent that contains 40 percent more phosphates than the ordinary kitchen detergent, claiming that it's indispensable to the functioning of those energy-gulping machines!)

FOOD DISPOSAL

Wasteful habits in purchasing food are easily corrected, but disposing of garbage can be a troublesome problem.

If you have a yard and if the yard is large enough for a compost heap and if you can afford to build a proper pit that seals out rodents, you could almost dismiss your garbage collector. It's truly miraculous to build a pile of garden clippings, to add fruit and vegetable parings, egg shells, coffee grounds, all table scraps, add wood and charcoal ashes, available manure or a little dry manure, then to turn this pile a few times—and to find a mound of rich humus, smelling as sweet as lilacs, after just a few months. When used on flower or vegetable beds, compost makes all other fertilizers unnecessary. (The Department of Agriculture supplies complete information.)

If you don't have the space in which to compost, be sure to use up scraps until they're fit only for garbage.

ENERGY

I'm sure you need no further facts about wasting energy or using your appliances sparingly. There's only one piece of misinformation I'd like to correct. I've heard claims that ovens do not need to be preheated to ensure proper cooking. Balderdash! But I do try to use the oven for more than one thing at a time to make maximum use of the heat.

The original Seven Deadly Sins are supposed to bring on the destruction of one's soul. I've composed an altered list and mounted them on my kitchen wall as a reminder that committing them can help to bring about the destruction of our universe.

THE SEVEN DEADLY KITCHEN SINS

Ignorance
Irresponsibility
Greed
Gluttony
Waste
Sloth
Impatience

If we all pitch in to help, I'm convinced we can enjoy our lives, still eat beautifully, and pass on a good world to our children.

Index